CONTRACTING FOR CHANGE

CONTRACTING FOR CHANGE

Contracts in Health, Social Care, and Other Local Government Services

KIERON WALSH, NICHOLAS DEAKIN, PAULA SMITH,
PETER SPURGEON, AND NEIL THOMAS

OXFORD UNIVERSITY PRESS

1997

Oxford University Press, Great Clarendon Street, Oxford OX2 6DP
Oxford New York
Athens Auckland Bangkok Bogota Bombay
Buenos Aires Calcutta Cape Town Dar es Salaam
Delhi Florence Hong Kong Istanbul Karachi
Kuala Lumpur Madras Madrid Melbourne
Mexico City Nairobi Paris Singapore
Taipei Tokyo Toronto
and associated companies in
Berlin Ibadan

Oxford is a trade mark of Oxford University Press

Published in the United States by
Oxford University Press Inc., New York

British Library Cataloguing in Publication Data
Data available

Library of Congress Cataloging in Publication Data
Data available

ISBN 0–19–828945–6

1 3 5 7 9 10 8 6 4 2

Typeset by Graphicraft Typesetters Ltd., Hong Kong
Printed in Great Britain by Biddles Ltd., Guildford & King's Lynn

CONTENTS

LIST OF FIGURES

LIST OF TABLES

PREFACE

Kieron Walsh, whose name appears first on the title page of this book by the unanimous decision of the other authors, died in May 1995 while the book was still in the course of being written. However, placing his name at the head of this list is not merely a sentimental gesture. From the beginning of the project on which the book is based, Kieron was the main driving force in the enterprise, leading from the front in the inspirational—and it must be said occasionally maddening—way that was his trade mark.

The original research project from which the book derives formed part of the Economic and Social Research Council's Contracts and Competition research programme. Four of the authors came together from different parts of the same parent university to put forward a successful application for funding under the programme, which enabled them to appoint the fifth as research officer. Our project was intended to provide an insight into the role of contracting in the British public services—in contrast to the other projects in the programme, which were mostly oriented towards developments in the private sector. Work on our project benefited substantially from the engagement with other projects in the programme—especially joint seminars—for which we would like to record our thanks to Jonathan Michie (as programme coordinator) and also to colleagues on other projects with whom we shared ideas as the programme evolved, especially Rob Flynn and his colleagues at the University of Salford. The research project itself was completed in April 1995 and a final report has been lodged with the ESRC [ref. L114251007].

During the life-span of the project we published a sequence of articles and gave a number of conference papers; we also held an international seminar reviewing experience with contracts in other countries. These events gave us further opportunities to compare ideas and test and evolve our own interpretation of events in Britain.

This book represents an attempt to set our research findings in a broader context—the framework of policy developments as they have affected the public services over the past decade—and interpret them in the light of other recent academic work. It is here that the loss of Kieron Walsh at a crucial point in the preparation of the draft has been particularly poignant. He had been one of the pioneers in the analysis of change in the British public services; and in his other writings had built a consistent critique of these developments, most notably in his last book, *Public Services and Market Mechanisms* (Macmillan, 1995).

We have been able to take advantage of this published work, much of which he discussed with us either individually or at team seminars. More importantly for our present purposes, Kieron left a series of drafts which were intended for the present book. Two chapters for which he had taken primary responsibility were in complete draft form (they form Chapters 2 and 8 of this book, in amended versions) and he left substantial fragments of material intended as contributions to the presentation and interpretation of the empirical material that forms the centre-piece of the book. We have been able to incorporate some of this material into the final versions; but we have not had the benefit of his reflections on seeing the complete final analysis of the fieldwork material. We have also lost the chance of hearing what would certainly have been his trenchant criticisms of our own final drafts—though much of the material in them is based on ideas hammered out in team discussions in which he was a prime mover.

Apart from our intellectual (and practical) debts to Kieron, we would like to acknowledge: Tina Hearn and Mary Straker, the other researchers who worked on the project; our respondents—those who helped us with access and all those whom we saw during the case studies; Jonathan Michie as ESRC programme coordinator; David Musson as our editor at OUP (who showed patience and understanding when it mattered); John Stewart for timely help at draft stage; Sue Gilbert and Elaine Gallagher for help with production.

Nicholas Deakin
Paula Smith
Peter Spurgeon
Neil Thomas

University of Birmingham

ABBREVIATIONS

CCT	compulsory competitive tendering
CHC	community health council
CIPFA	Chartered Institute of Public Finance and Accountancy
CTC	competitive tendering and contracting (Australia)
DHA	district health authority
DLO	direct labour organization
DMU	directly managed unit
DoH	Department of Health
DSO	direct service organization
DSS	Department of Social Security
ECR	extra-contractual referral
ESRC	Economic and Social Research Council
FHSA	family health services authority
FMI	financial management initiative
GMS	grant maintained status
GP	general practitioner
HA	health authority
LMS	local management of schools
MBO	management buy-out
NAHAT	National Association of Health Authorities and Trusts
NHS	National Health Service
NHSME	National Health Service Management Executive
NPM	new public management
OECD	Organization for Economic Cooperation and Development
RHA	regional health authority
SSD	social services department
STG	special transitional grant
TUPE	Transfer of Undertakings (Protection of Employment)

Introduction

The central focus of the present book is on the process of change in the public services in the UK. More specifically, it is about the use of a particular device, contracts. In the studies on which the book is largely based, we have set out to explore the different purposes to which contracts have been put, their significance in a set of different situations, and the consequences of their introduction for the organizations involved, their managers and staff, and for the users of these services.

We shall suggest that for their advocates contracts have had both a symbolic and a practical significance. Symbolically, they have been presented as standing for the virtues of market-based management in its purest form—simplicity built on a financial foundation, with clear allocation of responsibilities and remedies for non-performance. Practically, they have come to be seen as the key device in the management tool-kit, whose introduction across a whole series of different services has helped to push along the reforms in the public sector over the past decade and a half.

Equally, for critics of the change process and its outcomes, contracts have come to stand for what are seen as the excesses of the Conservative government's reforms, with commercial values threatening the 'public sector ethos' or 'voluntary sector values' (the phrase 'the contract culture' is often employed in this sense). And in the same way, the contract itself becomes the epitome of the intrusion of these values, with their emphasis on financial criteria, apparently to the exclusion of all others, and involving excessive 'bureaucracy' in implementation. Most important of all, the operation of the contract-based system has come to be seen as the ultimate test of whether the reforms to the public services have actually improved the quality of the services delivered.

We have chosen to look at three service sectors in greater detail. The first consists of those local government services that are delivered through structures and procedures that have changed as a result of the introduction of compulsory competitive tendering (CCT). The second is the National Health Service; and the third social care. By this term, we mean chiefly the delivery of services to particular groups (the elderly, the mentally ill, those with learning and physical disabilities), both in institutions and in their homes, as part of the process of providing 'community care'.

The changes that have been introduced in these sectors have taken place at different times and have assumed significantly different forms. The selection of these three service sectors was based chiefly on the opportunity that choosing them would provide to make comparisons between them, focusing on contracts at different stages in the development of new policies, in terms both of the procedures adopted and their outcomes. Comparison between the different experiences in different sectors should help to illuminate the purpose of contracting, the form it has taken, and its consequences.

In addition, this selection has meant that different members of the team could bring to the research their existing expertise in the different service areas: Kieron Walsh in local government, Peter Spurgeon and Paula Smith in the health service, and Neil Thomas in social care.

The process of contracting is furthest advanced, at least in terms of time, in local government. During the 1980s, local authorities had to adjust to a sequence of statutory requirements to put an increasing number of local services out to tender. At the same time they had to reorganize their own internal structures to split the functions of purchasing and providing services. They had to do so against the background of continued pressure on resources and political conflict (often intense) between central and local government, culminating at the end of the decade in the failed attempt at radical reform of local finances (the 'poll tax' episode). Nevertheless, the contracting process itself in this sector is relatively straightforward, reflecting the nature of the services being provided.

In the health service, the introduction of the internal market and the change of status of the health authorities (who became the purchasers) and what were to become the NHS trusts (the future providers) was the outcome of a single parliamentary Act. Although certain elements in these reforms (the role of fund-holding GPs, for example) took time to assume their final form, in essence the change was a 'big bang', with all the fall-out that this image might lead one to expect. In other respects, too, the dynamics of the reform process were different (there is no locally elected element in the NHS); and the nature of services being provided is also far more complex.

The reforms in the social care sector have been the most recent of all; indeed, they were barely in place when we started our research at the beginning of 1994. Although they stem from the same legislation as the NHS reforms, their implementation was delayed as a result of the need to cope with the fall-out from the 'poll tax' episode. Their introduction into a service where responsibility for provision rests with elected local authorities has raised some of the same issues as those that emerged as a result of experience in local government with CCT. However, a major difference in this sector is the multiplicity of specialized agencies operating within it and their different characteristics. Some of these are voluntary organizations and their encounters with what for most of them has been an unfamiliar culture involving new and challenging procedures—the 'contract culture'—has highlighted a whole range of additional issues.

Throughout the research, our primary interest has been in how services are managed, employing contracts as a 'tracer' device. We have been concerned with three basic categories of issue:

- the nature of the organizational strategy and specifically the approach adopted towards the division of functions between purchaser and provider of services;

- the characteristics and patterns of organization and in particular the institutional cultures that are emerging;
- the nature of the organizational processes, the nature of the transactions that take place, and in particular the way in which transaction costs have been dealt with.

The first of these, the investigation of organizational strategies, has focused particularly on the approach that organizations have adopted to the introduction of market process. We have been concerned, for reasons that will shortly be apparent, with the way in which internal hierarchies and professional values and practices have been affected by these changes. We have also been concerned with the emergence of networks and the significance that these have had both within and between organizations.

One key concept in the analysis of the way in which individual organizations work and relate to one another has been that of trust. This, in turn, is reflected in the approach that different organizations have taken to the task of contract management. The strategies that have been adopted range widely across the spectrum from punishment to reward and all points in between. The contrasts between different service sectors and different agencies have proved particularly illuminating here.

In the main body of our text, we also try to show, among other things:

- which types of contract and which aspects of the contracting process are applicable generally in the public sector and which are specific to particular services, institutions, and circumstances;
- what forms contracts have taken in different service areas and how they have been managed there and the reasons for any variations;
- how far the contracts employed correspond to the ideal image of contracts and contracting (both positive and negative, as set out above) or whether they tend in practice to become something less dramatic—in some cases, merely a convenient means of preserving the status quo;
- the place they have occupied in the structural reforms in each service sector; and the impact their introduction has had both on managers, staff, and the users of services; and
- whose interests their introduction has served.

The plan of the book is as follows:

In Chapter 1, we provide a brief general description of the ways in which change has been introduced into the public services in the UK over the past fifteen years, focusing particularly on developments in local government CCT, health, and social care. Chapter 2 sets out and explains the main theoretical concepts that we will be employing in our detailed analysis of public service change and the role of contracting within it. This is followed in Chapter 3 by a discussion of the nature of contracts themselves, how they have been defined, and the different objectives that they have served. This discussion is supplemented by reference to a detailed analysis which has been made of a large number of contracts in the three services (more than 350 in all). These chapters (which form the first part of the book) are based mainly on recent studies of change in government, including work by the authors.

The second part of the book is based specifically on research undertaken by the authors for the ESRC's contracts and competition programme initiative. It is mainly based on the twelve case studies that have been undertaken, four in each of the three selected service sectors (local government CCT, health, and social care). This section of the book is made up of five chapters; Chapter 4 sets the scene by describing the case studies and putting them in context; and the following three explore the experience of change in the case study areas from a variety of different perspectives. Finally, Chapter 8 summarizes the contrasting experience of contracting in action in the field, drawing also upon the results of a questionnaire distributed to over 500 people involved in the contracting process, designed to establish their perceptions of the impact of the introduction of contracts.

The final part of the book sets the results of these intensive investigations in a wider context, drawing on experience internationally and on other studies of contracting to reach conclusions about the issues identified at the outset and to try to draw up a balance sheet of experience in the UK public services to date.

1

The Experience of Change in the UK Public Services

THE FRAMING CONCEPTS

What has been attempted in the UK over the past two decades is nothing less than a wholesale transformation of public services, involving radical organizational and cultural change. This transformation (sometimes referred to as 'reinventing government') has been based on the introduction of measures derived from market principles.

As Flynn (1990) has described it, the approach has four objectives:

- market mechanisms should be used wherever possible, even if there cannot be an unrestricted market for the service;
- competition should be established between providers of services, and consumers should be allowed to opt out of state provision to sharpen that competition;
- individual choice and interests should take priority over collective ones; and
- state provision should be kept wherever possible to a minimum.

This fundamental change of approach has been based on the belief that the state —more specifically the Keynesian welfare state as it emerged during the postwar period—has failed in its main task, to deliver steady economic growth in stable social conditions. This perception of failure surfaced in many developed Western countries during the course of the 1970s—though most strikingly in the Anglo-Saxon countries (Walsh 1995a). It rests mainly on what are seen as fundamental deficiencies in the functioning and performance of the public sector in managing and delivering public services.

Theories of Change

The critique of the public sector is associated predominantly (though not exclusively) with the political right and theories of 'public choice' (Dunleavy 1991). This holds that the state, together with the bureaucratic structures that have been created to discharge its expanded functions and the 'bureau-professionals' that those structures have nurtured and sheltered, is a fundamental source of problems, not a means of providing solutions. In particular, the vested interests of professional bureaucracies exert a powerful influence on the side of inertia and, if not counteracted, will secure the retention of existing frameworks in the face of pressures for change.

The ideology that has underpinned this critique as it has been developed in the UK is derived from these public choice theories in economics and a body of neo-liberal and libertarian social philosophy (Hayek 1978; Buchanan 1986; Niskanen 1971; Willetts 1992). From these sources stems the view that public bureaucracies will always exhibit the following characteristics:

- bureau maximization, seen as an inevitable development, given managers' basic motivation, self-interest;
- inability to meet objectives, in the absence of market disciplines; and in particular lack of proper capacity to exercise effective cost control;
- waste; 'x-inefficiency', caused by lack of effective monitoring of performance;
- distortions of delivery systems by the interests of producers (either professionals or trade unions).

Those characteristics of the public sector (these critics have argued) reflect basic deficiencies in the operating culture of state agencies. These include the difficulty of exerting political control over their activities, problems of ensuring that proper cost disciplines are observed and quality of output achieved without financial penalties for overrunning on expenditure; and the danger of producer dominance exercised by public sector unions. All these characteristics will inevitably make them insensitive to consumer needs and secretive about their performance. In addition, it has been asserted that the way in which state provision in welfare operates stifles enterprise and has helped to create and sustain a 'dependency culture' (Ridley 1992; Adam Smith Institute 1994).

In fact, not all these propositions have been empirically validated (Dunleavy 1991). Indeed, some of them have been convincingly disproved (Walsh 1995a). Arguments about the value of the contribution made by the public sector and the distinctive ethos of those working within it have been advanced to counter assertions about the culture prevailing there (Stewart and Ranson 1994). There is ample evidence of the positive functions that can be performed by welfare-state institutions in providing a resource for those excluded from the labour market and a springboard for them to re-enter it (Donnison 1990).

None the less, the critics have been extremely influential. Their ideas entered the political arena in the UK as a result of the economic crisis of the mid-1970s, which appeared to provide them with the necessary legitimation (Deakin 1994). The national-corporatist solutions of the postwar period had by then apparently proved inadequate to cope either with internal changes in the structure of the economy and society or with developments internationally, notably the shift to new styles of organization and service delivery brought about by the introduction of new technologies: the arrival of what is sometimes called 'post-Fordism' (Hoggett 1990).

The Politics of Change

The critique of the existing public sector passed into the political mainstream as a direct result of the change in the leadership of the Conservative Party in

1975, when Margaret Thatcher succeeded Edward Heath (Young 1990) and became a key element in the programme of radical reform that the Conservative Party refined in opposition (Willetts 1992).

However, despite the claims made by former Conservative ministers in retrospect (Baker 1993; Lawson 1992; Ridley 1992), the public sector reform project was never entirely coherent as an enterprise. Parts of it were inherited from the 1970–4 Conservative administration, with its 'quiet revolution' in the public sector, which also drew upon private sector models (Bruce-Gardyne 1974). The managerial elements in the new programme were marked by the experience of those who had held office under Edward Heath, notably Michael Heseltine and (more briefly) Kenneth Baker. But the enterprise was also strongly influenced by neo-liberal theory, in particular the views advanced by Keith Joseph after his 'reconversion to Conservatism' in 1974 and propagated by the think tanks he then helped to set up (Halcrow 1989).

These neo-liberal views, and the parallel campaign conducted by Nicholas Ridley and vividly described in his autobiography, exerted a particularly strong influence on the new leader, Margaret Thatcher, although her own autobiography is very short on evidence: the sole entry on the public services in the index of her autobiography simply says 'insatiable'. Nicholas Ridley (1992: 80–1) asserts on her behalf that she:

never believed that it was either possible or desirable to bring standards in the public service up to the highest level in the private sector: to do so would be enormously expensive. It would also destroy an area of choice, an ambition for which to strive and restore an element of the dependency culture. She would prefer to see more and more people opting for private provision, leaving the state services as a safety net for those who can't afford to opt out. This is very different from the current search for public services which are so good that no one will want to use the private sector.

In the second half of the 1970s, Margaret Thatcher's concerns about the public sector began to find an increasing resonance with public opinion. In this way, a programme emerged, by stages—not for nothing was the term 'stepping stones' employed by the Shadow Cabinet to describe the process they proposed to embark upon in government. The outlines of this programme were in turn filled in and developed by 'learning on the job' once power had been secured through victory at the general election in 1979.

A Programme for Change

There have been three core elements in the public service reform programme pursued by Conservative ministers in office. These have been to cut down government *expenditure*, reduce government *functions* (and staff), and change government's *values* and the ways in which they are reflected in all its remaining activities.

The first objective was set out in the White Paper published by the government immediately upon obtaining office in 1979 (Young 1990) and has been pursued by a variety of different techniques ever since, though with only limited success (Hutton 1995). Although these devices and the uses to which they have been put are not our main theme, it is important to be aware of this dimension to the programme. The Treasury has been constantly concerned to use the power that the system confers upon it at the macro-level to impose this agenda upon the levels below it—specifically, local authorities who lack the constitutional protection that other systems confer upon subordinate units of government. Thus, the issue of the cost of public services remains continually relevant in setting the conditions for change.

However, it is the other two objectives—modifying the functions of government and changing its style of work—that provide the main focus for us, since they define the key 'framing' elements in the process of change.

New Approaches to Management

The concept of 'management' is of central importance in the present context, because it relates both to the objective of transforming values and is directly relevant to the attempt to change outcomes. However, the term has tended to be blurred both in outline and outcome. It is less than an ideology but more than a simple description of an activity.

In the recent past, management in government has tended to be associated with two contrasting approaches. The first is the 'Taylorist' approach, based on the work of the pioneer management theorist F. W. Taylor. Subsequent variations on Taylor's theme of scientific management have sometimes been termed 'neo-Taylorism' (Pollitt 1990).

Taylorist management techniques are derived from industrial production engineering. They are tight and closed, resting on detailed specification of activities, systematic separation of different elements within them, and strong central control over both resources and functions. The activities of front-line staff are closely controlled—responsibility for innovation rests at the centre, which both devises the tools and controls their use.

By contrast, a second approach to management has emerged which also forms part of what has been termed the 'New Public Management'. This is based on decentralization rather than concentration of authority. The procedures introduced are loose and open; they encourage experiment and innovation by local managers and front-line staff, who have much greater responsibility (in every sense). The centre is kept as small as possible and its functions are cut to the essential minimum of strategic direction. The key resource is human—hence, the emphasis placed on techniques for motivating and rewarding staff. This type of change has made a particular impact on women, as front-line staff, both in terms of the changes in style and the rewards and penalties attached to them.

The two approaches are distinguishable but not incompatible: both can be used at the same time for controlling different types of work and the people performing it. Tight control systems can none the less allow a substantial amount of freedom to 'new wave' managers operating at a lower level. The role of audit and inspection is important here, in providing the centre with the essential link with events in the periphery, which enables it to continue to exercise overall management control. Strategy, in this approach, becomes a means of exercising control at a distance.

However, a common feature of both approaches is a belief in the applicability of market mechanisms and the tools developed in the private sector for budgeting and control of financial and human resources. Prominent among these tools are contracts. As one of us has written elsewhere (Walsh 1995*a*: pp. xvii–xviii):

Contract has become, along with the concept of customer, a fundamental metaphor for the changes that are being made in the public service. It is as likely to be used to characterise relationships within the organisation as those with private providers. Authority relations are being redefined as contracts . . . Contract is allied with performance measurement to produce an individual focus on the public sector worker, making the employment contract more like that for purchase on the market. The public service is becoming a 'nexus of contracts', rather than a bureaucratic hierarchy.

Implementing the Agenda

The UK experience reflects the influence of both these approaches to management, together with elements from the other enterprise of cost containment. This is distinguishable both in concept and execution from the main management agenda, because it is essentially concerned with the expense of managing public enterprises and securing 'value for money' from their operation, not with their objectives or the non-financial outcomes of their actions. In the implementation of the Conservative agenda since 1979, it is possible to identify and disentangle most of the different strands already described in this chapter. Essentially, it is a *hybrid* enterprise.

Among the main actions taken have been:

- the imposition of new management devices on central government departments through the financial management initiative (FMI);
- the hiving off of many of the executive functions of central government into semi-independent agencies: the 'next steps' programme;
- the straightforward abolition of some middle-level state agencies (local authorities—GLC and metropolitan countries) and creation of new ones (non-departmental public bodies or 'quangos') to take on part of their functions;
- the privatization of some functions; and the *threat* of privatization of others (the device known as 'market testing');
- restructuring of agencies that remain in the public sector and the introduction in them of new management techniques, often through the bringing in of managers from the private sector;
- the introduction of a new vocabulary in which the objectives of agencies can be translated into market terms;

- the creation of new devices for inspection and regulation and the collection of information intended to be used for the evaluation of performance; and
- the promulgation of the virtues of value change through the publicizing of results of evaluations (often in comparative form) and rewarding 'role models', as part of what has become known as the 'Charter movement', after the government's Citizen's Charter (1991).

The Citizen's Charter represents the most coherent statement of the government's aspirations for public sector reform. As John Major, whose personal initiative it is, described it in 1992, the Charter principles: '. . . give the citizen published standards and results: competition as a spur to quality improvement; responsiveness; and value for money to get the best possible service within the resources that the nation can afford. They give more power to the citizen and more freedom to choose' (quoted Walsh 1995*a*: p. xxi).

Objectives of Policy Changes

Despite all this activity, there is a certain lack of complete clarity about what the desired final outcome of these drastic changes should be. The key concept is of the 'enabling state', based on a permanent separation between the traditional roles of the public sector, so that regulation and taxation are kept but direct provision is split away, and the function of purchasing services developed in its place.

One important issue here is the potential for fragmentation; to rely on achieving coherence in policy priorities and coordination in service delivery through the 'nexus of contracts' (Walsh 1995*a*) may not be sufficient. The centre's control of events is constantly at risk—either from independent initiatives taken at the periphery or failures that occur there. In this context, concentrating on 'strategy' and the separation of functions between policy and implementation can become a defensive measure, designed to ensure that politicians at the centre do not have to accept blame for operational failures.

Another issue is the question of the desired 'end state' and whether the enterprise should have a fixed end-point. The true believers see no reason for pausing while some delivery functions are still even partly in the public sector. 'Marketization' is a self-evidently desirable process and market failures are presented as either grossly exaggerated or easily compensated. This is the main significance of the government's current programme of 'market testing', in which outside agencies are invited to bid to take over the responsibilities of parts of the public sector in competition with the units currently responsible for them (HM Treasury 1992).

Others accept that there are functions that still properly belong in the public domain. But where does the boundary fall? Can it be identified with any degree of consistency once the basic propositions set out above are accepted? As has often been pointed out, this means that the public sector is in a state of permanent revolution—which can either be rationalized as a dynamic principle, stimulating innovation and encouraging better performance or else criticized as highly demotivating for managers.

Some Implementation Issues

The nature of the enterprise has been tested by the experience of introducing the reforms and some of the inconsistencies and internal contradiction within the enterprise itself have been exposed as a result (cf. Marsh and Rhodes 1992).

One problem is that the language of the enterprise is 'hollow'—which is to say that it is often non-specific and sometimes merely rhetorical and therefore leaves spaces that can be colonized by those with different objectives, or with none except self-interest.

Another issue is the potential contradiction between the declared sovereign virtue of competition (in principle) and the urgent necessity for cooperation (in practice). There is also a tension between the centralizing elements in the programme and decentralization, which is a key objective of the new public management. This exposes important issues about responsibility and accountability.

Further conflict may arise between different objectives derived from different starting positions—one key example is value for money against quality; another is pressure on staff, asked to accept a trade-off between greater independence and staff cuts; those cuts may in turn jeopardize other policy objectives, like economic regeneration.

There are also issues about the extent to which new approaches can be genuinely open ('transparent'), given both the strong tradition of secrecy in British governance and the intrusion of the new 'commercial confidentiality' through the creation of quasi-private agencies, which seek to protect their position against competition from rivals by restricting access to financial information.

There is a general question of the relationship between innovation in different service sectors and the need for effective collaboration and joint planning between these sectors (this includes difficulties stemming from the existence of different information systems). There is also a debate about the continuing significance (if any) of a competing 'public sector ethos' and the feasibility of undertaking a complete cultural 'transplant' of private sector values. Also, success in doing so, if it is achieved, may have implications for 'non-commercial' values and policies based on them—for example, equal opportunities programmes.

The place of the user, or 'consumer'—there is an important issue around definitions employed here and how they relate to the action taken—in the enterprise remains in doubt: is the priority accorded to them purely rhetorical or genuinely central to the process of change? How far can they exercise any independent influence over the course of events?

Finally, there is a question about the stability of the whole enterprise; the extent to which even a quasi-market will develop its own dynamic and produce outcomes that can only be addressed by reversing the 'hands off' principle and intervening directly from the centre.

Most of these themes (and some others) are present in the three specific service sectors which for reasons described in the introduction we have selected for closer examination, local government (specifically those services affected by compulsory competitive tendering); the health service, and social care.

The Breeding of a Hybrid

Within the broad framework of the overall policy objectives set out at the beginning of this chapter, there have been some substantial divergencies in the different service sectors we have chosen to examine. This is because, as we have already suggested, the enterprise itself is a hybrid. The main response is that the government itself has had different objectives for different services, within its overall policy agenda. These differences have sometimes even extended to pursuing competing objectives within individual service areas, like health and social care. The three distinct dimensions of policy—financial, structural, and cultural—on which stress has been laid at various times (see above) have been given higher or lower priority at different moments during the Conservative government's period in office.

The government's agenda also has different implications for the individual sectors to which it has been applied. Change has been refracted through a set of different patterns of organization, in which power and responsibility are distributed in a range of contrasting ways. It has also taken place in environments in which there are different sets of values (personal, professional, and institutional) and a variety of operational priorities.

Furthermore, within each service sector, pressure groups and policy brokers exert influence in different ways and with varying degrees of effectiveness. The government's freedom of action is further limited by other external constraints —political, economic, and social—and by the climate of public opinion. These factors, too, can have different effects in each service area.

The task of implementing policies for change is therefore of necessity going to take a different form in each sector; the choice of means will also be different and we should expect the outcomes to be so as well. However, the circumstances of their introduction are likely to be broadly similar, because there are certain common factors that apply through the period during which these changes were first introduced.

From May 1979 to the general election of 1992, the government was in firm control of both the executive ('Whitehall') and the legislative machinery ('Westminster'), with a safe majority in the House of Commons. During its period in office, the government has also succeeded in achieving a substantial measure of additional centralization of power. This has been secured through diminishing the range of independent functions performed by local government and creating quangos specifically designed to implement the government's new innovations in policy (Jenkins 1995). As part of this process, Ministers have 'planted' a number of outside individuals sympathetic to their programme in key positions within government, from the Cabinet downwards. These measures have in part been made possible by the absence of any constitutional restrictions on the executive and the reluctance until recently of Parliament or members of the public to take an active interest in these developments.

All these factors have helped to make the task of implementing policies for change that the government has taken on considerably easier. But it does not necessarily follow that the government has always been successful in translating all its policies unamended into action. Some institutions or professional groups have put up a stiff resistance to change and have succeeded in delaying or changing the government's original proposals; though others have crumbled virtually without a struggle. The existence of such obstacles has been reflected in the timing of introduction of different reforms. In addition, very clear 'electoral rhythms' can be detected throughout this period, with controversial measures held back until after elections and radical reforms hurriedly undertaken once a fresh period of office has been secured.

REFORM WITHIN THE SECTORS

Reforms have been introduced into different services at different levels in the system. This means that there is a perpetual problem of consistency and linkages between them. For the purposes of our research, we have chosen three particular service areas and explored them in greater detail. These are:

* local government services (CCT);
* health services;
* social care.

As described in the Introduction, by 'local government services' we mean here those services for which local authorities have overall responsibility in building, highways construction and maintenance, refuse collection, street cleaning, building cleaning, catering, schools and welfare catering, vehicle and ground maintenance, which have been affected by government legislation requiring compulsory competitive tendering (CCT). 'Health services' covers the totality of the operation of the National Health Service; and 'social care' relates to the services provided under the rubric of 'community care', for which local authorities have a key coordinating responsibility.

Changes were introduced in these three areas at different stages in the overall reform programme described in the first part of this chapter. The character of the changes, the nature of the participants in the process, and the pace of change have also been very different. So it is hardly surprising that, although all the evidence is not yet available, it is already evident that they are having widely differing outcomes. At the same time, there are some obvious similarities, in terms of the overall objectives of policy, which help to make comparisons meaningful. For example, a central objective has been to remove politics from the process of service delivery. As one of strongest advocates of contracting, Graham Mather (1989), has put it:

It reduces the public choice phenomenon of lobbying for bureaucratic expansion by introducing built-in competitive pressures. It facilitates review of policy objectives by requiring regular reassessment and respecification within a democratic framework. It strengthens opportunities for quality control and concentration of resources on supervision and compliance. It regularises relationships between local authorities and competing agencies. It is a force for transparency of funding.

In the next section, we consider the three selected sectors in sequence and in some detail.

Local Government

The reform of local government was addressed very early in the government's first term in office. Initially, this represented an attempt to obtain control over a potentially deviant segment of the machinery of government, which was largely responsible for implementation of policy and (even more significantly) for the expenditure of public funds over a wide range of policy areas. In this latter capacity, local government had long been the object of Treasury concern and the subject of a sequence of measures designed to bring local spending under tighter central control (Travers 1986; Butler *et al*. 1994). Ministerial concern was further heightened, as the 1980s advanced, when local authorities fell increasingly under the control of opposition political parties, who proceeded to pursue their own directly contradictory policy agenda, for which they invoked the concept of the 'local mandate'. These developments greatly enhanced the government's motivation to intervene.

After 1983 the policy mix became more complex. Concern with economy and effectiveness in local authority spending had prompted the creation of the semi-independent Audit Commission with power of oversight. Compulsory competitive tendering (CCT) for certain functions of local authorities (highways construction and maintenance) had been introduced as early as 1981, but had not made much initial impact. However, from this stage onwards, the government's intentions began to alter. Another way forward began to emerge, through the injection of market values and reduction or modification in local authority functions. Blunt instrument expenditure controls ('capping') and the sanction of abolition (as in the case of the GLC and metropolitan counties) were still employed but the search for more sophisticated alternatives was under way, with the new-right think tanks, with their direct access to Ministers, acting as the principal change agents (Cockett 1994).

From 1987 onwards, a 'marketization' agenda begins to predominate. The poll tax was promoted as the main device for achieving it, by securing the accountability of authorities to their electorates for expenditure through transparency in operation (Ridley 1992; Butler *et al*. 1994). However, the Treasury regarded the tax (launched as the 'community charge') as ineffective and confusing (Lawson 1992). The wholesale restructuring of some key local government services (housing and education) and the further extension of compulsory competitive tendering, designed to reinforce the division of functions between purchasing and providing, was followed after the failure of the poll tax by new financial reforms which have further reduced both the amount of resources raised locally and local discretion over how they are spent.

Issues on Local Government Services   So far, the government has enjoyed limited success on the expenditure agenda overall—a reduction in the extent of local discretion has been secured, though at the cost of greatly increasing the contribution from the centre (Commission on Local Democracy 1995).

By contrast, significant progress has been made on the structural change agenda. This is reflected in the rapid spread of the internal purchaser/provider split, introduced by many local authorities as their basic tool for managing change. As the market element in the agenda has begun to establish itself, contracts have become a central feature of the change process, after the extension in the Local Government Act of 1988 of the requirement to put a range of services out to tender.

Despite these developments, the government's third priority, cultural change, remains a contested area: public sector values are still presented as a significant factor in the equation that differentiates what takes place within local government from 'pure' market activities.

Health Service

By contrast with local government, reform in this sector came relatively late in the Conservative government's reform programme; though when it came it was far-reaching—in most respects more so than in local government.

In the early 1980s, the government was relatively timid in its approach, though some action was taken which foreshadowed later developments. For example, there was some tinkering with the administrative structure (the abolition of a tier of administration, the area health authorities); more significantly, the first steps were taken towards the introduction of the new management culture, with the first appearance of General managers. However, until the mid-1980s the government was held back by its perception of the strength of the professional lobby in medicine and evidence of the popularity of the existing National Health Service 'free at point of delivery' and the media's willingness to reflect public concern in their coverage of health service issues.

There was also a difficulty in identifying savings in expenditure. The NHS has traditionally employed time successfully as a rationing device to produce excellent value for the taxpayers' money, by international standards, although this has been achieved at the cost of restricting choice and delaying the treatment of non-life-threatening conditions.

This was the background to Mrs Thatcher's hasty retreat from radicalism after the fiasco of the leak of some tentative proposals for reform in a 1982 report by the Central Policy Review Staff (shortly thereafter abolished). The subsequent election was fought on the Prime Minister's personal assurance that 'the NHS is safe in our hands'; and subsequent changes, promoted by Sir Roy Griffiths's report with its censure of consensus management and advocacy of cost centres, were relatively modest and their revolutionary potential was concealed behind clouds of rhetoric about concern for patients.

However, the continued use by the medical profession of the rhetoric of crisis to try to squeeze out more resources and the publicity given to an individual case of a child refused heart surgery eventually helped to precipitate more decisive action. General election victory in 1987 enabled the government to put forward a radical reform package. This had been assembled in secret (with no academics or medical professionals involved) and embodied a basic change of approach—the creation of a managed internal market.

This new approach is summed up in the White Paper that followed: *Working for Patients* (1989). Some key features of this document are:

- the separation of functions at the centre by the creation of a management structure which would devolve administration to a management executive while retaining political oversight;
- the transforming of health authorities into purchasers of health care, and the larger GP practices also to enjoy that status as 'fundholders';
- on the providing side, hospitals would be given the opportunity to become self-governing trusts and would compete with private sector hospitals and with those still directly managed in the public sector for the custom of purchasers.

The whole system 'would be regulated by contracts which would vary in their specificity and in subjection to legal determination, but which would specify the normal parameters of commercial intercourse—cost, volume, quality, timeliness, and so forth' (Butler *et al.* 1994).

Although the legislation that followed (the NHS and Community Care Act 1990) proved intensely controversial, the result of the 1992 election ended immediate political uncertainty around the future of the NHS and liberated the government to pursue their reforms. Since then, events have moved rapidly on, with the result that trust status for almost all hospitals is now effectively irreversible; the commissioning system has become 'real' and contracts have gained depth and explicitness. In the process, purchasers have been developing a greater understanding of the nature of their task. This has exposed the question of the balance to be struck between short-term imperatives of contract management and broader health-care goals. Meanwhile, fundholding GPs have developed unexpected muscle as their capacity to manage their budgets to their patients' best advantage has developed (Glennerster *et al.* 1994) and, critics would add, a two-tier system is developing *de facto* as a result, with patients of practices without that status enjoying less favourable access to hospital treatment.

In addition, the Patient's Charter (one of the suite of service-specific documents produced in the wake of the Prime Minister's 1991 Citizen's Charter) has provided a focus for policies designed to monitor quality and improve performance. The focus on waiting lists as a key device for measurement and the Charter's reference to the right of every individual 'to receive health care on the basis of clinical need' has also had the effect of exposing issues about the allocation of resources for health care and the priorities given to different forms of treatment. As Petchey has commented, the reform programme (1993: 198):

has resulted in marked extension of direct and indirect state control over the NHS at the expense of clinical autonomy. It has also placed health care rationing firmly on the political agenda. Instead of treatment being allocated, as hitherto, largely covertly and by clinicians according to priorities that were either undisclosed or else justified by reference to generally unquestioned clinical criteria, in the internal market it will be purchasers rather than providers who will be responsible for deciding on what (and effectively on whom) the limited health care budget will be spent.

Issues on Health Service It is difficult to be specific on the financial aspects of reform. Cost reduction has always been on the agenda—as in the case of long-standing Treasury concern about costs of prescribing drugs. But increased spending overall in this sector is a sign of virtue, not vice (electorally, at least). And despite the use of the language of the market the vast majority of the resources will still come from public funds, for the foreseeable future.

The structural changes are still bedding down. Government attempts to push operational responsibility away from the centre are unlikely to be wholly successful while rationing issues have such political salience. But the market agenda has conferred more control over detailed operations to local managers, who are clear about the gains that can be made, from their perspective.

However, the extent of the change in culture is still contested; and is capable of provoking ferocious debate—for example, when 'difficult' cases around the rationing of expensive treatment crop up.

In all these developments, contracts have had a central role, though their form and function is still evolving.

Social Care

Change in this sector came even later; but when it did so, it was more radical still, in that it involved creating an external market, with a variety of players from outside entering the existing system and competing with agencies already present. The funding of care lay at the root of the measures taken in social care: in particular, the rapidly rising cost of providing residential care, driven by the perverse incentive of the social security budget taking responsibility for funding it (Wistow *et al.* 1994). Also crucial in determining the character of the changes eventually made, was frustration at the inability of the existing agencies involved to contrive effective measures in collaboration (cf. House of Commons Social Services Select Committee 1985; Audit Commission 1986).

The concept of 'community care' has deep historical roots; its promotion as a policy was by no means a novelty (Titmuss 1969). The concept of a 'mixed economy of care' and that of an 'enabling authority' was also well established (see above). It had been made explicit in the context of provision of social care by Norman Fowler (then Secretary of State for Social Services) in his speech in Buxton, in 1984.

The introduction of full-blown market devices represented a sharp break with postwar experience. However, reform had become inevitable because of a combination of pressures:

• the deinstitutionalization/normalization movement, which had led to the discharge of substantial numbers of patients from long-stay institutions;
• demographic pressures and in particular the rapid increase in the numbers of the very old;
• the failure of the local authority social services departments set up after the Seebohm Report to cope with these pressures; and
• cost pressures.

Sir Roy Griffiths was commissioned by the government to produce a report which would address these issues. He produced a 'tight' model with ring-fenced funding and clear lines of accountability from Minister of Community Care to local authorities, who would be entrusted with responsibility for managing local markets but at the price of surrendering the provider role. In effect, their retention of a central role would be conditional upon a wholesale structural and cultural transformation.

As Wistow and colleagues comment (1994: 19): 'the publication of Griffiths' report marked the beginning of a shift towards a definition of enabling far less compatible with the established values of social work and social care but far more consistent with the promotion of market mechanisms elsewhere in the public sector'. But although this approach fitted other current thinking about the role of local authorities it did not match the government's agenda. There was therefore some considerable delay before the publication of the White Paper, *Caring for People* (1989). This provided for a modified Griffiths structure with a strong emphasis on the situation of users. Three of the primary objectives were to provide opportunities for people to live in their own homes, wherever possible; to provide practical support for carers, and through care assessment procedures to secure the best possible quality of care. The White Paper also laid particular emphasis on developing the role of the 'independent' sector (i.e. voluntary organizations and for-profits agencies). Funds for community care were not to be ring-fenced but there would be a progressive transfer of relevant elements in the social security budget to local authorities.

The local authorities' role was defined as market management and market *development*; the contract was to be one key device but there was also a requirement to plan for meeting local need through the production of community care plans, on which local consultation was to take place. At the same time, the emphasis on needs assessments on health issues underlines the increased importance of the public health role. Availability of information was to be a particular issue.

Legislation in 1990 combined reform of the NHS with the new provisions for community care. However, there was further delay in implementation. In part, this was because of the problem of funding the replacement for the discredited poll tax, in part because of the destabilizing potential of the NHS changes and also the impact of other additional responsibilities being laid upon social services departments, for example those in the Children Act. The interval was devoted by the Department of Health at the centre to producing blueprints for implementation by stages; full implementation of the reforms eventually took place on 1 April 1993; and despite the delay some problems remained unresolved. For example:

- in many instances, there were too few suppliers in local markets; and those that were already present or put in an early appearance were often ill-equipped to cope or not disposed to enter the 'contract culture';
- there has often been an uneven distribution of information as between purchasers and providers and shortages of skills and relevant experience among purchasers.
- the Department of Health requires that 85 per cent of the transferred resources should be allocated to the 'independent sector'—that is, non-statutory sector providers, including for-profit organizations. This necessarily implies greatly increased participation by voluntary organizations; how far does local market management help or hinder their involvement? There is also a potential 'cultural' barrier to their full participation (Gutch 1992).

Finally, there have also been significant practical problems of setting up new procedures in a politically contested area. Many Labour-controlled local authorities were ideologically predisposed against market-based solutions; and local authority staff are suspicious of the motives of private sector providers.

Issues on Social Care   On the financial agenda, it is still unclear how far cost savings can be achieved, except at the expense of quality. The rationing of resources provided from the centre has already raised questions about how the services can be maintained; for-profits organizations are also concerned about whether they are being allowed to compete fairly for these resources.

On structure, there are unresolved questions about the ability of local authorities to implement and adapt to the new division in their functions—the purchaser/provider split.

The role of contracts has been central. The new allocation of functions and in particular the market-management responsibility placed upon local authorities puts purchasers in the position of having to devise contracts that will give expression to their overall strategy. So far, this often appears to take the form of cooperation with the voluntary sector and tough sanctions on the for-profit organizations.

Change in the UK Public Services

TABLE 1.1. Organizational change by service area

	Health	Social Care	Local Government
External markets	weak	strong	medium
Internal markets	strong	weak	strong
Trading accounts	medium	weak	strong
Tendering	weak	medium	strong
User choice	medium	strong	weak
Commissioning	strong	medium	weak
Link to service planning	medium	strong	weak
Financial targets	medium	weak	strong
Contracting out	weak	strong	medium
Purchaser/provider split	strong	weak	strong/medium

SUMMARY

The changes discussed above are the consequences of a sequence of varied interventions from central government, undertaken at different points in time, but over a fairly brief period. The key common elements are: operation through markets (external or internal); the use of trading accounts; tendering procedures; the emphasis on commissioning; providing a degree of choice for the user; the link to service planning; the setting of financial targets; the degree to which contracting out is required; and the separation between client and contractor or purchaser and provider.

These changes affect existing organizations in different ways, depending on the focus for action adopted in different service areas. The situation described earlier in the chapter could be summarized as in Table 1.1. The changes are related to and dependent upon each other. Change also generates different relationships between the various actors involved, both those already *in situ* and those entering the arena for the first time, by altering the terms of existing linkages and creating new ones. The outcomes could be represented as a continuum (see Figure 1.1).

partnerships   informal alliances   competition

      cooperation   truces   conflicts

<<<<<<<<<<<<<<<<– – – – – – – – – – – – –>>>>>>>>>>>>>>>>

FIG. 1.1. Continuum of outcomes of change

These different patterns will be (in part, at least) the result of the way in which reforms have been introduced and the strength of the positions of the various actors after central government has intervened—existing institutions, professional organizations, pressure groups, and policy brokers.

The common outcome in all cases is some sort of market-like situation but with very different sets of dynamics. In operation, these 'managed' markets can be harmonious, 'gritty', or entirely seized up. In all these market situations, the role of *contracts*, both as a metaphor for the changes that are taking place and a principal means of achieving them, has been central.

2

Understanding the Process of Public Service Management Change

INTRODUCTION

The purpose of this chapter is to develop a framework of concepts that can be used to analyse the nature of the change in public service organizations. In doing so, we will draw upon a range of thinking and analysis in social and organizational theory, but particularly on institutional theory. This theoretical approach takes a number of forms. The emphasis in the economic theories of institutions is on the way that they operate to create efficient forms of organization in different disciplines (Williamson 1975; 1985). In sociological theories of institutions there is more concern for the way that norms and incentives operate to structure action, and the role of language (Di Maggio and Powell 1983). In political science the focus tends to be upon the way that political 'institutions' influence social systems (March and Olsen 1989).

In spite of these differences there is a common core to the institutional approach, in that it is concerned to explain both action and structure and to encompass change and continuity. The basic form of our approach is to understand organizational change as taking place within an existing framework of institutions. Our analysis therefore starts with a definition of institutions, as they operate in the field of public management.

DEFINING INSTITUTIONS

North (1990) takes an approach to the understanding of institutions that emphasizes both change and continuity, and structure as well as process. This understanding incorporates a reflexive approach to social life, conceiving people as both the source of rules and as being constrained by them. North defines institutions as:

the rules of the game in a society or, more formally [are] the humanly devised constraints that shape human interaction. In consequence they structure incentives in human exchange, whether political, social, or economic. Institutional change shapes the way societies evolve through time and hence is the key to understanding social change.

It is important to distinguish between institutions and organizations, since the two ideas are often used interchangeably. Knight (1921) states the difference as follows:

Whereas institutions are sets of rules that structure interactions among actors, organisations are collective actors who might be subject to institutional constraint. Organisations generally have an internal structure, an institutional framework governing the interactions of those persons who constitute the organisation.

Organizations are then the outcome or expression of the results of rule-governed patterns of action. The framework that constitutes the organization is based upon the rules involved and the way that they relate to each other, and action within organizations may be seen as a set of 'games' that are governed by the institutional rules.

Three fundamental levels of institutional influence may be distinguished for our purposes. First, there are macro-institutions operating at the societal level, and providing a framework within which all other institutions must operate, examples of such institutions include the way that money operates, or basic understandings about property rights. It is these framing institutions that make social interaction and continuity possible at all, and give it its specific cultural character. The way that markets operate, for example, will be dependent on the way that property rights are defined and the nature of rules about exchange (Davis 1992).

Secondly, there are meso-level institutions which influence how particular social and economic sectors operate, such as the requirement for contract in the public service. Contract will have to be defined within the prior concepts of property and exchange, and its acceptability to professionals and the public will partly depend upon the ability to define it in ways that are consonant with macro-understandings of the nature of public services. Thirdly, there are micro-institutions operating within specific organizational contexts, such as informal rules about how contract failures are to be dealt with or the use of particular accounting mechanisms. The implementation of new policies in the public service can be seen as a chain of rule-making and institutional development, at each of these three levels.

In general, macro-institutional change will have much more fundamental effects than change at the micro-level, since it is more pervasive in its impact. It is much easier to introduce changes in micro-institutions, such as accounting procedures than to change people's understanding of the nature of exchange. The introduction of markets in the public service in Eastern Europe and Russia is more challenging than in the USA since both macro- and micro-institutions are affected. In the public service, the extent to which change has involved the macro-institutional level has varied from one sector to another.

Rules and their Significance

Action takes place within a structuring framework of institutional rules that is both constraining and enabling. The framework of rules acts as a constraint in setting limits to action and influencing its outcome, as much through the way that other actors behave, as by enforcing any particular action. Rules define the set of choices that are available to actors. Frameworks of rules are enabling in the sense that they make coherent and coordinated action possible. Numerous studies have shown the way that frameworks of rules operate to make even simple everyday action possible through creating confidence that actions will produce expected results, and through creating a diffuse pattern of social trust (Giddens 1985). The nature of the rule system will determine the extent to which new patterns of action can emerge within existing organizational frameworks. The obvious analogy is with mathematics or chess, in both of which relatively simple sets of rules make possible extensive creative development.

However, there is a need for some redundancy, duplication, or slack in organizational systems if they are to be able to cope with change (Campbell 1992; Colson 1975). Ambiguity is necessary to adaptation and to the ability of the organization to cope with unexpected events. Highly structured sets of rules that are tightly interrelated are likely to make it difficult to produce innovation. Where regulations are too tight, then one can expect a cycle of rule-making as the organization, or those who control it, try to deal with unexpected emergent events. The alternative to ever tighter rules is a system based upon trust. We will argue that the contractual systems that have been adopted in the public service have different levels of tightness and interrelationship, but that this process of 'regulation inflation' can clearly be seen to be at work. Trust is likely to be eroded.

It is useful to distinguish between rules of action, and constitutional rules (Brennan and Buchanan 1985; Ostrom 1990). Rules of action govern everyday behaviour and are the means of ensuring organizational continuity. They might be rules about who can talk to whom, hours of work, or the way that money can be spent. Constitutional rules are those that set the conditions that govern what everyday rules are possible and acceptable, that is, rules for the system, rather than rules within the system. Examples of such constitutional rules would include macro-institutions, at the societal level, such as property rights, or general principles such as the rule of law, but there will also be constitutional rules at the level of the organization, for example that it should operate as a bureaucracy or like a market. Ostrom distinguishes a third type of rule, namely collective choice rules which determine which action rules are chosen in particular cases. An example of such a rule would be that budgets are normally to be prepared on an incremental basis except for trading accounts, that performance should be measured, or that contracts with voluntary bodies are different from those with the private sector.

Collective choice rules would also govern the sort of contract that is chosen in particular circumstances, for example that the risk should, where possible, be shifted to the contractor, or that it should be borne jointly by client and contractor. The combination of rules that operates in any particular instance can be seen as a rule regime. It need not be the case that the rule regime is consistent, and we will argue that one of the bases of change is that rules may conflict with one another. The more this is the case the more difficult it will be for members of the organization to form expectations. In analysing this process it is important to distinguish between conflicts of rules that operate at the same institutional level, and those that operate between levels. The first is illustrated by the possible conflict between an understanding of the public service as based on a public service ethic, as opposed to the market. The second might involve rules about information exchange making it difficult to operate a contract-based system, or the difference between European and British regulations about how contracts are to be let.

Attachment to Institutions

Institutions may operate in a variety of ways, which will influence and be influenced by the values, interests and power of organizational actors. People will pursue strategies that are likely to forward their interests and give effect to their views about how the organization should operate. Etzioni's (1993) and Gouldner's (1964) classic studies of the operation of bureaucratic systems illustrate the possibilities. Etzioni distinguished three patterns of attachment of individuals to organizations: coercive, calculative, and moral. The first involved direct control of the actions of individuals by those with power over them in a situation of value conflict, and the use of force, pressure, or sanctions for transgression. The most obvious examples of such organizations are total institutions, such as prisons or, perhaps, long-stay mental institutions. Calculative involvement is based upon the notion of people acting in particular ways because of the rewards that they will receive for doing so, or the losses that they will avoid. This is the dominant *mode of attachment* in commercial organizations. Moral involvement is based upon the idea that people will act as they do because of their belief that what they do is the right thing to do in itself, and because they are committed to the values of the organization. This form of attachment may be expected to occur more often in voluntary organizations. A key issue will be the appropriateness of different types of attachment in different circumstances.

As we shall see, contracts in the public service assume involvement or attachment to some degree, and this is reflected in the way that contracts are structured, the way that default or disagreement is dealt with, or the nature of contract monitoring.

Change and the External Environment

Meyer and Rowan (1977) argue that organizations will frequently adopt particular structures and practices because that is seen to be the way to achieve legitimacy with external agencies, such as central government, which may have funding or legitimating powers. The public sector, they argue, is particularly subject to this sort of pressure because it tends to have high dependency for funding and finds it difficult to demonstrate its efficiency and effectiveness. In order to show that they are effective, public organizations must adopt the organizational approaches that are taken as the hallmark of good practice. This process is apparent in the way that some public service organizations have responded to the introduction of markets and contracts, with the need to show that the changes being required by government are being followed. The formal structure is used to demonstrate conformity to external agencies, while the real pattern of organization is 'decoupled' from the formal. This argument has been extended to maintain that much change is purely surface and ritual (Brunsson and Olsen 1993), but it is quite possible for conformity to have real results. The nature and level of commitment to particular rule systems can be expected to have effects on the way that they will operate, and their impact on outcomes.

The world of organizations is clearly not one of unlimited continuity and stability; they obviously change, while at the same time maintaining a continuity of identity. Change may occur at any of three levels: constitutional, operational, and collective action. Technological change may make particular actions unnecessary, or a rule can simply fall out of favour or become unfashionable. This process can be seen as the normal evolutionary process of change that is always going on to a greater or lesser degree. Change in constitutional or collective choice rules are much more significant, likely to happen less often, and more likely to be the result of conscious action. Such changes are likely to happen for three main reasons. First, they result from breakdowns in the existing system, as in the case of the collapse of the communist regimes of Eastern Europe and Russia, making conscious institutional creation necessary. Though organizations, particularly in the public sector, may only rarely go completely out of business, government action can abolish particular bodies, such as the metropolitan counties and the Greater London Council.

The second reason for constitutional or collective-choice changes is because of shifts of power, with the newly powerful trying to reinforce their position in the organization. The third reason, and the one that has been most important in the public sector in Britain in the last decade, is the imposition of change from outside. This last source of change is particularly important in highly institutionalized environments. In such cases, the nature of organizations is influenced primarily by regulation or normative pressure exercised by external authority. The most obvious example of such influence is the use of statutory powers by government. It has been argued by Di Maggio and Powell (1983) that this process results in the 'isomorphism' of organizational structures and processes (i.e. different organizations performing similar roles developing similar characteristics). We will be concerned to investigate the extent to which a common institutional environment does lead to isomorphism, particularly in the case of a common approach to contracting.

Generally, one would expect that constitutional or collective choice changes are more likely at a time of significant disruption of accepted understandings and patterns of behaviour, or changes in the organizational context, for example severe financial constraint. Accepted everyday patterns of activity are not easily abandoned. They are likely to be made easier by the replacement of existing staff particularly at the decision-making level, and it is noticeable that the rate of staff turnover at senior level in public organizations has increased over the last ten years. Shifts of power from professionals to managers have also played a part.

We will argue that the changes that have followed from the marketization of the public service have reflected all three processes. Traditional bearers of organizational values have to some degree disappeared, and power structures have changed. The most influential factor has been the increase in the influence of the institutional context imposing change. Change has been internally generated as values have changed or individuals have seen different ways of pursuing their interests.

When there is constitutional and collective action change then there is likely to be a change in the basis of everyday action. Patterns of behaviour that are accepted relatively unthinkingly are likely to become matters of contention and debate. Lowndes (1994) has developed this argument, maintaining that at times of institutional stability, action is more likely to be norm-governed than during times of institutional change, when rational, strategic action is more likely. When institutions are stable, people are likely to operate in terms of taken-for-granted, everyday understandings, not questioning rules and traditional methods of operation. At times of change, everyday action may come to have much wider significance, and matters which have raised little interest or concern in the past are likely to be questioned because they become linked to the more general institutional framework of constitutional and collective choice rules. Individuals and organizational groups are more likely to become aware of their interests and how they are affected by organizational procedures.

To take an example from the public service in the last few years, there is now great concern and conflict about how overhead costs are to be dealt with. Until the 1980s this was a matter to which the members of public organizations gave little concern; now they are matters of great conflict since they affect operational budgets and contract prices. The reason for this is the way that the collective choice and constitutional rules that define property rights, and therefore resources and rewards, have changed. Relations with voluntary organizations provide another example, with relatively informal grant-based relationships being challenged, in favour of more formalized contractual approaches, which are seen as the proper way to do things and as allowing clearer responsibility and firmer control.

Major change serves to disrupt existing power structures and make clearer the interest structure of the organization. Dominant interests must face up to challenging interests (Alford 1975). It is for this reason that strategic action by organizational members is more likely at a time of change and disruption. We cannot assume that others will behave as they have in the past and their action cannot be taken for granted. In 'normal times' people can be seen as playing a game against nature, that is the natural operation of the organization. At times of change they are playing a game against others, whose actions may affect outcomes. Major change is likely to challenge existing power structures, though, at the same time, those in power will have the ability to resist change. The powerful may try either to ensure that change does not affect them or that they can structure change in such a way that it operates in their interests.

Dunleavy (1991), building on public choice theories, has argued that public service bureaucrats will try to shape organizations in a way that suits their interests, and we will argue that this process has been at work in contracting. People's ability to shape organizational change in a way that reflects their interests will be influenced by the level of uncertainty. If the results of the introduction of a particular rule are difficult to predict, then they are likely to act to minimize the risk that they face. This would suggest that organizations will be structured not only to enhance power and interests, but to minimize the effect of unforeseen events. Contracts are likely to be written in a defensive way to try to cover every contingency. Generally public organizations have adopted risk-avoidance approaches to contracting.

As Pettigrew has put it: 'the management of strategic change involves consideration of not only the content of a chosen strategy, or even of the analytical process which reveals various content alternatives, but also the management of the process of change and the contexts within which it occurs' (1987: 5). Following this we can see the context for radical change as either external to or internal to the organizational system with which we are concerned (Pettigrew *et al.* 1992). The external context can be those individuals and organizations that can set the rules of the game to one degree or another, notably central government as lawmaker and controller. We have illustrated the importance of central government in changing the nature of public service management, but it can also be important in setting detailed rules. The number of rules and regulations published on the detailed regulation of competition in health, social care, and local government has been enormous. The second aspect of the external context of the organization is the context of work, for example the market within which an organization must operate. Studies have shown the way that market stability and predictability influence organizational structures and strategies. A further aspect of the work context of the organization is the interorganizational field in which it must operate. As theorists have argued, the operation of networks is central to much contemporary organizational development. This factor is increasingly significant in the public service, where cross-organizational working is unavoidable.

Finally, one of the ways in which organizations will deal with the requirement to introduce new modes of operation will be to decouple the different elements. In the case of contracts they may separate out the contract-based elements from the rest of the organization, but this will be more difficult to do where the organization is tightly coupled and the influence of contracts is more pervasive. A key issue will be the extent to which change impacts on many or few aspects of organizational functioning.

Language

Language plays a central role in the way that change happens in organizations. Typically, change, particularly of the fundamental sort with which we are concerned, will involve the introduction or development of a new language. The attempt to express and understand a new reality is likely to require a new vocabulary.

This has clearly been the case in the public service, where the language of the professional bureaucracy has been challenged by the language of the market. To some extent, change is a matter of getting people to speak a new language as much as of getting them to act in a different way. This is particularly so in the case of public services, where there may be less opportunity to influence through automation of work processes.

In this context, Newman (1994) has shown how the introduction of the new business language and the managerial agenda with which it has been associated has crucially shifted the basis on which equal opportunities policies have been introduced into the public sector. At the same time, she argues, the terms in which these policies have been articulated has glossed over more fundamental concerns about jobs, pay, and conditions of service for women. Another example she cites is the use of the concept of 'quality' as one whose flexibility makes it susceptible of adaptation to a wider variety of different agendas (but see also Gaster 1995).

Language expresses new forms of the categorization of activity, which form the basis for new patterns of interaction, and new modes of control. A change, for example, from service planning to business planning reflects a change from professional autonomy to managerial control. The language of the organization is likely to be driven by the dominant ideas that inform change. The more radical the change the more we would expect this to be expressed in language change.

MARKETS AND PUBLIC SERVICES

In the language of institutions, then, we have seen a major reorientation of constitutional and collective action rules in order to introduce new values of entrepreneurial managerialism into the public sector. The governing norms, values, and beliefs of public servants and the metaphors and language they use to make sense of the world are being transformed. The structures within which they work have been reconfigured, first to forge a more direct and transparent link with the interests of users and citizens and, secondly, to align the incentives obtaining to those likely to create productive efficiency. A concomitant of this is to replace authoritative hierarchical planning with the hidden hand of market-price mechanisms, linked to the exercise of influence.

One element of the challenge facing public servants is that the language of markets has a highly elaborated code and the rules of action emanating from it are equally highly contingent. Simple metaphors derived from the ABC of perfect competition are, then, unlikely to suffice. This section attempts to raise some initial questions about the nature of the conditions which are likely to be faced within public sector markets and their resultant consequences. These questions will form the basis of our analyses of market conditions in case study sites.

The Maximization of Utilities at the Margin

In markets, individual consumers are said to maximize their marginal utilities through their purchasing decisions. Their preferences can therefore be inferred from their behaviour and there is no need to enquire further. This process in turn leads to productive efficiency in which the cost of any aggregate balance of quality and quality so desired is minimized.

Of course many have questioned these assumptions. Self (1993: ch. 7), for example, argues that we need a political theory of markets, in which normative and coercive means of motivation and attachment and the exercise of power are given proper regard. Leaving these issues aside, there are difficulties in applying such assumptions to quasi-markets in general and also to the particular ones created for the services with which we are concerned.

To illustrate the general point, we may examine the avowed purposes of the reforms. Bartlett and Le Grand (1994) characterize these as responsiveness to users, choice, equity, and productive efficiency. Hood (1991) argues that these values overlay, rather than replace, other principles of public services connected to the need for legitimacy and probity, on the one hand, and robustness and the avoidance of market failure, on the other. There are thus a variety of preferences, but it is not clear how these are to be balanced—what premiums might be paid above market definitions of productive efficiency. What we do know is that these goods are to be free or subsidized at the point of use. Economic theory suggests that this has a marked impact on user preferences and thus their expectations in relation to choice and responsiveness. The tensions between these and the notion of equity—construed in the policy as the optimal balance between 'needs' and use, within the bounds of what the citizenry is deemed willing to pay—are never explored.

A related issue concerns the nature of the services themselves. Heginbotham (1993) suggests that welfare-consuming differs from market-consuming because many of the goods are experience goods, with an element of co-production, and that experience itself is often conditioned by a need to consume them rather than by pleasure in their consumption. At the extreme, of course, there is a strong element of public good rather than individual good involved in their consumption. The net effect is that some standard means of expressing preference, such as choice at the point of entry, may not be sufficient. Certainly, many of the goods are complex and multidimensional and it is not always clear that collective purchasers will have the same marginal preferences as the aggregate of their users. In health, for example, users may place a higher value on local pride, accessibility, and ease of use than health purchasers concerned to maximize productive efficiency and the availability of technical expertise.

A further element of the complexity of the goods concerns the possibility and cost of specifying and monitoring outcomes. We return to this issue shortly in our discussion of contracts. However, it is important to note at this point the consequences of the particular reforms imposed upon local purchasing agents.

Webb and Wistow (1982) argue that effective implementation of policies by sub-governments depends upon the congruence between policy streams about governance, resources, and services. What is remarkable about these reforms is the tightness of their injunctions about governance and resources and the looseness of those about services. The locus of political decisions about service priorities and about the means of achieving them often rests with local professionals and managers as a result of a serial process of decentralization (of blame?).

Following this line of argument, there is a 'democratic deficit' in relation to the setting of service priorities, while the restrictions over governance and resources will inhibit the maximization of utilities at the margin. An illustration concerns decisions about whether to internalize or externalize the production of particular services, under conditions of uncertainty. Williamson (1975) argues that:

The internal organisation of productive activities permits parties to . . . deal with uncertainty and complexity in an adaptive and sequential pattern . . . Decisions taken within an organisation may deal with the existence of bounded rationality more efficiently than the market . . . because future contingent prices do not have to be specified in advance.

Thus, under competitive conditions, rational decisions would evolve among a range of actors having the freedom to make them. Local purchasers in our quasi-markets are not subject to competition. Patently, too, their freedom is markedly constrained: *some* health decision-makers are forbidden to internalize services, whereas others are not; some of the costs of externalization, such as duplicated management and contract specification, have to be met before local government (CCT) services can be internalized; there are severe disincentives to the internalization of social services. We will need to explore the practical impacts of these constraints.

Market Motivations and Structures

A precondition of market operations is that competition exists or is possible. Of course, the ideal is that market structure should be sufficiently diverse that neither individual purchasers nor individual providers can exert a significant effect upon it. This might apply to cleaning services in our case. Our empirical studies explore the extent of local competition, but it is evident from the outset that public authorities are significant if not monopsonistic purchasers of services which themselves tend to monopoly in provision. This is not least because of the requirement for local consumption of goods, many of which contain high levels of asset specificity in equipment or expertise, and many of which are subject to considerable economies of scale and scope. The clearest case is of hospitals, especially with the growing demand for centres of excellence. As a result, there may not be a great deal of competition *within* any local field. The less stringent condition is of serial competition *for* the field, informed by behaviour in similar fields elsewhere—or, at the very least, contestability. One difficulty in making judgements on these issues is that the reforms are too recent to judge their dynamic impact in creating competition. Thus our focus will largely be upon the prospects for competition and the signs of its emergence. It is worth noting, however, that experience elsewhere is mixed. Propper (1992), for example, suggests that US health-care systems are becoming less competitive, not least owing to the nature of the good and the way that the conditions of entry favour the incumbents. We must also be aware of signs of collusion among providers in ostensibly competitive positions.

One interpretation is that collusion between purchaser and provider is also to be avoided. This is more evident in the CCT reforms and local government standing orders than elsewhere. The theoretical argument here belongs to a whole series of second-order propositions as to how to apply the law of second best when competition is less than perfect. To take one example, it may be best to counterpose monopoly on the provider side with monopoly on the purchaser side. This is especially the case where conditions are uncertain and the cost of specifying services, subject to varied contingencies, is high, as is the cost of monitoring outcomes and the risk of opportunism. Hence, close relations based on a combination of trust and high penalties for its abuse might be appropriate.

Another example concerns the motivations of actors. A precondition is that all providers are motivated at least in part by financial considerations and are subject to hard budget constraints, risking their own demise unless they achieve reasonable levels of efficiency. Again, however, where the chances of opportunism are high it may be important to constrain utilitarian motives by normative ones.

In all of these instances, however, it will be the beliefs of actors about the world, rather than its objective state, which will be important and those beliefs will not yet be leavened by extensive experience. Thus, we shall be concerned to explore the attempts by both purchasers and providers to behave competitively—and what they mean by that term—whether or not their structural position is conducive to such behaviour.

Quasi-Markets

We have already raised some of the questions arising from the fact that purchasers are acting on behalf of users. (Are collective citizens/taxpayer interests the same as the sum of user preferences? Are lay and expert preferences similar?) Additionally, we might ask whether purchasing agents are sufficiently in touch with users' preferences that they can judge how to maximize marginal utilities. This arises especially in cases of bilateral monopoly, where large-scale purchasers are distant from their constituents and at risk of developing cosy relationships with major providers. However, it is not limited to these situations. Gronbjerg (1993) argues that providers of US welfare services incur high transaction costs for the sake of high opportunity gains. Purchasers are content to absorb these costs on users' behalf, for the sake of their own gains in convenience and legitimation. Thus the diagnosis by public choice theorists may hold good in the case of some of their own prescriptions.

A further question concerns access to information. Does the purchasing agent have better access to a wider range of relevant information than users? If not, the argument for having an agent is weakened. One case in point is the use of the local authority as the purchasing agent for school cleaning. In this case the rules allow schools to internalize their own contracting and our later analysis explores the outcome of such discretion. Normally, however, relevant information of varying types and levels of generality is dispersed among users and a variety of staff within purchasing and providing organizations. This is a significant complication in applying the theory of principals and agents, as we shall see.

Quasi-markets may also be subject to the problems of adverse selection, especially under conditions where service requirements are uncertain or indistinct, while resource constraints are severe. The relative costs of general or specialist surgical facilities or arguments about the staffing of welfare services are cases in point. Here the arrangements for regulation and evaluation become important.

Finally, we must enquire about the extent of cream-skimming—provider selection of the most promising, most convenient, and most profitable of users—which the incentives and safeguards allow.

THE NATURE OF CONTRACT

Contract, in its traditional, neoclassical, form is a relatively impersonal process in which the parties to an agreement state their formal commitments to each other. They may be held to these commitments and, should they fail to honour them, sanctions may be brought to bear. The law stands behind the agreement, as the means of resolving differences. The contract serves to allocate risks, responsibilities, and rewards precisely between the parties to the contract. The relationship between client and contractor is limited to matters specifically concerned with the exchange. The time limit of the contract is strictly defined. Terms and conditions of contract are written, detailed, and cover the substantive issues.

This approach to contracting fits with the world of neoclassical economics; as Campbell and Harris (1993: 166) argue, it assumes:

contractual promises to be the legal expression of rational utility-maximising individuals making discrete exchanges in perfectly competitive markets. There is a strong implication bound up in this assumption that the parties to a contract would rapidly alter their allocative decisions should changed circumstances offer them the possibility of realising profits in excess of those to be realised by performance of the existing contract.

Contracts are seen as complete, and ambiguity to be avoided. The obligations of parties to the contract are seen as absolute, and opportunism is to be assumed. Economic criteria provide the basis of judgement of the value of contracts. This understanding of the nature of contract can be seen as inadequate in two ways: it does not represent the reality of the great majority of contractual relationships, and it is inadequate in its understanding of the nature of contract. Empirical studies of contracting have found that the classical understanding of the nature of contract simply misrepresents what actually happens (Macauley 1963; Beale and Dugdale 1973). It is common for contracts to be vague about risks and responsibilities, to ignore sanctions that are available for failure to perform, and to be imprecise about time. Contracts are deliberately left incomplete in many cases. Contracting parties are highly likely to behave in ways that have little to do with, or contradict, what the contract states. Gordon (1985: 659) argues the role of contract is to act as a bounding mechanism; the objective of contract is not primarily to allocate risks, but to signify a willingness to cooperate.

It is the social process of contracting that is important, not the contract itself, about which the parties to the relationship may be relatively ignorant. The result is that the distinction between 'market', the world of contract, and 'hierarchy' (Williamson 1978; 1985), the world of organization and authority, is far from clear (Stinchcombe 1990; Stinchcombe and Heimer 1985). As Richardson (1972: 884, quoted by Loasby 1991: 84), says: 'by looking at industrial reality in terms of a sharp dichotomy between firm and market we obtain a distorted view of how the system works'. People contracting on the market are likely to behave as if they are in a continuing organizational relationship, and as we shall see, people in organizations may behave as if they were in formal contract relationships.

Classical concepts of contract are inadequate to the understanding of more complex relationships. As Macneil (1980: 45) argues, contracts are more to do with relationships than with what is to be exchanged: 'planning how to do things and how to structure operating relations, rather than simply defining what is to be exchanged has come to dominate a great deal of modern contract'. The purpose of contract is to make the future more tractable by developing both mechanisms for dealing with unforeseen events, and through establishing patterns of social relationship and communication that will be robust. Highly formalistic approaches to contracts may be seen as preventing the development of precisely those social relationships that are necessary to make them work. As Hirsch (1977) has argued for the social system more generally, there is a danger that the world of contract is dependent, for its effective operation, on a value base that it itself tends to erode. Uncertainty is inevitable, and ambiguity may have value as a means of ensuring the possibility of adaptation.

'Relational' Contracts and Enforcement

The argument of 'relational' contract theorists is that the contract must be socially as well as technically sufficient (Heimer 1985). It must be able to cope with unforeseen circumstances. It must also be able to deal with problems of observability, information asymmetry and the possibility of opportunism. The argument that is made increasingly strongly is that trust is basic to the effective operation of contracts, as, indeed, it is to that of organizations (Fox 1974; Miller 1992; Arrow 1974). Vagueness and ambiguity may contribute positively to the development of trust by creating the need for interaction and negotiation (Colson 1975).

Theorists of relational contracting are concerned with how contracts work in practice, not with the detail of what they say. The courts, too, have been increasingly concerned with what contracts are intended to do, rather than what they say (Atiyah 1979; Reiter 1981). If the role of contracts is to establish relationships, then they may deliberately be left vague, and formal legal institutions should be wary of interpreting them strictly or implying terms (Trakman 1983).

In extreme cases, contracts may be self-enforcing, requiring no process of monitoring by the contractor. This may happen where the output is immediately observable, and responsibility for failure clear and apparent. In such cases the client/purchaser can simply not pay for poor work or work not done. Such obvious cases are rare. Output, even in simple services, may be hard to observe. Responsibility may not be clear. The contractors may have done their best, but circumstances may have been against them. Absolute responsibility and absolute liability may be difficult to determine and allocate. Self-enforcement is possible even where the output cannot be observed. Clients may, for example, rely on a degree of self-enforcement where contractors have a great deal to lose should they be found to fail. Where reputation is important then contractors are likely to be more careful of their performance. The 'shadow of the future' will be important here, in that whether contractors will cheat will depend upon whether a one-off failure in quality will damage long-term income. Self-enforcing conditions are more likely to arise in continuing that one-off relationship, since the relationship itself will be valued (Axelrod 1984).

Where self-enforcement is not likely, then the client is thrown back on sanctions, incentives, or values. Sanctions may involve the deduction of money, requirement to repeat or actually to perform the work, delay in payment, termination of contract, or refusal to work with a contractor again. Incentives may be more appropriate than penalties, especially where output depends on the commitment of the contractor. Many purchasing relationships (Sako 1992) emphasize the importance of the parties to contracts operating with common norms and values. Even if the argument for contract is based on purely utilitarian principles, rather than promise or duty, commonly held values may have benefits. Economists have increasingly seen organization culture as allowing more effective communication and control (Casson 1991; Miller 1992; Kreps 1990), and the same is true of contracts.

The argument for relational contracts does not imply the abandonment of sanctions. Clauses allowing the deduction of money for failure by the contractor may fulfil a function that goes further than simply allowing the client to punish the contractor. Clauses that may be enforceable in law, as constituting penalties, may be valuable in conveying information about contractors. Those who are confident of their ability to provide good service are more likely to be confident of their ability to avoid penalties (Klein 1980). More firmly established contractors may be confident of their ability to bear sanctions.

Quality

Quality is related crucially to issues of information asymmetry and observability. Where quality is immediately apparent objective contract monitoring is possible. Even then it may not be possible to measure performance qualitatively, and this creates difficulties in the use of sanctions for breach of contract. Detailed assessment of quality may be difficult even in the case of simple material goods as studies of diamonds and fish markets have shown (Kenney and Klein 1983, Wilson 1980). In the case of services the definition of quality is difficult, because of their intangibility. If the assessment of quality cannot be based on a grading system then the danger is that purchasers are reduced to the decision of whether the service is acceptable or unacceptable. Quality may then fall to the lowest acceptable level, the situation analysed by Akerlof in the study of the market for 'lemons' (Akerlof 1984).

Inputs and Outputs

It may also be difficult to observe inputs to the contract, that is the 'effort' which is made by the contractor to provide an effective service. It will often be difficult to determine whether the contractors simply did not try hard enough, or circumstances were against them. Where more than one party is involved then it may be difficult to determine relative contributions (Alchian and Demsetz 1972). Economists have argued that where it is difficult to monitor inputs, then the best approach is to base assessment simply on outputs: 'Where monitoring is very costly, and effort and state of the world are "effectively" unobservable, contracts will depend upon the outcome alone' (Ricketts 1987: 145). The problem, though, is that the output may also be unobservable, for example in the case of personal services.

In practice it seems just as likely that products will be treated as 'credence' goods, in which we must have faith in the producer. The observability of inputs, outputs, and the relationship between the two, is related to the extent to which the liability of contractors can be seen as absolute or qualified. It would seem unfair to hold contractors absolutely liable for their performance if they have little ability to control outcomes, because they cannot easily monitor it. In the extreme, neither client nor contractor may be very clear about what is happening in complex and ill-understood technologies (Strauss *et al.* 1985).

The purchaser may oppress the provider as much as the provider may behave opportunistically. This is particularly likely where outcomes are a matter of judgement, rather than being strictly measurable. Barber (1989: 61) discussing the management of building contracts argues:

Contractors may, however, be limited and responsibilities may even be affected by the frequent reference in the standard form of contract to the 'satisfaction of the supervising officer'. Are contractors expected to be psychic and anticipate what standard will satisfy the supervising officer's subjective opinion of the matter . . . such references probably require no more than compliance with the specification applied objectively. The confusion would be avoided if the myriad references to the supervising officer's satisfaction were removed, and replaced (except where specifically intended) by a general term empowering him to reject and require removal of work not complying with the specification.

An approach based upon 'removal' of poor work, and rectification, cannot be operated in many cases. Since services frequently go out of existence as they are produced, they may not be amenable to correction. Poor work by doctors, lawyers, and other professionals may not be reversible.

Reputation

Where observation of inputs or outputs is difficult then the reputation of the provider is likely to be important. If reputation is important to the contractor's competitive position in the market, then contract failure may be more significant in damaging that reputation. It may be difficult to observe output, but, if failure is observed, it may have more severe consequences than the provision of a poor batch of material goods. Even a low chance of observation of poor work or shirking may provide incentive to those for whom the importance of reputation is high. Reputation will depend upon the commitment of the contractor to the particular market. If a provider has invested in equipment or skills which cannot easily be transferred to another use, then exit from the market is difficult. Reputation will also be important in contestable markets (Baumol *et al.* 1982). Purchasers may increase the importance of reputation by tying providers into markets.

Information problems mean that a contract can never be complete, covering all eventualities. Even if it were possible completely to describe the work to be done, and the relationship between client and contractor, it would often be hugely expensive to do so. The costs of preparing contracts and specifications which are relatively incomplete are commonly 5 to 10 per cent of the overall contract value. Coping with an uncertain future may best be done by deliberately leaving the contract incomplete, as is done with the labour contract, allowing direction of staff as circumstances change. Contracts will often contain variation clauses enabling the parties to deal with changing circumstances. Major changes may be dealt with by break clauses that allow periodic renegotiation of the terms of the relationship.

Transaction Costs

These various difficulties in the contract relationship create transaction costs, that is, costs of preparing contracts and specifications, letting contracts, and managing contract performance. Williamson (1985) has argued that it is transaction costs that will determine the nature of the governance of economic transactions. Organizations are seen as being established on the basis of the search for efficiency. It is not necessary to accept this argument to see the notion of transaction costs as significant in assessing the effectiveness of different modes of economic organizations. Particular contract approaches are likely to reflect the relative power of clients and contractors, but also the cost of creating detailed contracts and work specifications. In cases where the investment is low it is not likely to be worth writing detailed contracts and specifications.

Identities and Relationships

Traditional contract approaches imply that the identities of the client and contractor are clear, and that the world is one of principals and agents. In complex contracts there are likely to be more than two partners to the exchange. The world is not so much one of principals and agents, but a world of intertwined principal and agent relationships. Contract rights and relationships may be difficult to define in certain cases. It may also be difficult precisely to identify who the parties to the contract are, for example where there is extensive use of subcontracting, or where there are subsidiaries and parent companies. As we shall argue this is a particular issue in the case of contracts in local government and social care.

The contrast between 'markets' and 'hierarchies' is not easily drawn. In practice, organization has strong elements of contract, and the contractor/client relationship may look very like the organizational relationship of employer and employee. As Stinchcombe and Heimer (1985: 126) argue:

A structure with legitimate authority, with a manipulable incentive system for adjusting costs, quantities and prices, with a structure for dispute resolution and with a set of standard operating relationships, works very much like a hierarchy, very little like a competitive market. Yet all these features of hierarchy are routinely obtained by contracts between firms in the same sector of the market.

The difficulty of distinguishing market and hierarchy will be greater the more there is an extensive nexus of contracts or treaties (Aoki *et al.* 1990). There is a dimension from pure hierarchy to pure markets, that might look something like Figure 2.1.

The relationship between client and contractor will be influenced by all the

Employment Contract and Hierarchy
↓
De-centralized Accountability and Authority
↓
Devolved Budgetary Control
↓
Joint Enterprise
↓
Preferred Suppliers
↓
Trust-based Contracts
↓
Spot Market

FIG. 2.1. A continuum of relationships

factors discussed above, namely risk, trust, the observability of inputs and outputs, the extent to which quality can be defined, the time-span of the relationship, and the extent to which client and contractor can be precisely identified.

SUMMARY AND CONCLUSIONS

In this chapter we have introduced and described our approach to the main issues, through the study of institutions. First, we have defined what they are and identified the different levels at which they function. Next, we have explored the significance of the rules under which they operate and the way in which these rules affect the attachment of people to organizations. The significance of change and the ways in which pressures from the external environment in which institutions function impact upon them provides the context for the introduction of 'marketization' into the public sector. This has brought with it significant changes in the content and use of language. Finally—and crucially—we have described and evaluated the nature of contracts, and begun the process of identifying the key issues arising from their introduction.

In Chapter 3, we will describe how contracts came to be introduced into the public sector and take up a number of the key issues: risk, trust, quality, how inputs and outputs can be identified, and the costs of contracting and default. All these themes are then followed through in greater detail in the case studies that form the meat of our study.

3

The Introduction of Contracts

In this chapter, our focus is on contracts as such. We will draw upon work we have done on contracting in the three selected service areas (local government (CCT), health, and social care), for, as a general rule, it is the institutional context that will exercise a decisive influence on the way in which contracts are introduced into public organizations and the impact that they have within them. The traditional approach to the organization of the public service has involved relatively open-ended and incomplete contracts of employment, which the organization completes by the exercise of authority. The introduction of the 'new public management', with its logic of action drawn from private-sector models, involves the development of contracts that are more complete and closed. The type of contract that has been introduced can be seen as varying along three dimensions: focus, form, and content.

The *focus* of the contract refers to whether it is specified in terms of inputs, methods, or performance; that is, what is required to do the work, how the work is to be done, or what are the results to be achieved. We would expect a closer focus on results where the nature of the work is difficult to specify. It is also important, in this context, whether the contracts are broadly or narrowly focused. Refuse collection is an example of an area where contracts will be narrowly drawn; acute specialities in health is one where they will characteristically be broad.

The *form* of the contract refers to level of formality, whether the contract is based on a fixed or variable price, and how it deals with the relationship between quantity and price. These choices will be affected by the legal context, but also by the way that purchasers and providers approach risk.

The *content* of the contract deals with issues of how the services are to be provided, how they are defined, and the nature of contract conditions covering such issues as arbitration, variation, and default.

The various different approaches to contracting involve contractors in taking up different positions on a number of practical issues thrown up by the introduction of the contracting process into the service sectors which we have chosen to study. Among the most important of these are three linked issues to which we will be devoting particular attention in this chapter. These are: methods of dealing with *risk,* problems of ensuring *quality,* and the use of *default* to cope with problems of unsatisfactory performance.

On risk, as we saw in Chapter 2, the general tendency has been for the client, who is naturally highly risk-averse, to write the contract so that it is the provider who bears the greater risk. This applies even where it might seem to be more efficient for the client to do so, as in the case of voluntary organizations bidding for small contracts in social care (Walsh 1995*a*). The economics of public service contracting suggests that government should be an efficient bearer of risk (McAfee and McMillan 1988). But setting fixed price contracts, which might appear to minimize risk, may lead to a decline in the next key area, that of quality. For example, in the USA there is some evidence that this practice leads to more early discharges from hospital, with the result that patients go home 'quicker and sicker' (Walsh 1995*a*).

Quality is liable to pose particular problems where it cannot easily be defined and may be difficult to observe. These problems have led in turn to pressure to install more effective machinery for monitoring both the process of service delivery and outcomes. Here, much will depend upon the character of the information that is available and the way in which access to it is distributed—whether providers have more information than purchasers (Propper 1992). In some cases, the service will have been relatively simple to specify before the contract is let and it will be easy to establish whether performance has been satisfactory. In others, monitoring may involve adopting a variety of elaborate procedures for surveillance and evaluation (see Gaster 1995: ch. 7).

An alternative approach in the sectors we have studied involves attempting to reinforce the commitment of the contractor by aligning their values more closely to those of the client or choosing contractors who are believed to share the same values. As one of us has written elsewhere:

in the case of contracts for community care, a great deal of attention is typically given to ensuring that the contractor's philosophy is in line with that of the purchaser. Internal contracts tend to rely more upon the alignment of values than those with external providers, and the internal contractor may be required to follow defined policies on matters such as equal opportunities, training or staff conditions . . . It is easier to ensure commonality of values in long term contracts and if the contracting organisation is not primarily oriented to profit. (Walsh 1995*a*: 128)

The issue of default arises where it has been established that performance is deficient. The purchaser will then need to consider whether to make some form of direct intervention. Many contracts in these service areas contain provisions allowing the client to exercise sanctions; these can take a variety of forms, ranging from deductions from or delays to payment, hiring substitute labour and charging the contractor for it, or, at the extreme, terminating the contract. However, the use of these sanctions by way of default procedures poses a number of legal and practical difficulties, which is why the general emphasis in contract management in the areas studied has tended to be on maintaining good relations with the contractor.

All these contract variables will be affected both by external pressures and by the internal context of the organization responsible for them. For example, in the case of local government the way that contracts are to be specified has been partly laid down in government and other regulations. In the health field, the National Health Service Management Executive has given guidance on how contracts should be written. A key feature of the external context will be the nature of the market, notably the degree of competition and the rate of change and stability. The internal context of change will be important, notably the balance between professionalism and managerialism and the attitudes towards contracting and markets. The nature of the service will have a key influence, through the impact on the degree to which the service can be specified, and the ease with which performance can be monitored. The management of contracting will also be affected by the content of change—the various elements that go to make up the new market approach—and the way in which they interact with each other. In sum, the impact of contracts needs to be understood within the total institutional context within which they operate. We return to these issues when reviewing our case study material in Chapter 8.

CONTRACTS IN CONTEXT

The three specific sectors that we have selected for further examination (selected local government services, health, and social care) present instructive contrasts in terms of the functions that contracts have been introduced to perform. They are employed in contrasting environments, where markets function differently and different regulatory frameworks are in place. Thus, it is not surprising that the three sectors being considered differ in the degree to which enforceable contracts have been introduced. In the National Health Service, the vast majority of contracts are internal quasi-contracts which are not enforceable in law, though there is a limited tendency to move towards external, enforceable contracts. In social care, the introduction of the mixed economy of care largely involves external enforceable contracts with voluntary and private providers. There has been relatively little development of internal quasi-contracts (Wistow *et al.* 1994). In local government, there are both external, enforceable contracts and internal quasi-contracts. Within the local authority there is strong enforcement of an internal, contract-based, trading regime; direct services and direct labour organizations must behave as if they were private providers and win tenders for work. This regime is considerably more rigid than that prevailing in health. Given these differences one would expect contracts to vary in form and content from one sector to another. In this section we consider the overall character of contracts in each sector, and the way in which they deal with issues of risk, quality, and default. We also touch upon the important issue of users and their interests. The discussion is intended to give a broad flavour of the nature of contracts as an introduction to our case studies, rather than to provide a detailed account.

However, we have also been able to draw upon our own detailed analyses of contracts in two of the three service areas, health and social care. These are based on a sampling of contracts in these areas; the results have already been published elsewhere (Smith and Thomas 1993; P. Smith 1994). Our case studies also yielded interview material on which we drew here. In the case of local government, we have had access to work previously undertaken and to the Local Government Management Board's database on contracts.

Local Government Contracts

Local authority contracts are typically highly detailed, involving hundreds or even thousands of pages of documentation, and often more than fifty contract conditions. There has been some pressure to introduce performance or output-based contracts, but there have up to now been few practical developments, despite pressure from the Audit Commission (1993a). As contracting is extended to white-collar, professional services, notably housing management, there is more emphasis upon the general philosophy of service as opposed to performance contracting. One housing contract says, for example, that the aim is:

To provide high quality services that are

responsive—to what local people want and need
sensitive—to people as individuals: this means valuing people as customers, citizens and employees; and providing services in a caring manner
high standard—every job is well done with attention to quality
effective—in their impact, meeting needs and satisfying customers
efficient—in their organization, giving value for money.

Such statements are also common in leisure management contracts, but, overall, the emphasis is still strongly on inputs and methods of work, which are fairly clear for such services as refuse collection.

Approaches to risk vary, but the general emphasis is on shifting risk to the contractors, for example through making them responsible for coping with variations in the quantity of work or the impact of external factors such as the weather (see Chapter 7). As one client-side officer said:

We aim to be perfectly candid with the contractor. We say for example that we are going to provide public events in parks. You will find it difficult to do the maintenance work because of that, but that's just tough. You have to do it.

Monitoring procedures that may lead to default have sometimes been introduced: these specify both levels of performance (for example the proportion of streetlights that are in working order) and the sanctions taken if the standard is not met.

These issues are likely to affect all the different types of service providers: both external contractors and the internal direct service and direct labour organizations (DSO/DLO). For example, one respondent commented: 'The DLO do feel that they are at risk and the client side is at no risk.'

However, it is not necessarily the case that the contractor bears all the risk in practice, even if clients may want that to be so. Here, the feasibility of codifying information and symmetry in access to it will be crucial. The contractor, for example, may have significant information advantages:

The problem of the contract was that it was a new service and we did not know very much. We really did too heavy a specification. Only the catering manager on the contractor side was able to look at the specification when he got it and point out that it was too high. We wanted five hot meals but that would have been too expensive.

The actual distribution of risk will be the result of a complex interaction of factors including the nature of the work, the form of the contract, the impact of external events, and the availability of information. It will also include cultural factors to do with the legacy of past relationships. For example, DSOs are seen on the one hand as contractors but on the other as linked to the council and therefore under an obligation to 'give extra'. The way that this is dealt with will depend upon patterns of risk neutrality and risk aversion in the agencies involved.

The introduction of contracts has led to a clearer focus on the quality of services in local government. In some cases, such as refuse collection, it is relatively easy to state the meaning of quality. In many cases, though, it is difficult to state what quality involves, especially as contracting moves to more complex professional services such as housing and finance. A high proportion of contracts are adopting formalistic approaches to quality, involving the adoption of certificated systems of assurance, such as the BS 5750 'kitemark', although this is becoming less frequent. There is a great deal of debate about the effectiveness of such systems and they may do no more than emphasize formal commitment to quality (Gaster 1995).

Local authority contracts involve complex processes for dealing with default, using a combination of rectification of work, payment delay, warning notices, and deductions from payment. The use of sanctions is common, though levels of deduction of money are relatively low in practice (Walsh and Davis 1993). There is still much argument about the effectiveness of sanctions as against incentives, and over the extent to which a trust-based approach may be developed so that contracts may in effect become self-monitoring. Only in the case of leisure contracts have incentives been extensively developed, with profit-sharing mechanisms. There do not seem to be many significant differences between internal and external contractors in this respect.

Until recently, local authority contracting could be seen as being relatively simple to develop and manage compared with the other cases with which we are concerned. It is comparatively straightforward to assess outputs in most cases, though it may involve high monitoring costs, sometimes as high as 10 per cent of the annual value of the contract. However, this situation is changing as contracting is extended to more complex services such as information technology and housing management. This change will influence the way that responsibility can be allocated. In the case of, say, refuse collection or building maintenance, the test of performance may be relatively objective. However, it should be remembered that performance, as such, is not always the focus of attention— for example, cleaning contracts may be about how many times a room is dusted, not whether it is actually clean. When dealing with contracts for professional services, assessments of performance are necessarily more subjective. There will necessarily be more debate over how effectively providers can be held to account.

As far as the interests of the users of services are concerned, there may be a tendency to omit consultation because the nature of the work is simple and easily observable. However, the environment in which some services are delivered (to schools, for example) is becoming highly politicized, and user interests cannot be overlooked. We develop some of these issues further in Chapters 5 and 7.

Health Contracts

In this section, we will draw upon an analysis of contracts in the health service carried out as part of our ESRC research programme (P. Smith 1994). This analysis is based on a total of 176 contracts, drawn from the first and third waves of contracting in the NHS. In general, contracts in the different parts of the health service vary widely in their form, their objectives, and their emphasis— whether they stress input measures or attempt to define results.

As far as form is concerned, the contracts studied fell into three different categories: block contracts, where the contractor pays an annual fee in return for a defined range of service; cost-per-case, where the price of each individual treatment is specified; and cost and volume contracts, where a baseline level is funded on a block basis and all funding after that is on a cost-per-case basis. In the first wave sample (1991–2), the majority of contracts analysed were block contracts. These contracts varied widely in their sophistication and level of detail.

On content, contracts for health tend to be much less detailed than in local government, especially in the case of contracts let by GP fundholders, which will sometimes (though not invariably) be no more than statements of procedures and prices. Contracts are much more likely to be stated in output terms, for example the number of interventions to be carried out, although these output measures tend to be very unsophisticated (Appleby 1994). Contracts are becoming more developed over time and there is pressure to become more prescriptive, focusing upon the effectiveness of different approaches: 'Purchasers need to be more determined to target resources on clinically effective procedures' (Stockford 1993).

The nature of contract documents differs from local government in being less legalistic and less detailed. They are more likely to be written in everyday language, and to be less precise in defining the work to be done.

Much of the approach to contracting has been affected by constraints upon information. As one purchasing manager said:

We started off with block contracts for most of the output. Data for the preceding two years was sketchy and awful. You could have cost and volume for most of the output but the trouble would be getting the information, which would be difficult.

Problems of information asymmetry are a common feature of the health scene, with the providers usually having privileged knowledge (Kerrison 1993). As a result, there is a great deal of conflict between purchasers and providers over information issues, reflecting the crucial role that these play in the purchasers' activities.

The pattern of risk-bearing in contracts in the NHS is dependent upon the nature of the work, the form and content of contracts, and the impact of external events. Of the different main types of contract used in the NHS, fundholding GPs are likelier to use the more sophisticated 'cost-per-case' contracts (P. Smith 1994; Glennerster *et al.* 1994). These contracts leave most of the risk with providers, unlike block contracts. Their use reflects not only the relative power exercised by fundholding GPs but also the fact that the contracts themselves cover discrete areas of activity which can be more precisely specified than those block contracts which include all or most of the specialities provided. By contrast, the way that risk is distributed in block contracts is dependent upon the accuracy of the assumptions that are built into the specification about workload and the way that variation is dealt with. The contracts normally allow for some variation around assessed workloads, with trigger levels which have to be reached before prices change. In some cases the trigger may be very high; in the past, there were examples of a variation of as much as 15 per cent in workload having been accepted before payments changed. Generally, these contracts involve some degree of risk-sharing but the fact that they treat the reduction and increase of the level of demand similarly would suggest that they would be more favoured by the risk-neutral than the risk-averse. This may well have implications for pricing. The use of marginal cost for deductions for changed amounts of work favours the provider, though there are examples of full-cost deduction.

Risk is increased in health by the fact that contracts are generally for one year, so that it is difficult to manage variations in workload. There have been some cases of flexible contracting through allowing credits or debits for over- and under-performance against plans, but the nature of financing makes such innovations difficult. Of the three sectors it is in health that issues of risk are most difficult to deal with (we return to this theme in Chapter 7).

Health contracts do generally have sections on quality, which tend to emphasize the need for a cooperative, incremental, approach involving both client and contractor. These sections vary from simple statements—such as those cited below—to the inclusion of more detailed declarations about quality, which tend to focus on the environment for care, rather than care itself.

Purchasers and providers have a common interest in continually improving the quality of care.

It is necessary that an incremental approach to quality of service is taken and it is expected that . . . the Authority will work with the unit to determine and agree measures and indicators of quality in services which will be acceptable to the Authority and possible for the unit to achieve.

This may simply be a reflection of the clinicians' dominance of information (Kerrison 1993). As one interviewee, on the purchaser side, said: 'Really it's the provider that does most of the measuring and monitoring of quality at the detailed level, with the purchaser doing very little.' It is natural to attempt to develop methods that can ensure self-monitoring by providers, perhaps through quality-assurance systems.

Although, over time, there has been greater emphasis on sanctions, default measures are only specifically addressed in just over 50 per cent of health contracts examined in our study. Failure was seen as incurring financial deduction in only 15 per cent of contracts. Only 19 per cent of health contracts made specific provision for contract termination for failure of performance (P. Smith 1994). However, as we have seen, 'performance' in this area tends to be defined not in terms of the quality of care actually delivered but by measures like waiting times and achievement of financial targets and 'efficiency savings'. The National Health Service Management Executive has encouraged the 'greater use of sanctions and incentives', though within the 'context of "shared risk"'. Sanctions are most commonly operated when there is failure to supply appropriate information, and failure to meet relatively precise targets such as waiting times. This has been an emphasis that has developed over time and has been sharpened by the impact of the Patient's Charter, which has also provided a focus for the specification of quality and the development of monitoring measures.

The nature of contracting in health reflects the fact that purchasers and providers have very different power bases. The purchaser has the money, but poor information and little detailed understanding of the work. Providers have significant information advantages, but cannot easily demonstrate their effectiveness. The relationship can be seen as taking the form of a set of 'nested games' (Tsebelis 1991).

In summary, contracts for health care are broadly focused, with a primary emphasis on results—though with the development of more effective procedures this may be changing. The main form is still block contracts, though there are various degrees of sophistication within this form. However, the key factor in determining the nature of contracts for health care is the context of the 'managed market', within which they function. This term 'instantly conveys the ambiguities and tensions inherent in the particular process of contracting for health (and social) care' (P. Smith 1994: 22).

Social Care Contracts

To underpin our description of the main characteristics of contracting in this service sector, we can call upon our own earlier analysis of contracts in this area (Smith and Thomas 1993). In this preliminary study, we examined seventy contracts, fifty of them for residential care and the rest for a variety of services.

The form of contracts varied as between the residential and non-residential services. For example, although most of the residential contracts were 'cost-for-case', they are, in effect, 'agreements to trade', which are only activated when an eligible person wishes to enter care. By contrast, non-residential contracts were typically block contracts, usually with a single voluntary organization. Several of these contracts convey a strong flavour of the two agencies 'playing at shops' (Common *et al.* 1992). These contracts reflect a situation in which there are no competing providers and the parties are well known to each other.

On content, social care contracts are typically less detailed than those for other local government services, with fewer legal conditions and limited specifications, though they are tending to become more complex. They are typically more detailed and more legalistic than health contracts. Where there are fewer providers in a local area, however, contracts tend to be less detailed: customer and contractor are likely to be already well acquainted. But the contract relationship in social care is complex because of the involvement of purchasers, providers, users, and, perhaps, even third parties who may contribute to meeting the cost by 'topping up'. There is much debate over whether three-way (or conceivably even four-way) contracts are possible. It is often unclear how the care plan for the individual fits in with the formal contract and how far the commitment in the plan extends (Smith and Thomas 1993). The interaction between the different powers of the parties involved is also often unclear.

In general, social care contracts tend to focus more upon outputs than inputs and methods, sometimes reflecting a lack of detailed knowledge about how services are provided or, in other cases, a different set of priorities. As Ricketts (1994) argues, where monitoring is difficult, the tendency is to focus on outcomes. In contrast to the majority of those in local government, social care contracts typically state broad aims, for example:

The basic aim of this contract is to offer older people the opportunity to enhance the quality of life by providing a safe, manageable and comfortable environment, plus support and stimulation to help them to maximise their potential physical, intellectual, emotional and social capacities.

It is common to emphasize the importance of the general philosophy of the service, implied, for example, in such issues as rights to privacy, dignity, independence, and citizenship, although this raises issues about the form and extent of monitoring. It is easier to rely on general output statements when there is trust in the relationship with the provider, as there is presumed to be with most voluntary organizations.

Risk is more likely to be shared in social care than in local government contracting more generally. Payment for work may be made in advance, or partly in advance and partly in arrears, and may continue for a period after the death of the user. Payment may be made when users are absent. Prepayment is particularly likely to be made in contracts with voluntary organizations. These are generally prone to take a different form, in part determined by past relationships with these organizations (Deakin 1996).

Those authorities with the most providers, who are operating in circumstances approximating to market conditions, are the most likely to operate tight conditions that leave the risk with the provider. This is most obvious in the case of the level of payment, which is lowest where provision is highest. Notice of termination of the contract without reason is more likely in social care than local government. Such powers create difficulties for providers, and purchasers with many providers are likely to claim such a right without also allowing the provider a similar right to withdraw from the contract.

It is difficult for the purchasers to monitor actual quality in social care despite loudly proclaimed intentions to the contrary. Our interviews suggest that little effective monitoring has actually taken place so far, although improved procedures were being set in place during the term of our research. There are two main approaches to securing quality in social care. The first is to require that providers have a quality assurance system that they can demonstrate to the purchasers. Secondly, for example in domiciliary care, purchasers tend to use select-listing procedures, requiring providers to pass tests of their capacity to deliver quality services before being allowed to become one of the organizations eligible to provide. The right to inspection is also important in this context. Contracts in social care do sometimes specify quality standards over and above those required for registration, but it is difficult to impose these in practice, given choice on the part of the users (see Chapter 5).

The references to quality in social care contracts often devote considerable attention to attempting to define quality. Some purchasers adopt very general statements, such as 'To create an atmosphere which is as ordinary and normal as possible'. Some are more precise: 'The scale, style, furniture and equipment of the home will be of a normal domestic character rather than of an establishment nature.' These difficulties in defining quality create the kind of problems for monitoring described at the start of this chapter; in addition, some quality systems may actually have a distorting effect on the service delivery process.

What is also distinctive about the social care sector is the level of interest in the consequences for users of the introduction of contracting (see for example Flynn and Common 1992; Lewis 1993). The closer involvement of users in the actual process of service delivery in the community care field (in contrast to the position in the other two sectors) may help to explain this marked difference.

Many social care contracts make almost no mention of default. Those that do so tend to depend for remedies on a combination of rectification periods, holding back part of the payment, defraying the added cost of alternative provision onto the provider, or immediate termination. The possibility of making financial deductions is not generally written into the contract, though it is somewhat more likely in shire counties with the highest levels of provision. In practice there has been very little deduction of money from contractors since the community care legislation came into effect. This may be partly owing to the difficulty of defining exactly when and how default has occurred, which in turn stems from the nature of the product itself.

Social care contracts tend not to be legalistic in form, though recent developments are towards greater legalism. The legal status of many of the contracts is unclear, and much debated. In practice it would seem that little notice has been taken of the contract detail, though pressure for clarity from providers is leading towards a situation in which contracts are seen as more central.

At the same time, the steady development of the 'contract culture' gives local authorities, with their continuing central role in this field (see Chapter 1), the opportunity to consider some broader strategic questions about the nature of the market in which they are operating and the changes that they wish to try to bring about in it. The extent to which this has been realized in practice and the effects on relationships between local authorities and provider agencies are key features of the case studies reported in the second half of this book.

CONCLUSION

At the start of this chapter, we set out three different dimensions on which the contracts in our three service sectors could be categorized: focus, form, and content. On all these dimensions, the contrast between the three sectors often proved to be marked.

For example, on content it was noteworthy that both social care and health contracts are typically incomplete, in contrast to those employed for the selected local government services.

Two other striking contrasts are the uneven development of processes for monitoring contracts and ensuring quality, and the different levels of involvement of (or indeed concern for) users and their interests. However, these findings need to be seen against the backdrop of the particular character of the services concerned.

Generally, contracts have been found to be more appropriate in some specific circumstances than others, depending upon uncertainty, asset specificity and opportunism (among other factors). However, no matter how appropriate they may appear to be, the simple contrast that is sometimes made between a managerial world organized through a hierarchy which operates by imposing solutions by authority and a market world operating by contract and automatic adjustment to changing circumstances is simply not valid. Both the organizations and the contract system exist within a regulated structure—they are 'embedded' in an institutional framework. The way that contract functions in each individual situation depends on the way in which those institutional frameworks have been set in place and function.

We have accordingly focused our main effort on analysing the impact of contracts on the ground, through case studies of contracting in the three service areas in various localities. It is to these case studies and our findings from them that we now turn.

4

The Research Investigation

INTRODUCTION

Previous chapters have examined changes in the public sector, in particular the introduction and use of contracts, from a conceptual and theoretical perspective. The discussion has purposely been multisectoral and has sought to explore the origins and influences upon policy development. It is clear that different sectors of the public services have been directed to these policy issues at different times and that the rate of introduction has varied considerably. Therefore, although this project involves a comparative study, it is concerned primarily with the implications of implementation rather than an explicit evaluation of service outcome.

The emphasis of the study, outlined in this chapter, is thus upon tracing the process of change resulting from the introduction of contracting, from policy formulation to operational implementation. We *are* interested in the patterns of response at both an organizational and managerial level. The desire to understand the implications of change at this level and across different sectors suggests that one is inevitably going to encounter a range of forms of implementation. Just as the literature would suggest that there is no single ideal organizational structure (Spurgeon and Barwell 1992) and that managerial behaviours are significantly influenced by external and internal factors (Flanagan and Spurgeon 1995), so the response of different organizations and managers both within and across different sectors to major policy changes will exhibit a variety of forms. The research methodology adopted must be capable of describing and interpreting the richness and diversity of these responses.

There were quantitative aspects to the overall research process adopted, most notably the analysis of a large database of contracts and a survey of attitudes and perceptions of the contracting process. However, the openness, unevenness, and relative novelty of the research canvas confronting us suggested that a case study approach was likely to be most appropriate and most fruitful. Keen and Packwood (1996) advocate this approach as suitable when one is trying to determine the features and relationships that explain the input of a particular intervention or policy initiative.

CASE STUDY METHODOLOGY

Traditionally, the case study method has been viewed as a rather weak approach to scientific enquiry offering somewhat tentative conclusions and limited degrees of generalizability. However, this perspective focuses upon statistical generalizability only. It also derives from a highly positivistic conception of the nature of science, a stance made increasingly untenable by exploration of the philosophy of science; Chalmers (1982) effectively refutes the notion that science is based upon a objective set of facts derived from a detached and pure process of observation.

More positively, Lincoln and Guba (1985) suggest that case study approaches with their emphasis upon qualitative methods:

a) validate and build upon the tacit knowledge the investigator brings to the enquiry;
b) allow for purposive sampling whereby informed choices of site or location enhance understanding of the process being investigated;
c) incorporate the notion that the focus of the design can be adjusted as the process unfolds and issues of particular interest are identified.

A most important feature supporting the choice of case studies in the present study is the capacity of the method to enable a current phenomenon (contracting) to be examined in context. Given the diverse organizational and managerial response predicted, this opportunity to contextualize the pattern observed was critical.

There are, though, other strengths to the case study approach which make its use here entirely appropriate. An effective multiple-site case study requires a coherent framework in order to maximize the learning from different sites. The derivation of this framework is typically via theoretical models about the topic under investigation. In this instance analysis of the theoretical and conceptual material in the previous chapters identified key research questions and hence provided the essential link between the conceptual framework of contracting and implementation in a variety of organizational settings.

Secondly, the framework, by highlighting the key learning issues to be derived from the case study sites, provided a basis for analytic generalizability (as opposed to statistical generalizability), thus facilitating comparison between sites within and across sectors on the key areas. These issues are examined in some depth in the discussion of the case studies in Chapter 8. In keeping with this approach, the case study reports adopt a multisectoral approach and are organized around a number of key issues—structures for contracting, market relationships, contract management, and how these aspects are addressed by each sector.

These major issues are of course reflected in a number of different aspects of both organizational and managerial behaviour. The case study approach affords the opportunity to explore multiple, overlapping issues such as the way policy has been implemented, the structures developed to support implementation, the ways in which the culture of the organization has adapted to new processes, and the roles and relationships played by individuals within it.

Consistency in approach to exploring these issues was obtained through the development of a structured interview schedule built around the issues identified earlier in the theoretical discussion. On-site interviews were supplemented by analysis of supporting documents and contracts themselves.

CASE STUDY SITE SELECTION

A total of twelve case study sites were selected with four each in the health service, local government, and social care. In selecting sites across the sectors, it was important to recognize that local government has had much longer experience and exposure to contracting even if on a specific and limited scale. Social care in contrast has had the least experience of contracting, with the health service somewhere between the other two. Additionally, it was recognized that the structure of the health service with regional health organizations probably contains a more distinct regional flavour than either of the other services.

Recognizing that statistical generalizability was not possible, it was necessary to maximize the positive sampling opportunity by seeking a balance between typicality and authorities which might be described as innovative or interesting. Each site is described briefly below, but in such a way as to preserve its anonymity.

Health Service: Purchaser Authority Case Study Sites

The critical variables in choosing sites were size (budget), rural or urban location, ethnic mix, and sites of 'interest' within a mix of regions. Three regions were represented.

Site A   The authority came into being on 1 April 1992 as an amalgamation of the old DHA with the FHSA. It identifies its key function as to identify the health needs and requirements of the local population and to commission a range of services within the available resources in order to secure the greatest improvements in health possible with the highest quality services. A five-year strategy to enable the authority to deliver its key function and purpose has been laid out in a consultation document, *Strategy for Health and Healthcare Purchasing 1994 to 1999*, where eleven key priorities are identified.

It is one of the smaller health authorities in both geographical and revenue terms, with a population of approximately 293,000 and a budget for 1994/5 of £111m. It is coterminous with the local authority, which is one of the outer London boroughs. Over the last ten years there has been an increase in the very young (0–4 years) and the very elderly (over 85 years) and these two age groups represent the highest users of health services, with the forecasts indicationg increasing usage. It is a relatively healthy area although there are pockets of deprivation around the borough.

The authority presents itself as a 'progressive organization with an open and honest culture'. Its staff are young, relatively inexperienced in substantial management within the health services, but are enthusiastic and ready to try new ways of working towards and learning about their key purpose. There is clear leadership at the top and within the organization to help them work towards commissioning the most appropriate health care for the population, within the resources available. Relationships with the main providers are tense but are steadily maturing as they each become more sure of the contracting process, its impact on their organizations' development needs, and the need to move to a more rational basis for commissioning services.

A key principle for the authority in the commissioning and contracting of health care lies in their intention to 'build up' resources for improving primary care services rather than 'switch from' resourcing acute care services. Consequently, they are building up their knowledge and understanding of primary care, particularly in terms of GP services, with the intention of supporting this with a good research and information base. Attention is also being placed on establishing and developing alternative primary and community-based services, for example community pharmacy, as well as actively involving and consulting local people and groups in the health-needs assessment programme. Joint work with other agencies, particularly social services, is also progressing although the health authority is clearly playing the key enabling role in this process.

Areas which need attention and improvement in this developing process of identifying and refining the contracting process are the effective and efficient capturing of relevant data and information to support both commissioning and contracting and the establishment of a more robust system for monitoring the contracts and integrating this information with the emerging quality assurance processes and standards.

Site B   The health authority has been working towards developing its profile and culture as an integrated Health Commission over a number of years. The chief executives of the DHA and the FHSA agreed upon a joint strategy to achieve a smooth transition at an early stage. A joint commissioning executive which draws in social services has been in existence for a while and the FHSA chief executive now works alongside the chief executive as the deputy chief executive of the joint authority. In order to sustain the transition the authority adopted a much leaner and more tightly structured organization than the other case study sites.

Its 1994/5 budget shows £70m. for acute services, £53m. for primary care services, £19m. for mental health and learning disability and £8m. for maternity services with GP fundholders currently spending around £20m., with a population between 300,000 and 350,000. Key purchasing and contracting decisions are made by two teams for primary and secondary commissioning, although a decision has now been made to relocate all managerial responsibility for commissioning under one directorate. Special attention still needs to be given to the level of the delivery of primary health care as this has had a minimal profile to date and it is likely that separate structures will be maintained for a while within the new directorate to help to achieve this.

The authority presents as a well-managed organization, although there is a still a tendency to lean towards a more bureaucratic style of management, as with older-style DHAs. Energy has been put into getting structures and systems in place to achieve integration and to establish contracting mechanisms and dead-lines to meet the requirements for health commissioning. However, clear evid-ence of the work which has been done on the organization's strategic direction is not as obvious. This has encouraged an introspective approach to contracting to be adopted, in that the organization and the teams tend to look within for ideas and approaches rather than relating the issues to wider environmental analysis.

The top team appear to be considerably distanced from the experiences of the contracting process. Relations with main providers appear to be weak, with the providers feeling that the purchasers act autonomously and that their views are not listened to and valued. Owing to the tight management structure, more junior staff are involved in the contract negotiations than in the teams from the providers. This has caused tension and has been viewed as representing a lack of capability and competence on the purchasers' behalf. As these staff do not always possess sufficient executive authority to make agreements, contracting negotiations have been unnecessarily elongated as validation of these agree-ments has had to be brought back into the organization.

However, locality commissioning is emerging in a positive way. Key people from within the organization act as locality links, which enables an important channel of communication to exist between the joint executive group and the contracting teams. This will now need supporting by effective management in-formation systems as there is no real base within the organization to capture and use data to support the contracting process.

Site C   The health authority was formed in April 1993 as an amalgamation of three HAs and the FHSA. Its brief is to work towards bringing services together on a unified basis across the three districts and the FHSA in order to commis-sion effective and efficient health services.

The authority has a culturally diverse population of 586,500 which stretches across three boroughs. It is pictured as a young, mobile, and growing popula-tion, with higher than average birth rates which throws a wide range of needs and requirements onto the financial resources of the HA. The budget for 1994/5 is approximately £200m.

The authority presents as an intellectually strong organization with many ideas about commissioning, service development, and innovative ways of delivering the new purchaser role. This approach to building a 'thinking' organization is led by the chief executive, although it will be necessary to ensure that ideas are convertible into practice and that they are capable of implementation. A more clearly defined purchasing strategy or five-year plan, as in other case study sites, would help with the implementation of the ideas.

The HA sits as a 'captive audience' for its main providers. It serves one of the poorest population areas in the country and thus its main objective is to maintain and sustain the best possible local services.

Working with the main providers, their clinicians, and bringing the GPs into the highly politicized debate has dominated the formation of the authority's process of commissioning and contracting. This has led to a strong reliance upon the capabilities of individual managers, often in the middle tier, to deal with difficult provider negotiations as well as the complex political forces. This will need to be reinforced by devolving executive authority, along with the management of the process, to the contract managers in the future in order to build credibility with the providers and enhance their capability.

While it has approached the contracting process in a highly mechanistic way, as with other case study sites, the authority has developed both a highly sophisticated information-capture system and a well-structured approach to quality issues to support the contracting process. This has also allowed clearer quality standards to be identified and agreed and for the HA to identify the information it wishes its providers to supply in the contract monitoring process.

Site D   The health authority is undergoing significant change in both its strategic direction and structure and in the style in which it is managed and led. A new joint chief executive was appointed in April 1994 with the brief to move the management of the area's health and social care in a more integrated direction, by bringing the DHA together with the FHSA and balancing the provision of acute services with the building up of primary and social care services. This intention was formally reinforced by the publication of a consultation document, *Purchasing for Health 1994–2000*, in May 1994. This represents a five-year purchasing strategy for the authority, highlighting two major themes for development which are concerned with bringing services closer to people's homes and providing sufficient resources to promote more effective technological acute care.

The health authority is one of the largest in England and Wales with a resident population of 520,000. Its budget for 1994/5 is £330m. representing the authority's medical, pharmaceutical, and optical responsibilities. It is coterminous with the local authority and works in partnership with the city council, CHC (community health council), and local voluntary, trade union, and business umbrella organizations. This initiative represents a city-wide concern for collective action on major issues like community safety, alcohol and drug and substance abuse. However, the city council's zero-growth financial state may present the health authority with additional financial responsibilities in order to ensure that national and local strategies and targets are achieved.

The new chief executive is aiming to open up the organization to change in order to enable it to be more 'fit' for its purpose. This will mean reviewing some of its bureaucratic organizational structures and processes. Planning and implementation groups were formed a few years ago with the intention of giving a more 'matrix' feel to the delivery of the core business. However, in practice, this was integration on the surface with the groups acting as the mechanism for drawing together participants of the DHA and the FHSA with other agencies to consider commissioning and contracting. One consequence was a cross-cutting mixture of participants from both provider and purchaser organizations with little clarity about role and responsibility. Although these issues have now been resolved, attention is being focused on the appropriateness of the groups continuing with both their planning and purchasing roles. Separating the strategic issues of commissioning from the operational issues of contracting is seen as a potential way forward.

Over the years the health authority has placed a heavy investment in acute care and hospital sites such that there is now a need to create a balance across the delivery of all health and social care services in the city. To achieve this a rationalization of the various hospital sites is required in order to maximize their use and release valuable monies for alternative services. The key to success lies in convincing all the stakeholders of the need to break the historical patterns of the delivery of acute services and to relocate resources to areas which more truly represent the population's pressing health needs. This will require the purchasers and providers in the area to work together on common outcomes.

Local Government: Local Authority Case Study Sites

Case-study sites were selected to provide illustrations of experiences of contracting in a range of contexts. The critical variables in choosing sites were

- *size and type of authority*: for example whether the authority was a county, metropolitan district, or non-metropolitan district council;
- *the approach taken to the separation of client and contractor functions*: which are the terms used in local government in relation to compulsory competitive tendering (CCT) to cover users and purchasers (clients/client agents) and providers (contractors). Walsh and Davis (1993) identify a number of approaches, including a *lead client approach* where the 'client agent' role is taken on by the major user of a particular service, who carries out the client (or purchaser) function both for itself and on behalf of all other clients (or users) who may be located in a number of different departments; and more *integrated approaches* (where clients, and contractors, are located in a single department);
- *the extent to which contracting out was a feature*: including authorities where all contracts had been retained in-house through to authorities adopting an enabling role, with delivery functions being transferred to external contractors.

Site E Site E, a Labour-controlled, metropolitan district council had, at the time of the research, retained all contracts, for services subject to CCT under the 1988 Act, in-house. Initially, the emphasis in this authority was on keeping client and contractor functions as close together as permissible and a lead-client approach was adopted. In-house contractors or direct service organizations (DSOs) were located in the same department as the lead client. A client/contractor split was implemented at chief officer level with the latter taking a 'twin-hatted' role.

Later, client and contractor functions in various departments were integrated: most client functions were amalgamated into one single organization and most contractor functions into another single organization.

Site F Site F, a medium-sized county council, spread out over a large geographical area, had a tradition of Conservative control. However, at the time of the research, and following the 1993 local elections, the authority was Labour-controlled. Site F had also adopted a lead-client approach and, as with Site E, contractors were situated in the same department as the lead client, with the client/contractor split at chief officer level.

At the time of the research, some contracts had been lost: three grounds maintenance contracts in the second round of tendering and two building cleaning contracts in the first round. The latter, however, were subsequently awarded to the DSO when the lowest tenderer withdrew.

Site G Site G, a fairly small non-metropolitan district council in terms of population and budget size, although geographically large, had experienced similar patterns of political control to Site F. The tradition of Conservative control was replaced, following the 1994 local elections, with, effectively, Liberal Democrat control. However, prior to this there had been a gradual erosion of Conservative control which had produced an increase in cross-party working.

This authority was an 'enabling' authority in that all 1988 Act services had been contracted out, originally via a management buy-out although services were subsequently tendered and awarded to various other providers (including both private companies and other authorities' DSOs). Prior to the management buy-out, a client/contractor split had been introduced within the technical and amenities department. An integrated client function for all 1988 Act services remained a feature after the buy-out.

Site H Site H, a metropolitan borough council, was politically volatile with swings between Labour control and coalitions (of Conservatives and others). At the time of the research, political control, following the 1993 local elections, shifted from a Conservative/Liberal Democrat alliance to a minority Conservative administration when this alliance broke down.

Decisions on where to locate client and contractor functions were loosely based on the department of major use (a lead-client approach), although there had been some tinkering with this. Approaches to the client/contractor split varied between departments but generally relations were close, with the split either at chief officer level or second-tier level.

All contracts for 1988 Act services (with the exception of two grounds maintenance contracts) had been won in-house at the time of the research.

Social Services: Purchaser Authority Case Study Sites

Case-study sites were selected according to two main criteria:

a) *the size and type of authority*: two county councils and two metropolitan districts were chosen, incorporating one small, two medium-sized, and one large authority. Size was taken as an indicator of organizational complexity and elaboration, with larger authorities being able to allocate more specialist resources to managing changes but facing greater implementation problems owing to the complexity of the existing arrangements;

b) *the approach taken to 'enabling'*, including attitudes towards the independent sector and the approach taken to separating purchaser (client) and provider (contractor) functions. Wistow *et al.* (1992) isolate a range of positions from 'committed enthusiasts' through to 'conscientious objectors'. While we had no representation at the very extremes of this range—especially of the enthusiasm for externalizing services found in some London boroughs —our sample authorities did occupy a variety of positions on it.

Site I Site I is a medium-sized county council, bordering on a conurbation. Overall the age and social structure of its population is unremarkable, and indicators suggest that there are no significantly large instances of social need. This average picture masks a very considerable variety in the social make-up of particular settlements, which includes poor and declining industrial areas, tourist and retirement centres, commercial centres, and market towns. The location of market alternatives to public social services also varies, from virtually nil to over-abundance.

The management of the social services department had in the past been grounded in these different localities. In anticipation of the NHS and Community Care Act, and in line with a county-wide strategy to develop a market-oriented organization, radical change occurred: some services were externalized, and local management was curtailed to allow a purchaser/provider split and more centralized control. However, past financial caution by the Conservative administration was not rewarded, the authority losing out under the charge-capping rules. Thus, the changes were introduced under severe financial stringency leaving the structural changes without concomitant process and cultural changes. A Labour victory, a new director, and the problems arising from the change have led to a retreat from radicalism and a return to more localized and integrated management. While the authority is prepared to work collaboratively with the commercial sector, there remains a preference for public and familiar voluntary sector suppliers and a stronger belief in the ability to develop community resources than in the ability to influence markets.

Site J Site J is a small metropolitan district council. Statistics suggesting that, overall, its social make-up is unremarkable are deceptive, since they conceal marked geographical differences between affluent commuter areas with an established social fabric and impoverished populations almost devoid of formal and informal supports.

The department's modest budget is, none the less, well in excess of that allowed for in the standard spending-assessment calculations, reflecting strong support for social services in an authority in which Conservatives remain a major force. In recent years, however, straitened financial circumstances have meant that the only sources of growth have been specific central government grants, notably the special transitional grant (STG).

The advantages and disadvantages of small size are evident in J, where at least at its strategic apex, the attitude towards the changes can best be characterized as enthusiastic incrementalism. The advantages can be seen in attempts, led by the director, to develop a coherent and systematic range of strategic initiatives towards the creation of an 'enabling authority'. Explicit policy documents —avowing a belief in social care markets as a means of improving choice, responsiveness, and value for money, and an equal belief that these can and will be managed through open partnerships—have received formal political approval. Elements of the strategy include:

- treating users as consumers, by giving them information about services, access criteria, and charges, by accrediting services for them to purchase, by involving them in planning and auditing services;
- 'even-handed' treatment of commercial, voluntary, and in-house services;
- promoting market diversity to allow choice between types of service;
- long-term consultative arrangements with provider and user groups and a commitment to giving early market signals;
- joint planning, commissioning, and market influence with health purchasers;
- other corporate initiatives, such as benefit campaigns and housing strategies, which complement this process;
- the development of information, quality assurance, and performance-monitoring systems.

Contracting is seen as one mechanism by which these strategic relationships can be expressed in the form of explicit agreements. It is also seen as a potential means of managing originally in-house services, whether or not they are formally externalized from the authority which has occurred in some instances and is due to occur in others.

Site K   This is a county council, relatively small in population (400,000) but covering a large geographical area. There are two major urban developments— the county town and a new urban area whose population and industrial base are both due to inward migration. Beyond these, there are a number of small market towns with substantial rural hinterlands. Other than in its dispersion, age and social structures of the population are not remarkable and overall indicators suggest average or below average levels of need.

In the past, the authority was Conservative-controlled and the social services

department's approach was traditional, parsimonious, and localist, with for example, relatively low levels of professionally trained staff and limited development of specialist services. The advent of a Labour administration in the late
1980s coincided with management changes and a commitment to expand services, within financial constraints. The department moved from a structure which
offered 'generic' services based on localities to one which specialized according
to client groups. The expansion occurred within these specialisms and in close
conjunction with the health authority. With the advent of the NHS and Community Care Act this relationship has been formalized into a joint commissioning executive, but some sections of the department have equally close links
with NHS trusts. While the close link with health represents a strategic choice,
the department has not invested heavily in developing clear, overall statements
and directions. Much of its approach has been tactical and incremental, and
for good reason: the authority has been under constant threat of being charge-
capped; its future as a single entity has been brought into question by the Local
Government Commission; and there remains a strong political commitment to
public services so that marketization and the contraction of in-house services
are both viewed with great reluctance. Incremental change also enables any tensions between managers to be contained, since the team contains members with,
variously, traditionalist, professionalized, and managerialist tendencies.

This incrementalism does not prevent imaginative solutions being taken to
particular problems. Indeed, the overall climate is cautiously optimistic, with
managers accepting both the constraints and the opportunities of the new arrangements to develop or refashion services. This has entailed a willingness to work
with a range of organizations outside the department and to encourage other
enterprises into the area to fill perceived gaps. New money from hospital resettlement schemes and from the special transitional grant has been an important
catalyst of change and development. The latter grant was relatively generous
to begin with, owing to its initial link with the size of the independent residential sector, which is large in K. (However, that factor merely emphasizes the
size of the challenge to move from residential to community-based services.)
At over £4m it provided some temporary relief from the constraints on the baseline budget: this was about £32m, just above the standard spending assessment
for social services.

Site L This metropolitan district council serves a large population within a
conurbation. It contains areas of very considerable deprivation and social stress
and its overall scores on need indicators are high. Poverty, unemployment, home-
lessness, urban renewal, and, especially, the regeneration of its economic base
have preoccupied policy-makers in the once marginal but now well-established
Labour administration. These have caused it to modify its traditional antipathy
towards markets and to work in partnership with the commercial sector in some
policy areas. However, there remains a strong belief in a welfare state made
up of civic services and an equally strong antipathy towards 'welfare for profit',

so that partnership and mixed economics in welfare have been actively resisted. 'Contracting' has normally been associated with 'out' and is therefore to be avoided wherever possible. L displays many of the features of 'conscientious objection' depicted in the typology of Wistow *et al.* (1992).

The explicitness of internal management arrangements based upon contracts has also represented a threat to traditional means of managing the problems of integration, control, and boundary management which are inherent in large politically controlled public service bureaucracies. The social services department alone employs several thousand people, mostly in direct service provision.

That size allows for the creation of specialized teams to develop adaptive mechanisms and also for the containment of various initiatives and strategies, not all of which are coherent or complementary and not all of which permeate the rest of the department. Indeed, the response to the demands of the NHS and Community Care Act was initially fragmented. Much work was done to establish an assessment, rationing, and service brokerage function, separate from direct provision, and to develop access criteria and financial control systems for the purchase of residential care. However, managers of this function also managed direct services and their power to purchase or commission other services was limited and ambiguous. These developments occurred in relative isolation from technical work on contracting, for which a specialist team was assembled, but whose purview was limited to existing service level agreements with the voluntary sector and contracts for residential and nursing home care. Both of the above developments also occurred in relative isolation from the construction of strategic plans for services.

Overall, then, adaptations to the demand for the development of a strategically coherent enabling authority have been partial, loosely coupled, and faced with political vetoes over the encouragement of mixed economies. A new director and management team, stressing the need for new structures, strategies, and attitudes has meant that the changes have gained greater coherence and visibility of late, but tensions between traditional approaches and the 'new realism' are a particular feature of L.

The large budget (well over £100m in revenue) is above the standard spending assessment, reflecting attempts to protect it over recent years. While the STG represents a smaller proportion of overall spending than in other case study sites, it and other specific grants (for mental illness, for example) have represented the major sources of growth, so that their conditions have had a significant effect on the direction of change. It is around those specific grants that most of the links with the NHS occur. Instability and financial crises within NHS authorities has certainly added to a climate in which relationships are occasionally fractious and normally limited to necessities.

5

Structures for and of Contracting

This chapter focuses on structures for and of contracting. In doing so it identifies both the informal, implicit, unacknowledged rules of the game that structure interactions between actors—North's (1990) 'institutions'—and the formal and explicit structures, which include regulations, purchaser/provider entities and organizations more generally.

It also recognizes that the structuring that occurs in relation to contracting takes place at different (macro-, meso-, and micro-) levels—or, put simply, contexts for change are internal and external to organizations—and that this is a reflection of the interactions between the formal and informal structures.

The chapter is organized into three sections: local government (CCT), health, and social care. Each section focuses on two elements which structure and are structured by contracting: the regulatory framework, which is the macro context (the way that the formal rules have been interpreted and applied), and the organizational structure (specifically, the approach taken to the purchaser/provider split in each case study site), which is one aspect of the micro context. This chapter is followed by two further empirical chapters which focus in more detail on other structuring factors (for example, markets and the nature of the good or service).

In this chapter we argue that our two areas—the regulatory framework and the purchaser/provider split—provide an opportunity to reflect on the nature of pre-existing institutions and the survival of these, in the light of the threat represented by the public sector reform agenda outlined in Chapter 1.

LOCAL GOVERNMENT CCT — THE FRAMEWORK FOR CONTRACTING

Reform in local government—specifically the introduction of compulsory competitive tendering (CCT)—came early on in the Conservative government's first term of office. In Chapter 1 we suggested that the key driver for change in this sector was the desire of central government to attain greater control over the financial spending of local authorities and more generally—as local authorities are increasingly dominated by opposition parties—to curtail the level of discretion at a local government level.

The dominance of control as a theme in this sector is seen both in the character of local government (CCT) contracts (see Chapter 3 for more details) and more generally in the regulatory framework for contracting. These tend to be legalistic, highly detailed contracts which are formally structured with contract conditions, specifications, and supporting documents such as bills of quantities. Although the balance between a performance emphasis and the specification of inputs/methods is changing in favour of the former, with the extension of CCT to white-collar services, there is still considerable emphasis on trying to cover every contingency.

More generally, the framework for contracting for local government services is highly prescriptive and increasingly legalistic. It covers the development of contract documentation, defining certain issues as non-commercial and therefore not appropriate for inclusion. It structures the approach to letting contracts including the advertisement of contracts and the process of eliciting expressions of interest, inviting and evaluating tenders, and awarding contracts.

It also influences the management of contractual relationships requiring that trading accounts are kept and a rate of return on capital achieved. Action that could be seen as being anti-competitive has also been outlawed. Anti-competitive action has been widely construed but includes, for example, packaging work in a way that makes it unattractive to private bidders and operating default systems which are penal (Walsh and Davis 1993).

The nature of these services as, broadly speaking, 'simple' services (Walsh 1994)—in that they are relatively easy to specify and monitor compared to more 'complex' services such as health and social care—also contributes to the tendency to focus on the detail (for example, how the floor is to be cleaned rather than that it should be clean) and on inputs to and methods of providing the service, rather than objectives. A further factor influencing the character of these contracts is that in contrast to contracts for health care, local government contracts are 'real' in the sense that, when awarded to private contractors, they are legally enforceable through the courts.

These factors have contributed to a particular momentum in local government (CCT) contracting whereby the contract and the contracting process can almost take on a life of its own. Although this is also true of the other sectors to some extent, it is particularly so for local government.

In most of our case study sites, there were tensions between the way that the authorities concerned wanted to approach contracting and the constraints imposed on their actual approach—particularly in terms of the ways that parties to the contract actually relate to each other in practice—as a result of the highly prescriptive framework for contracting for local government services.

For example, in Site E, there was a deliberate emphasis on the need for policy-driven contracting rather than contract-driven policy: 'The fundamental argument is that the contract should not dictate the service. Rather we have to have a political and policy approach that will structure the contract effectively to respond to people's perceived needs.' The desired approach was for contracts to be user-focused, user-responsive, and flexible, but where this was achieved, it was often in spite of contracts. For example, schools had complained that the professional language in which contract documents were written made them impenetrable and summaries of the main points were produced for these institutional users or clients as a result. It was also interesting that although quality was driving the approach in practice, the contract documents themselves contained virtually no references to the quality objectives of the authority.

In Site H, developing contract documentation entailed a huge cultural shift for some staff. The comments below would also have been fairly typical of the challenges facing DSOs in other authorities.

We estimated the number of illegal fly tips and found that it was always low. It turned out from talking to some of the DSO staff that one driver knew where the fly tips were and picked them up when he went down that road. He was doing that work on his own initiative but depriving the DSO of income. The message that he had to understand was to only do what the client pays for . . . . Within a short space of time the DSO got that mentality e.g. they'd say things like 'in the course of my travels I happened to notice a dead dog, would you give us a certificate to pick it up?' They have to get tickets before doing the work . . . . In the good old days, the DSO used to do the work and we'd never charge other departments. Now we have to.

One of the major areas for change was in the way that parties to the contract were to relate to each other. Before addressing some of the issues involved in this, it may be useful to describe the approaches taken by the case study sites to the purchaser/provider split.

Purchaser/Provider Functions

In local government (CCT) the purchasing function is known as the client-agent role and the providing function the contractor role. Internal contractors are known as direct service organizations (DSOs). The client agent—as the term implies—acts on behalf of users or clients who may be institutional (for example, schools and other departments) or council tax payers. Sometimes the client and client agent are the same entity.

Sites E and G both had an integrated client-agent function (i.e. the purchasing functions for most or all services were located in a single unit). This had not always been the case in Site E: the initial approach had been to keep purchaser and provider 'as close together as permissible' via a lead-client approach (i.e. where the client agent or purchasing role is taken on by the major user or client of a particular service and this role is also performed for other, minor clients). However perceptions by clients that client-agent/contractor relationships were too cosy, with contracts too responsive to contractor needs as opposed to user needs, contributed to a significant change in both officer and member structures.

Client-agent functions were moved to one department and contractor functions to another. Two subcommittees (of the Policy Advisory Committee on the client side and personnel and administration on the contractor side) were also established. (The latter eventually became a DSO board.) There was also a series of arrangements for linking to other departments and the chairs of all principal services committees were members of the client-agent subcommittee. This was a high profile committee and its membership was designed to facilitate decision-making and liaison with other committees.

In Site G, all client and contractor functions relating to 1988 Act services were located in a single department and a client/contractor split was established early. There was, however, at the time of the interviews, no integrated contractor organization since all 1988 Act services were externalized via a management buy-out (MBO). On the member side, arrangements were based on traditional models. There were three committees receiving progress reports on the services provided to local authority residents.

Sites F and H adopted a lead-client approach. In Site F, all services to schools were located in the education department with overall responsibility for these resting with a single manager. An initial problem with this approach was that the provider manager outranked the client-agent manager and this contributed in part to the perceived lack of clout for client-agent officers over contractors (together with the fact that client-agent units for individual services were often a 'one-man show').

In Site F, the split was at chief officer level. In Site H, arrangements were less clear. This was partly to do with the fact that the management style in the authority was departmentally determined, so there were variations between departments. It was also related to a desire on the one hand for the authority to be seen to be complying with Audit Commission and CIPFA (Chartered Institute of Public Finance and Accountancy) guidelines and on the other for close liaison between client and contractor and an emphasis on devolving responsibility to the lowest possible level.

In some cases the split was at chief officer level, in others at a second tier or 'general manager' level (a term adopted in this authority). In practice it was not always clear what hat each person was wearing and arrangements were, comparatively, quite complex. In refuse collection and street cleansing for example, both the chief officer and general manager were twin-hatted. The latter reported to and deputized for the chief officer and during the contract letting process wore a contractor hat only.

In Site H, there were no central units to support staff in departments. A former consultancy arm set up to coordinate client-agent functions—such as drawing up specifications and monitoring—was disbanded as part of the emphasis on decentralization. There was an integrated contractor committee but member structures on the client side were organized on a lead-client basis. For example, the Community Services Committee was the lead committee for grounds maintenance and was responsible for setting lengths of contract and so on. Although schools were a client of grounds maintenance, they were not the major client and therefore the Education Committee would not be involved in these functions.

The issue of whether or not to integrate further (i.e. in terms of client-side structures or DSOs) was live in the authority, with a number of different camps favouring different options for different reasons.

The different approaches taken by the case study authorities reflect:

- market conditions (for example Site G had no internal providers);
- the extent to which the authorities wanted to minimize the impact of contracting on the workings of the authority (for example in Site H, the client-agent role for some services moved between departments and this seemed to reflect a pragmatic approach, doing what needed to be done at the time) or (as for example in Site E) were determined not to let contracting get in the way of broader strategies; and
- wider beliefs in the authority about whether responsibility for contracting ought to be centralized or decentralized. This can also be seen as an issue of control/responsibility and where this lies. For example, in Site F, in addition to client agents based in departments, there were also a number of centrally based officers with a client-agent role, including the authority's consultancy arm, a competition team, an advisory group (relating to white-collar CCT), a steering group of chief officers, and client and contractor subcommittees of the Policy and Resources Committee (the latter of which became a DSO board during the course of the research). There was also a group of vehicle users.

The number of groups itself, not surprisingly, contributed to a perception of contracting as bureaucratic, but it was the tensions over the respective roles of the central client and departmental client agents, particularly the level of autonomy for the latter, which are of broader interest. The problems experienced in Site F, described as 'a corporate tension about the positioning of the client' and the difficulties in balancing the needs of individual users for specific services with the needs of the authority, reflect broad dilemmas in local government. In Site F, the dilemmas related to the discrepancy between the view from the centre that departmental 'client officers were tending to look at things solely from a technical point of view and they did not consider the broader issues and the knock-on effects elsewhere in the service', and at a departmental level, where although it was accepted that a central client-agent role would be complementary to a decentralized, user-focused client, there was concern that 'the centre is looking to take over the client'.

In other authorities, dilemmas have centred on the desire for choice about whether or not to buy into central support services to be extended to all parts of the authority—not just schools—with this being a particular issue for DSOs.

The approaches taken to the purchaser/provider split are not only a reflection of different contexts—specifically the interpretation of external guidance in the light of internal priorities—but also shaped the nature of purchaser/provider relationships in the authorities.

Purchaser/Provider Relationships

Attitudes to contractors varied between case study sites. In Site E, the DSO was the preferred contractor but there were conditions attached to this. DSOs had to make a cultural shift from being service-focused to being user-focused or they would lose their customers. User perceptions that relationships between client agent and contractor were too cosy, and an emphasis from the council on quality, led to the formal structural changes outlined earlier. The effect of these was to interpose between user and contractor, a third party: the client agent.

The client agent was to be firmly allied with the interests of the user but with a critical link to the contractor. The client agent's role was to be a change agent and to bring about a cultural shift perceived to be necessary not only to prevent users (mainly schools) from using their right to exit from the contract (either by opting for grant maintained status (GMS) or via the small-schools exemption rule under the local management of schools initiative (LMS)), but also to ensure DSO survival.

It was recognized that the client agent could be, and indeed was being, perceived as a threat to the DSO. The DSO was feeling extremely vulnerable, having to cope with these cultural changes in the kind of general environment which was hostile for DSOs (see Chapter 6).

Eventually, it was intended that the client agent which existed to bring about changes would, once these had been made, take a back-seat role and a 'fast track' link between user and contractor could be established. Judging when the time was right for this to happen was very difficult for the client agent. If the decision was made too early, users, many of whom were already fairly dissatisfied (a legacy from the former system), would be more inclined to exit from the contracts. If the decision was made too late the client agent could be seen as empire-building, no longer a change agent but institutionalized. (Ironically, if the DSO lost contracts this actually strengthened the position of the client agent.) Furthermore, under the current arrangements, the DSO was losing work opportunities and becoming more distanced from its users.

In this authority, the purchaser/provider split was seen as a lever for improving quality and was generally welcomed (although less by providers than users).

In Site F, there was more emphasis than in the other sites on being seen to be fair to all contractors. The phrase 'Chinese walls are up' was used to reflect the DSO perception that they were treated no differently to any other (i.e. an external) contractor, a perception for which there was some evidence. For example, DSOs were involved in developing the contract at the interview stage only (i.e. at the point at which all contractors bidding for the contracts were invited to comment on the documentation and on what would encourage/discourage them in bidding). Also trade unions believed that they were receiving less and less information on the contract process over time and papers relating to CCT were dealt with under the confidential part of committee meeting agendas.

The client-agent perception, however, was that the reality for DSOs was quite different to their perception of it. For example, a mainly DSO view was that some client agents based in departments had adopted a policing approach to the management of contracts. However, in reality, DSOs' perceptions had more to do with personality clashes since, for example, no defaults had ever been issued. Client-side officers felt that there was not enough 'policing' going on. Also, with regard to the level of information, the centre's view was that the trade union requirement for information had actually increased and that it was the increase which had not been met.

There was general agreement, however, that relationships between clients and contractors were poor. Some interviewees believed that this was because client agents did not have sufficient clout against the DSOs, others that departmental client agents had 'become extremely dogmatic and pernickety about detail, when those at a strategic level would be more pragmatic'.

Departmental client agents had a more positive view of relationships than contractors, though again these varied considerably from 'a good working relationship' in which 'the interests of the customer and the authority are uppermost over what the specification says or does not say' to a very negative view —mainly held, it appeared, because of a personality clash.

Provider views were more negative. Even in those areas where relationships were quite positive, providers emphasized the problems caused by Chinese walls; and of the other relationships it was reported that 'Client agents are either useless or downright nasty. Basically they are not people of sufficient calibre to do anything other than what they are told'. In Site G, there was an emphasis on partnership. The successful bidder would become the preferred contractor. Within certain parameters, extra work would be given to such contractors without tendering and extensions to contract were used where possible, particularly as an incentive for the contractor to invest in the service.

In spite of this, however, the authority had been criticized by the district auditor for being locked into a traditional monitoring system consisting of:

a programme of inspections determined by rigid prescriptive schedules which

- do not vary to reflect consumer input
- do not make any use of contractors' monitoring arrangements; and
- do not vary as experience of contractors' performance is gained.

The debate was essentially about trust. The authority was, according to the district auditor, not putting its words into actions (for example, showing it trusted its provider by using the provider's monitoring systems). However, this authority was arguing that a contract based on a good relationship nevertheless needed to retain certain safeguards. Experience had given weight to this argument following problems with a recently tendered contract which had taken eleven months to settle down (the authority would normally expect to have to allow two or three months for settling in) and where the level of complaints made and defaults issued had been high enough on a number of occasions to warrant termination of the contract.

Generally, however, client/contractor relationships in this authority were very good and both parties referred to the relationship as 'not them and us, just us. We are both trying to do the same thing at the end of the day. It's not a matter of each trying to put one past the other'.

Site G had worked hard to develop such relationships. It had over time, it appeared, achieved the right balance. It believed that the organizational distance involved in working solely with external contractors (as opposed to DSOs) was a distinct advantage. The authority had excellent working relationships with its contractors because, although 'we stress throughout that it is a partnership [and] if there is a problem it is not always a contractor's - it may also be ours', at the end of the day, the nature of the relationship meant that there was less 'empathy' than there would be with a DSO and that 'hard decisions' could still be made when necessary. The problem this authority was facing, however, was how to sustain those relationships through competition: 'if you have a good relationship then you may want to extend the contract period. You do have to re-tender at some point, but not very often.'

There were tensions between the perceived benefits of re-tendering (with members in particular being in favour of this following a recent tendering exercise which had produced savings of nearly half a million pounds per year over seven years) and alternative approaches such as long-term contracts (figures of five to twenty years were cited) in return for investment in the service.

In Site H, approaches varied across departments although there appeared to be two main styles. One emphasized close working between client and contractor. Although there was a client/contractor split, in reality it only existed during the contract-letting process. This model of relationships was adopted in relation to building cleaning, refuse collection, and street cleansing. In the departments responsible for these services there were competition groups. Members included client, contractor, trade union, personnel, legal services, and finance representatives. The role of such groups was to develop competition and contracting policy and they were also used as a forum for discussing specifications, staffing levels, utilization of resources, and service developments generally. Contractors were closely involved in contract preparation because departments 'wanted to make the best use of resources in putting the specification together and on pricing'. This was seen by the authority as effective client/contractor links.

In the other model, clients and contractors appeared almost to conform to caricatures of their roles. For example client agents were 'going to great lengths to knock pence off amounts claimed' but these efforts were a bit misguided since users complained that contracts were not needs-driven. Both contractors and users were bypassing the client agent.

Several people across the case study sites commented on the need for mature contractual relationships: 'people are still very petty about things, there is a lot of flexing of muscles. You need to develop a world of trust [and more use of] persuasive powers', and several made links between so-called immature relationships and the labels of client and contractor which reflect the logic of control and suspicion inherent in the contracting framework:

The day before CCT we were a team of people . . . who were, though they didn't realize it, client and contractor all mixed up, all in one team. All of a sudden, overnight, the client agent officers, from a DSO perspective, grew horns and a tail. There was a definite split. From a contractor point of view it was 'I'm going to screw you to the wall because

I'm a contractor' and from a client point of view it was 'oh no you won't, we're going to screw you and penalize you at every opportunity'. A lot of internal pressures resulted from that and consequently the purpose of what it was all about was lost and the service declined. The contracting arm did as little as they could and the client watched them with a magnifying glass and in the meantime the service was the third imperative.

Or as one officer put it:

In the public sector formality gets in the way of relationships. [In having] to show explicitly that you have been fair to all contractors [you are unable to adopt private sector models] which are based far more on negotiation than formal tendering [and are] more dependent on forming a relationship and developing trust and then documenting the agreement we have reached rather than the other way round.

To summarize, therefore, the framework for contracting in the local government (CCT) sector implies a logic of control. This is in part a result of having to be seen to be following the rules (for example, being fair in Site F) or covering every contingency, getting everything down, not being 'screwed' by contractors. This focus can lead to contracts becoming an end in themselves, rather than a means to an end.

The logic also influences the character of relationships and the balance maintained between a relationship based on trust and retaining the necessary control. Within the case study sites there are different models of relationships, not only according to whether the contractor is a DSO or an external contractor (see also Chapter 6) but also within these categories.

In local government (CCT), the emergence of a client-agent role can be viewed as a response to some of the challenges of the client/contractor split (for example, how does the client obtain the necessary independent advice on which to base its purchasing decisions). However, the need for client and contractor functions, once separated, to also relate back to each other means that there are tensions in achieving the appropriate balance between the extent to which the client agent is allied with the client (and hence contracts are needs-driven) and the extent to which contractors are involved in the planning of services (and hence contract objectives are achievable and sensible).

HEALTH—THE FRAMEWORK FOR CONTRACTING

The reforms of the health sector came much later than the introduction of CCT to local government but were more far-reaching, including a clear and mandatory purchaser/provider split with the introduction of NHS trust hospitals and purchaser authorities. Within the latter group, although explicit competition was not envisaged, a diversity of model was introduced with the creation of GP fund-holding as purchasers of health care. There was considerable emphasis placed upon the role of commissioning health care in part as a countervailing force against the traditional power of the provider, including the medical profession.

A broad, centrally influenced framework exists for structuring the process and pattern of setting contracts between purchaser and provider organizations. At either a national or regional level, there were broad guidelines as to the timing of contracting stages and the nature of contracts that are set and from this it should be immediately apparent that the level of prescription is far less than in the local government (CCT) sector.

Within the health sector, there is, at least on the surface, a sense of a similarity in the way organizations approach the task, but when examined in more detail, as in the opportunity provided by the case studies, some interesting differences emerge between case study sites within the sector.

The differences can be most clearly illustrated by a brief summary of the character of health contracts (see Chapter 3 for more details) which was rather different from that of local government contracts. Within the health sector, moreover, it was very difficult to talk about a typical health contract—variation was a key feature, for example in terms of length (number of pages), style, and content —although there is a tendency to slightly greater homogeneity over time.

Compared to local government (CCT) and social care contracts, these are generally less detailed—'specifications' for specialties can be two to three sides compared to tens and hundreds of pages for local government services—and hence shorter and though they may contain references to termination, variation, and so on, they are not organized as formally as contracts in the other two sectors. Little reference is made to the actual care with the emphasis being on crude output measures (although these are gradually becoming more sophisticated over time). Another key feature of health contracts is that they are deliberately incomplete with the emphasis in some cases on setting up, for example, quality monitoring arrangements, during the course of the contract term. Finally, health contracts may be block agreements covering a large number of specialties, compared to the single-service local government (CCT) contracts.

In contrast to the local government sector, the regulatory framework and advisory structure in health was much more general, perhaps only attempting to address the issue of time-scale for the publication of provider prices, indication of purchaser intentions, and a date for an agreement of contracts for the forthcoming year. There was very little detailed advice on the particular format or content of contracts, the degree of specificity, the overall length of contracts, or indeed possible clauses about default and so on. There are a number of reasons why this approach may have been appropriate for the health sector.

In part, we have to recognize the introduction of the purchaser/provider separation as a mandatory imposition. Much energy was devoted to devising trust configurations and determining the size and number of health authorities (purchasers). Having developed a new structure, the government then offered guidance that the first year of contracting should reflect 'steady-state' in an attempt to avoid further disruption. This was a crucial intervention as it led to the previous year's activity being carried forward into the first round of contracting. The existence of the contracts therefore became simply a mechanism for allocating the resource from purchaser to provider for much the same level of activity. The first year of contracting was therefore not very dramatic.

A slightly more cynical interpretation might be that central government was not entirely sure how health contracts should look or be used. It was felt that expertise would emerge from practice at a local level. A further deterrent to a strong regulatory framework was the range and considerable differences between the services covered. Some genialities such as elective surgery for specific interventions lend themselves to contracting for a defined 'good' whereas services such as mental health, multiple conditions, health promotion, and so on are much more difficult to deal with in terms of writing a contract. In the circumstances, it is not surprising that many contracts were broad-brush statements about service provision within an overall budget.

Gradually, change and innovation have emerged with increasing emphasis upon purchasing authorities developing their role as commissioners of health care, that is, devising purchasing intentions to reflect local and national priorities as well as clinical effectiveness and relative value for money. All these forces, and especially the desire to contract for health outcomes, have increased the sophistication of contracts. Some of these innovations in practice are reflected in the case study sites.

Whilst in local government the key objective of contracts appeared to be about having control, hence the specificity, in health it was more a political goal of changing the balance of power between providers and users (as represented by purchasers, for example) and evolving a system where change in service pattern might be accomplished.

A key aspect of the regulatory framework for contracting that has structured the nature of the contracts drawn up is the pace of change. In Site A, contracts have had to be delivered according to predetermined time-scales and yet the health commission is trying hard to ensure that contracts are used to reflect strategic goals and that processes such as needs assessment, user involvement, and setting outcome targets are incorporated into contracts. That they have been less than successful in this—because of the time constraints—is illustrated by this remark: 'Contracting is the housekeeping system of the commissioning process, it is the payment and monitoring system, no more no less'.

The pace of change has also produced a high level of individual responsibility placed on individual managers in Site A (although the different directorates attempt to work cooperatively and to ensure there is a good information exchange). Sometimes the intense pressure to conclude contract negotiations makes it difficult to ensure there is sufficient internal debate and alignment with strategic goals. At times, the separateness can inhibit development. For example, the desire for a more matrix-based approach is difficult to achieve. There are also internal tensions between professional and managerial values with the bureaucratic aspects of contracting appearing to rather overwhelm other clinical, patient-oriented concerns.

In Site C there is a slightly different emphasis. Here the intellectual orientation perhaps gives rise to a view of contracting as a highly mechanistic, possibly irksome requirement.

Unfortunately contracting has become the 'be all and end all' of our main activity when really it is only a means to an end and something we have to learn to shape how we want it in order to be able to get on with the more important job of developing services.

This emphasis upon the challenges of commissioning resulted in the organization being concerned to identify ways of changing the pattern of services. In part, this involves questioning the assumptions of providers as well as seeking to involve the public in setting priorities and reviewing clinical evidence about the value of certain procedures. These activities come to represent a set of tasks somewhat removed from contracting, focusing upon internal debate and discussion about what the commission is trying to achieve. Contracts can, in such an environment, be relegated to a somewhat mundane process of agreeing the budget and activity pattern. The real charge and stimulation for purchasing staff lies within the prior process of determining what, and what not, to purchase.

Purchaser/Provider Functions

At first sight, there appears to be greater clarity in the health sector in relation to the purchaser/provider split, with the creation of NHS trusts as providers and health authorities and GP fundholders as purchasers. In reality, the situation has been complicated by mergers between health authorities, between district health authorities (DHAs), and family health services authorities (FHSAs); and initiatives such as locality purchasing.

Site A represents a merging of DHA and FHSA with a relatively new chief executive for the new authority. As in a number of contexts, the arrival of a new senior executive has seen a high degree of turnover of other staff and therefore quite a new, young team are in place. This sense of newness and openness may in part account for the high profile given to the need to involve and reflect users in shaping purchasing decisions and to efforts to ensure purchasing decisions reflect a primary care orientation.

The strategic development of primary care is regarded as the key to effective and appropriate provision in health care. The main focus will be upon providing as much care as possible through the GP with staff, support, and resources being put behind this more and to drawing GPs into decisions on health care purchasing. The approach focuses upon the 'build-up' of resources in primary care, rather than switching or substituting resources. For example, community pharmacists are being given an extended role as part of the primary health care team.

We need to create a small group of people to focus on the primary care strategy and involve those who will be directly affected. In this way we will be able to create and implement the long-term vision for primary care which will help us get where we need to be. We've begun to involve the GPs and they are becoming much more responsive to the ideas behind locality commissioning. We need to work from this experience and build teams to go out and work for change actually in the surgeries.

The organization operates around four main directorates:

- Directorate of Healthcare Purchasing—all acute contracts, GP fundholder and locality development, as well as quality coordination;
- Directorate of Primary and Community Care—covering contracts for these two areas as well as responsibility for joint working with other agencies (local authority, voluntary sector);
- Finance Directorate—covering all financial services and information provision;
- Public Health Directorate—dealing with the primary/secondary care interface as well as needs assessment, health promotion, and the provision of professional advice.

The chief executive's office encompasses organizational strategy, public relations, performance review, and support to the authority chair and non-executives.

The separation in this site of acute sector from primary care purchasing is an interesting feature. It seems to provide a clear picture of the differences between the needs and the requirements of the respective service areas as well as being able to document clearly achievements and deficiencies in each. This may again reflect the priority given to primary care development. However, there is a counter-argument to suggest that this separation of responsibilities will not help in the movement to more integrated care provision where barriers between primary and secondary care are removed, or at least obscured.

On the whole providers in case study Site A have monopoly-supply status at least as currently configured as an acute unit and a community unit. There is a risk therefore of a degree of complacency and this may be why the purchaser has attempted to disturb the cosiness a little by considering putting services out to tender to neighbouring providers. This was a useful symbol, even if not fully and successfully implemented.

Providers do on the whole feel they are involved in the debate and discussion about contracts, although there is an issue for providers in getting their clinicians to be more responsive and involved in the negotiations. This is beginning to happen, and as most of the debate is a haggle over activity levels and the 'mix' of activity at varying costs, this is increasingly important. A view from the purchaser negotiating team is instructive: 'The really important aim of contracting is to pitch it so that you always have the providers over-performing. The providers always shift more in contract discussions than the purchaser.'

Site B was in the vanguard of the process of bringing DHA and FHSA together. This was a joint, mutually agreed process and has resulted in a high profile for general practice and joint commissioning. It has also evolved to being one of the leanest purchasing organizations. Each of the key roles of public health, finance, performance management, and quality are led by executive directors but with quite limited degrees of professional support. In addition to these functional directorates there are two commissioning directorates—primary care and hospital care. The separation of these areas again encompasses the advantage of focus but the limitation of making integration of care difficult. Additionally, the slim support structure places great reliance on public health for any clinical perspective on the planning and negotiation of contracts.

The integrated approach (DHA/FHSA and social services) seems largely to be a result of positive personal relationships between key individuals, and perhaps also because as a relatively isolated geographic authority there has been considerable stability of staff and therefore a trust and confidence in one another that may not always exist in the same way elsewhere.

This large, but relatively self-contained geographic patch creates an environment where two main acute providers are the focus of most of the authorities' contracts. The providers would on the whole prefer to maintain the status quo as relatively great travel distances put the delivery of local services at a premium. This may not be a scenario viewed as viable by the purchaser. Therefore increasing pressure is being applied to the two providers in terms of reducing costs, tendering for services, and seeking (voluntary) rationalization of services. Currently, the providers have responded in a very competitive, rather than collaborative, style. There is a need for more mature relationships in the longer term.

Site C is one of the newest health commissioning authorities and has had a major change agenda involving the merger not only of DHA/FHSA but also the bringing together of three previous DHAs. Not surprisingly, then, it has had to cope with a very diverse population and has evolved a strong locality focus to its purchasing based around previous district structures. One interesting advantage stemming from the amalgamation process is the priority given to information on the different populations, and as a consequence the development of an information base is rather more sophisticated than for most purchasing organizations.

In order to tackle the size aspects of the new authority a matrix management structure is proposed whereby senior managers work across a number of functional groups (strategy, policy planning, operational review, finance, locality teams, and contract advisory groups). Apart from public health, the other three directorates include the directorate of purchasing and planning responsible for contracting and commissioning, the quality and community relations directorate focusing upon quality and consumer issues, and the directorate of services including performance management, finance, and resources.

It is recognized that the task ahead requires that staff acquire new skills and the organization is developed. This process is addressed by a separate directorate of organization and employee development working directly to the chief executive. However at the time of the study, the structure was very new and therefore its success or drawbacks could not be explored.

The authority and its providers are caught in the midst of great change. Not only has the purchasing authority come together from previous authorities but the providers' configuration is still to become clear. An inner city and needy population must also be accommodated. It is therefore not surprising that there are tensions at present. Once again, the authority is really concerned with relationship-building rather than contracts. This was expressed firmly, if harshly: 'Unfortunately because contracts are tangible things people hang on to getting them to prove that they are really doing something. Really they are worthless documents because they are not real contracts but agreements formed on the basis of trust between two parties.'

Site D, a large urban, city-based authority faces a number of major challenges. A new chief executive appointed within the last year has the task of moving the organization forward from what might be described as a slightly stalled state. At the same time its city base is promoting a raft of city-wide initiatives from a range of other agencies. The need to respond is intense and yet the authority itself is in a no-growth state in terms of its financial resources.

The initial approach of the authority to the demand for joint commissioning was to establish strategic planning and purchasing groups involving representatives from DHA, FHSA, and local authority. However, despite positive intentions, the groups came to be seen as a rather mechanistic response, with the subgroups of organizations represented tending to continue to work in their old, traditional style. With individuals working to different agendas, the result was that despite good intentions about commissioning, contracting finally simply became a mechanism for fixing financial transfer. Higher-order goals relating to health care and change in patterns of care were somewhat sidelined. The new chief executive has proposed a new more functionally focused structure with four main directorates:

- Finance and Contracting—covering all financial and contracting responsibilities, as well as performance management;
- Policy and Research—incorporating public health, information, and leading on quality standards;
- Local Commissioning and Primary Care—which was aimed at giving individual managers direct responsibility for identified geographic sectors. In addition the directorate would cover all GP fundholder liaison, as well as quality assurance and contract monitoring;
- Strategic and Corporate Development—would cover strategic planning, the investment plan, acute provider development, and market management.

The change in chief executive of the purchaser authority, not too surprisingly, is reflected in the views of the providers as having been rather poorly treated. Largely, they do not feel that they have been sufficiently involved in discussions at an early enough stage. It does though have to be recognized that reconfiguration of the city's hospital structure is inevitably contentious, prompting resistance and rather negative attitudes. The new team at the authority will need to work hard to establish a collaborative and cooperative approach to the process of reconfiguration.

In summary, variations in the approach to contracting can on the whole be attributed to a number of factors, most notably:

a) the degree of change (upheaval) experienced by the purchaser organization. This may involve DHA/FHSA merger or the bringing together of previously distinct districts. Apart from the delay in creating a shared understanding about the culture and purpose of the organization there are added difficulties of new interpersonal relationships within the purchaser, as well as the need to acquire an understanding of the background and issues for different provider configurations;

b) the detail of how the commissioning authority organizes its functions, typically shaped by the philosophy and style of the chief executive as well as the balance between strategic and operational concerns;

c) the skills and expertise of staff in post, both within the commission as well as in provider units;

d) the manner in which the commission seeks to accommodate GP fundholding. Major differences in approach were observed at the outset where some commissions might be described as hostile, seeing GP fundholding as a threat to their own power base as opposed to other commissions who saw the facilitation of GP fundholder status as a positive index of their own role. Later, the ways in which the GP fundholder groups influenced and collaborated with district commissions led to a range of different structures.

e) the nature of purchaser/provider relationships including factors such as the number and size of provider units as well as the climate set for negotiations.

Purchaser/Provider Relationships

In the health sector, as in social care, there are not just purchaser/provider relationships to consider but purchaser/purchaser relationships. For example, in Site A the authority's desire to be proactive and to be seen at the leading edge does sometimes encounter resistance in others, notably in purchasing partners such as social services. Relationships between the commission and social services might be described as cordial and constructive but leading to little action. The health authority is seeking to test the realism of joint commissioning by seeking to jointly finance a programme, thus producing reciprocal commitment or at least forcing social services to declare their hand. As one member of the health authority's joint commissioning team said: 'The trouble is that trust seems to easily break down between Social Services and us. They are definitely lagging behind in their thinking and particularly in their action but they think that their perspective is the most important one because they deal with people and their everyday lives.' GP fundholding has not really developed at present (only one practice), but the authority clearly understands the need to capture the GP world, and initiatives through locality management and GP multi-funds suggest that this will be a major focus of future work.

In Site B, commissioning teams (primary and secondary) have the responsibility to set contracts. Whilst functional support staff work across both groups there is a feeling that the separation has led to the resources available being 'locked in' and the powerful hold of acute services being preserved rather than changed. This problem is one repeated frequently at a national level. In part it may reflect the continued power of hospital-based clinicians but also to some extent the immaturity of the purchasing process. With the continuing demand for treatment, not to mention fierce pressure to reduce waiting times, it is extremely difficult for purchasers to withdraw resources from the secondary sector and reinvest in the primary and community sectors. Community care-based contracts can often be perceived as very much subsequent to the acute contract.

A locality commissioning initiative may place even greater stress on this separation. Locality commissioning seeks to provide integrated care attuned to local needs. At present, a number of functional managers also have a geographic responsibility and therefore acquire 'two hats'—functional and geographic. This could be helpful but equally could produce difficulties if the two areas of responsibility come into conflict.

There is a strong executive lead in terms of strategy and direction; however there is a danger that this board-level thinking becomes divorced from the 'nitty-gritty' of contract negotiation. Providers have already raised concerns about contract discussions being with individuals without the power or authority to conclude negotiations. It is important that board-level strategy-makers are fully aware of the provider difficulties in delivering service goals.

For this relatively small authority, clarification of the national dilemma about the relationship between the DHA and GP fundholders would be of benefit. At present 40 per cent (and rising) of the population is covered by GP fundholding. The authority is working hard to bring fundholders into DHA strategy. One option is to allow a mixed economy of purchasing (DHA and GP fundholder) with some form of strategic alignment. Alternatively GP fundholding could be encouraged and promoted so that the DHA role is reduced to influencing and monitoring the locally based general practice.

Site C exists in a political minefield and has to deal with a very complex set of provider configurations. In this sense, the organization has developed a rather analytic and intellectual culture. A strong dominant acute provider (with financial problems) coupled with three pre-existing approaches to contracting has meant that it has proved difficult to establish a strong contracting approach across the whole authority. Perhaps because of the difficult main provider, the rest of the organization's contracting activity has been fairly pragmatic and aimed at minimizing further conflict.

In Site D, the key shift in thinking reflected in the proposed structure is greater emphasis upon primary and community care as well as trying to link the acute sector activities to the way in which the 'market' for health was to be shaped. A particular challenge is also the need to move the relationship with social services away from 'hand-to-hand' fighting. The epidemiological emphasis and population base of the health authority has revealed major differences in perspective from that of the social services which on the whole appears more focused on individually oriented diagnoses.

The structural changes also meant significant reappraisal in working style, for the staff of the organization who had been used to a rather more autocratic approach. Most staff appeared positive about the new culture of openness, but this 'honeymoon' period might mask an uncertainty about what the change really means.

There are major plans, as in many large cities, currently out for consultation. In particular, these include rationalizing the acute sites and giving much greater emphasis to primary care development. Inevitably, there is some resistance and defensiveness from the acute sector, and the community unit will need to feel more involved if the shift is to be managed smoothly. The old 'tell them' style must be replaced by a greater sense of mutual trust but this will take time: 'Primary-led purchasing is where we are now heading and that has to be a good thing now that we are getting over the restrictions and constraints which were placed upon us in the past.' The bureaucratic history of the authority tended to lead to contracts being seen as control mechanisms. Therefore relationships with providers were rather tense. This was especially so as one of the main providers was an early trust with a national reputation. Contract negotiations were therefore rather confrontational. This is now changing as the health authority adjusts its approach.

The growth of GP fundholding has been dramatic. In 1991 there were only two GP fundholders, but in 1995 45 per cent of the population were allocated to fundholding practices. This is of course part of a national trend but also here the GPs have increasingly wanted to influence the process of acute site rationalization as to where they placed their contracts. The notion of population grouping (PATCH) with a cluster of GP practices is being developed. This is thought to encourage primary and community services at a local level. It remains to be seen whether this movement will be compatible with the city-wide primary care strategy.

In summary, structures across sites (A and B in particular) reflect a tension between a clear separation between acute and community sectors (and the desire to enable a focus on community services) and the need for integrated commissioning across acute and community services—which is reduced by such a separation. Moreover, matrix structures which seem to be emerging in all sites can also produce tensions. In Site B particularly, there are indications that staff tend to either start to identify with their geographic patch, their professional function, or more corporate goals.

There is general uncertainty about the future DHA role. For example, should GP fundholding be developed to be the main purchaser with the DHA in an overview monitoring role, or should a mixed economy of DHA/GP fundholding be encouraged? It may be that this uncertainty has contributed to the lack of progress on joint commissioning, which is still not very strong anywhere with experience ranging from hand-to-hand fighting in Site D to testing the strength of commitment of its partners by Site A. Or it may be—given the comments above about the tensions inherent in matrix structures—that the reforms demand a new breed of managers who can work across organizational boundaries. Although recognized as a need, no clear development process to engender the development of these skills has emerged. In part, this reflects a continuing lack of understanding about the precise nature of skills required.

Finally, across all sites, contracting is seen as housekeeping, a mechanistic, control process, and not a driver of change. Corporate issues, commissioning issues, and the board-level strategy seem to be at odds with and irrelevant to the detail of time-constrained negotiations about contracts as well as in conflict with professional values.

SOCIAL CARE—THE FRAMEWORK FOR CONTRACTING

The programme of public sector reform unfolded in social care last among our three sectors, but in one sense it was the most radical of all: it created an external market—rather than a mainly internal one, as in the other two sectors. The notion of purchasing or enabling was further refined in this sector with community care planning and market making; and pressure on internal providers was created via financial levers, competition, and the emphasis on the voluntary sector as a kind of halfway house between public and private. Social care offers an interesting comparison to the other two sectors because it combines the apparent difficulties associated with a 'complex' good/service (Walsh 1994) with real competition, and all taking place in a local government environment normally controlled by opposition parties.

Social care contracts contain less detail than local government (CCT) contracts, with fewer legal conditions and limited specifications, but are more formally organized than health contracts with an emphasis on broad aims for the service in relation to a general philosophy about rights, privacy, independence, and so on. Attempts to define quality in relation to the actual service—rather than peripheral matters—have been more sustained than in health (Walsh 1994).

Organizing for contracting was part of a package of tasks facing social services departments (SSDs) in the 1990s and decisions about this issue were closely connected with those on other matters. SSDs were to have lead responsibility for people with substantial and continuing care needs, with the NHS drastically reducing its long-stay and continuing care beds and the Department of Social Security (DSS) withdrawing from the financing of new residential care. Thus, open-ended (DSS) and direct central funding (NHS) were to be replaced by cash-limited and indirect funding. This funding mechanism has been criticized as too uncertain, too tightly rationed, and poorly distributed in relation to needs (see for example Means and Smith 1994; Harding 1992). None the less, with this as a basis, SSDs were to create strategies to enable the long-term development of needs-led services. Those services were to be 'normalized'—based on ordinary living arrangements and with families as the first port of call: social services were to ensure that back-up support complemented and reinforced informal care in flexible and acceptable ways.

The core staff of the SSD, then, were those at the centre, planning and commissioning care and developing service systems, and those at local level assessing individual needs, judging priorities, and arranging care from a variety of potential suppliers. These core functions were seen as 'purchasing'.

Providing services is no longer seen as a core function in this model, so an organizational separation of purchasing (core) and providing (peripheral) is seen to be needed. Indeed, an increasing proportion of services were to be provided externally and it was the role of the core SSD to encourage the development of this mixed economy. In it, internal providers, community groups, voluntary organizations, and commercial ventures ought, ideally, to trade with SSD purchasers in similar ways—except that there were financial penalties to discourage the use of in-house residential care and rules to prohibit spending most of the new money internally. The mixed economy had to be managed in such a way as to ensure a smooth, 'steady-state' transition to the new financial arrangements and then fairly rapidly to shift from a residential bias (the commercial sector's strength) to one supporting ordinary living.

Among others, the Audit Commission were in no doubt as to the implications. 'A process of change has been set in motion which will turn organizations upside-down' (Audit Commission 1992: 19), they claimed, when advising how SSDs should try to order this 'cascade of change', and followed this with guidance on how to achieve a 'community revolution' (1993*b*).

However, if the change was to be revolutionary and systemic, guidance on what to do and how to do it came out incrementally and with varying degrees of imperative force. The process of achieving it was equally to be incremental and partial—indeed the key parts were delayed for two years. Thus, complaints procedures and inspection arrangements were to be in place by 1991 and community care plans by 1992, by which time substantial progress on determining and implementing a purchaser/provider split was expected. By 1993, arrangements for assessment and care management, including the purchase of new care which would previously have been financed by social security, had to be in force. There have been similar, if less imperative, targets for subsequent years.

However, local authorities could choose how to implement these changes from a variety of models which had been posited or sometimes demonstrated. Equally, they could choose how far to implicate the management of the rest of the department in consequential change or, conversely, to insulate it. For example, a requirement to spend 75 per cent of revenue outside the department only related to new money, so that SSDs could choose whether to continue to manage provision financed by baseline budgets in traditional ways, or whether to move towards internal trading. It should be borne in mind, too, that market models were far less prominent in the Children Act 1989, which SSDs were also seeking to implement.

Local authorities had a number of key organizational decisions to make. Most fundamental was the extent and depth of the structural separation between purchasers and providers and how far systems should be developed to move towards market relations between them. This was nowhere a simple task since this new dividing principle had to be permutated with others based on client groups, localities, and various functional specialisms. Other key decisions, closely related, concerned the location of new or enhanced functions, necessary for commissioning: these comprised, chiefly, the development of community care plans, the design and management of contracts, and the regulation and monitoring of external providers. Lastly, planning, consultative, or negotiating forums must be either reviewed or newly established with users, with external providers, and with commissioners of related services, notably health. Last, but by no means least, authorities had to decide whether and how to externalize some of their services, either by putting them out to tender or by creating arm's-length trusts.

Purchaser/Provider Functions

Site I, Conservative-controlled at the time of the research, was advised that central government would eventually insist on market relations for both in-house and external services. It therefore opted for a radical purchaser/provider split in readiness for the original 1991 target date. A centralized provider section was created with two geographically based purchasing sections: all three were to be managed at third-tier level. Services for children were included in this restructuring (see Table 5.1).

This was a radical change in structure and in style of working. In the old system, several local barons ran their divisions confidently on the basis of professional hierarchy, local partnership, and *ad hoc* problem-solving. Now an unfamiliar and more formalized set of working relations had to be established. Events conspired to stunt the growth of this new system. Nationally, the transfer of funds was delayed; the authority was charge-capped; the director, a leading supporter of the change, left to be replaced by one who was much less comfortable with its implications; and there was a change in political control.

In consequence, the funds available to develop the necessary infrastructure of skills and systems did not materialize and the enthusiasm for the change diminished. Some important elements of system and process were not in place by 1993, when the Act came fully into force, and the resultant difficulties reinforced pressures to revert to more familiar structures and systems.

As various managers said:

We have not developed our organizational arrangements to support the model we adopted. It has made it difficult for [the provider sector] to have a clear view of its future. (provider manager)

It was Mickey Mouse stuff . . . we left the money on the provider side and didn't even have a service agreement with them, so service gaps were exposed and purchasers had no resources to plug them. That was the biggest mistake we made. The amount of energy that has gone in to make sure people got a service, despite the split, has been crazy. (purchasing manager)

TABLE 5.1. The emergence of a purchaser/provider split in the operational management of SSDs, and the externalization of services[1]

Which Site?	Site I			Site J			Site K			Site L		
	Original structure	First, 1991	Proposed/ revised 1994/5	Original structure	First, 1991	Proposed/ revised	Original structure	First, 1990	Proposed/ revised 1994/5	Original structure	First, 1991	Proposed/ revised 1995
Which reorganization?[2]												
The level of organizational differentiation[3]												
First	G	F*, G	G	C	C	(no revision)	G	C	C	C	C	F*, C
Second	C	G, C	C, F*, G	F, G	F		C	C	C	G, C	G	G, C
Third	F				F*, C		C, F, G	G	F*	G, F	G, C	C
Fourth					G			F*			F*, G	
Highest level at which a purchaser/provider split emerges	—	1	2	—	3		—	4	3	—	4	1
What services, if any, are (to be) externalized?		substantial proportion of residential and some day care achieved			substantial proportion of residential planned. Limited transfer achieved	Incremental and more limited transfer of residential. Some community/ home based		None			None	

Notes:

1. Support services have been excluded from this analysis. All sites attempted to revise and increase support services, especially those concerned with financial control/purchasing, contracting, and information systems.
2. The original structure refers to that obtaining before the community care reforms.
3. This does not equate with tiers of management. In particular, it omits the levels of director and any second-tier deputy director. At lower levels of differentiation, the focus is on community care, rather than services for children.

Key:

F = differentiation based upon functional specialisms (e.g. residential/fieldwork services).
F* = differentiation in which a functional specialization between purchasing and providing is recognized, explicitly or implicitly (e.g. 'purchasing' may be called 'assessment and care management').
C = differentiation based on client or user groups (children, older adults, learning disability, etc.).
G = differentiation based on geography.

Notions of trading and competition were quickly replaced by notions of partnership and latterly the centralized provider unit has been abandoned in favour
of geographic divisions, in which a third-tier officer manages both 'assessment
and care management' and 'direct provision', rather than 'purchasers' and 'providers'. There will be no internal trading.

In Site J the move towards a purchaser/provider split was less radical initially. Third-tier officers remained in charge of children's and adult services
respectively and the split was at fourth tier in the adult-services division only.
Purchasing teams then specialized according to client groups, and it was here
that purchasing budgets (cash for most external services and units of service for
in-house and block-contract services) were held. Site J was also hampered by
financial stringency: there was a year's gap during which the two fourth-tier
purchasing posts were vacant, to be replaced by only one officer.

None the less, progress towards the full establishment of this separation including, eventually, formal trading relations for in-house services, has been made
more consistently than in Site I and there is also a closer link than elsewhere between these structural elements and other aspects of the changes—for example,
the hiving off of some services and the policy of even-handed, collaborative,
market development, which will be described later.

The close involvement of the director in this compact authority, along with
the absence of political upheaval or controversy, has contributed to this steady
development. Site J, therefore, represents the closest approximation among our
case study sites to the pure model outlined earlier.

The approach adopted in Site K was a good deal more incremental, reflecting its particular context. A Labour administration took over in the late 1980s
and embarked on a programme of service development to rectify past 'neglect'
in this dispersed authority with a long tradition of localism. A 1990 reorganization, with client-group specialisms at both third and fourth tiers was designed
to reinforce the development of professional services. The advent of the community care reforms brought a modification of structure, functions, and activities, rather than their wholesale replacement. Purchasing and providing were
initially seen as activities, rather than organizationally distinct roles.

Pressure to make a clearer division bore fruit in 1994 when distinct roles were
designated in each adult client group at the fifth tier. These changes, and their
gradual introduction, can be seen as a studied response, balancing the desire to
develop services—meeting the terms of central government grants in order to do
so—with the suspicion of market solutions which the Labour council displayed.

Such a balancing can also be detected in Site L, but the point of balance
was much more explicitly in the direction of hostility to markets. Thus, the initial changes were designed as the minimum necessary response to fulfil legislative requirements. The language of markets was taboo, and the concept of
a purchaser/provider split was not accepted as legitimate. Elements of such a
distinction did exist but were fuzzy and fragmented. At the periphery, social
workers made assessments which activated spot contracts and their line managers

were accountable for such budgets, while there were centralized officers providing technical support.

The latest reorganization proposals go much further to emphasize the distinction between the management of assessment and care management on the one hand and direct provision on the other. Equally, they strengthen strategic commissioning functions at the centre, while still avoiding the language of purchasing.

In none of our case study authorities has there been a strong ideological commitment to the widespread *externalization of services*, in which some Conservative-controlled councils have engaged. Any decisions to do so have therefore been based upon more pragmatic considerations.

Site J is the possible exception: here initial plans to contract for the management of the hotel (but not the care management) side of its residential accommodation were developed at a high corporate level but were subject to much delay and revision such that a much slower, incremental, and more limited transfer of both accommodation and staff has been occurring. The current rationale and the justification of past decisions have also been subject to alteration, as both changed external circumstances, hindsight, and continuing difficulties exert an influence: 'Members and senior officers are cautious and wholesale transfer is no longer advocated. The government has removed some of the incentives and closed the influence loopholes' (SSD officer). None the less there have been plans to develop community-based arm's-length trusts for both children's and adult services—the intention here being to expand services which are in short supply, avoiding the financial restriction on expanding in-house services, as well, perhaps, as some of their more generous conditions of service. Some home care services have also been market-tested, but with negative results.

It appears that the externalization of much of Site I's residential provision was done with more protective motives, rather than for immediate financial incentives. The initial contract, guaranteeing the purchase of a high proportion of the places at prices higher than those charged in the open market, was, unusually, financed through the baseline budget, with no charge on monies from the special transitional grant. Such a move avoided a legal challenge concerning unfair competition.

In Site K for example, the major contingencies have been a substantial oversupply of residential care, alongside severe financial constraint and some in-house provision which provided substandard facilities. There has been a gradual managed contraction of those in-house services—keeping the better homes and improving them—rather than their being floated off to compete in an over-supplied market. None the less, the eventual externalization of non-residential provision is contemplated by managers, at least once they are on a sufficiently competitive and business-like footing and provided financial incentives remain.

Site L, being opposed to market relations in social care, was naturally also opposed to the externalization of public services. Physical conditions in its own homes were often below the stringent registration standards it applied to the commercial sector, while its costs were high. The dilemma has been solved by a substantial reduction in the authority's own provision, using the savings to finance improvements elsewhere.

Regardless of the organizational form, certain *essential* functions had to be developed. In each of the case study sites similar responses were adopted to three of them:

- the setting up of a procedure to marry the assessment of people's individual needs with the financial control of purchasing budgets;
- connected to this was the need to ensure that a much wider range of external suppliers were paid appropriately. Since relationships with many of these were on the basis of spot contracts, a close link had to be forged with information about the work carried out;
- the development of and consultation on community care plans which involved a range of additional key actors such as the district health authority, service providers, and service users.

In the first case, systems were developed in support services teams but managed through the assessment and case management teams. The only differences concerned the location of budgetary control (which in the more elaborated structures, might involve second- as well as first-line managers) and the additional administrative support provided. Payment systems relating to external suppliers were normally managed through the central finance section, although in Site I the two geographic purchasing divisions undertook the work. The community care planning process was managed by the central planning sections, although the style of consultation and the involvement of other sections of the SSD varied. Local planning was emphasized in Site I for example, while in Sites K and L the focus tended to be on client groups.

There was greater variation in the way that other important activities were pursued, the key determinants being the range of specialist officers in the department and the extent to which contracting was welcomed as a core activity or disliked and kept as far apart from mainstream operations as possible.

Site J had no specialist staff to develop, let or manage contracts, or to develop the more sophisticated financial, information, and service-monitoring systems which were recognized to be desirable. Existing officers shared these tasks as best they could.

In all these developments, the director (promoted early in the reform process), supported by his new deputy and his assistant director (adults) took a very close interest. A range of policy documents were promoted in line with a model of the SSD 'enabling' by means of market development, preparing itself for competition, and establishing arm's-length trusts. The director has also played a leading role in managing relations with the existing trust providing residential care, although senior officers at the corporate core of the authority, as well as leading councillors, are also heavily involved.

In Site K, a similar process of modifying the roles of existing staff was undertaken, save for the importation of an assistant director to strengthen the financial management of the department. However, in both recent internal reorganizations (carried out in 1990 and 1994), operational tasks were amalgamated to free people to take on developmental roles, and the strategic responsibilities of senior managers have been increasingly stressed. A good deal of work was also done, especially in 1994, to separate the processes for managing commissioning from those for managing direct services, and then to link them within a strategic commissioning framework.

During this process of change, the planning and support sections have become increasingly important as sources of strategic ideas. It was the latter which was given the task of developing new contracts, since no specialist staff were recruited. This related especially to services for elderly people, since the divisions for mental health and learning disability services were already making extensive use of contracts they had developed for themselves.

One priority for future work was to develop business planning in the provider sections. Perhaps paradoxically, the development of business potential was concentrated on the external world. A short-life, externally funded, agency had been established to act as a catalyst for developing the range, quantity, and quality of commercial and voluntary services for people living at home. It has publicized service gaps and SSD purchasing plans; it has undertaken market research, assisted with business plans, tested pilot schemes, and sought funding on behalf of potential providers, as well as providing modest start-up and staff development grants.

The director's role in this site has been to manage the interface with the committee and with key outside agencies, such as the DHA and the social services inspectorate and to enable developments to occur. The strong stress has been upon the development of services, rather than on the development of markets in explicit terms, in order to balance financial stringency, a desire for service improvements, and political antipathy to market relations.

Overall, Site I has followed its tradition of sharing its developmental work among existing operational staff. The radical separation of purchasing and providing guided the division of tasks: the assistant director on the provider side was charged with setting those services onto a more business-like and competitive footing; the two purchasing assistant directors divided the development of systems to manage external relations (including contract design and negotiation) between them. Contracting with smaller agencies was devolved to local managers. We have already noted that these arrangements left a gap in the middle, concerning relations between purchasing and providing.

Later, there was some strengthening of technical support. An officer was appointed at a fairly senior level to develop information systems: these seem to envisage separate systems for in-house and external services, thus reinforcing the retreat from the pure model of the competitive council. Similarly, a contracts officer was recruited to assist in the revision of existing contracts and the construction of new ones. His role is purely technical and advisory, however, and there is no necessity for purchasing managers to consult him. Limited experience, technical expertise, and self-confidence among those managers means that providers remain in a fairly powerful position in the design of contracts— a process which is characterized by high levels of partnership and trust. Providers with experience of both contrast this with the more assertive and 'hard-nosed' approach of Site L, where the conduct of contractual relations is more centralized.

The final form of strengthening came in the recasting of the research and planning section into a commissioning section. This reflected its growing strategic role, but the title is somewhat misleading: it was to provide support for strategic purchasing decisions and to coordinate strategic planning. It has no budgets of its own nor power to take decisions (which continue to be made by the management team).

The more recent reorganization, however, marks a retreat from this hesitant centralization of strategic functions. Henceforward, the locus of much decision-making will be in the geographic divisions and the links between purchasing and in-house provision will be re-formed there in less formal and algorithmic ways: intermediate, professionally based technology has made a comeback. Authority-wide coordination and development work will be shared among those divisional managers.

Site L offers a stark contrast with the other case-study sites in that here, functions related to the development of contracting have been made much more differentiated and dispersed. This is partly owing to the size of this site, its complexity, and the inheritance of a range of specialist support staff. It also reflected the desire to insulate market relations from the rest of the department's work.

This feature is seen most markedly in the arrangements made to manage the special transitional grant (STG). For this, a commissioning section was brought together to develop contracts and manage day-to-day administrative relations with the commercial sector. It has gradually developed internal specialisms around client groups. It is located within the planning division, which is also responsible for community care plans and joint planning, as well as the development of information systems. Thus both specialization and hierarchic coordination of these activities was achieved under one assistant director. That officer took lead responsibility for relationships with the commercial sector.

Service managers, who controlled both direct services and most purchasing budgets and whose staff made individual purchasing decisions via assessment and case management, were responsible to a different assistant director. Those managers were involved in the forums with providers, but were of lower status and acting as representatives of their peers. Thus in the forums, the lead officer could truthfully disclaim responsibility for the behaviour of care managers since he was organizationally distant from them. Such a disclaimer would not have been possible in other authorities.

These arrangements minimized the impact of external actors upon internal activities and also enabled service managers to continue to adopt a low profile in order to get on with the job in a pressurized and politically sensitive environment. It remains to be seen whether the more explicit separation of direct services from assessment and care management will bring this latter function closer to the management of external contractual relations.

The *registration inspection function* also provides an example of the complexity of the structural and interpersonal relationships in this sector. In all sites except J, inspection units report directly to the director of social services. In Site J, the immediate line manager is the third-tier person responsible for all aspects of quality, standards, and evaluation.

The Registered Homes Act 1984 had extended the SSDs' inspection functions to residential care, imposing minimum standards of staffing, physical environment, and care. Nursing homes were registered and inspected by the health authority in similar ways. The 1990 Act extended inspections, but not registration to the local authority's own homes. To ensure impartiality inspection had to be at 'arm's length' from provision, with independent sector providers and lay people forming part of an overseeing committee. Since virtually all SSDs are prepared to enter into contracts with any registered home, inspection has played a vital part in the construction of arrangements for contracting.

A balance has had to be struck between the operational impartiality of the inspection section and the expertise it possesses to inform commissioning, contract management, and business planning. For example, should inspectors inform purchasers of concerns about homes in advance of moves to deregister them? Should inspection reports be available to enable informed choice by prospective residents? Initial negative answers to such questions—informed by a desire to establish confidence in the section's independence—have been modified by central government moves towards deregulation. Of late, then, inspectors have been edging back towards involvement in debates about commissioning and about quality, lest much of their role disappears.

Purchaser/Provider Relationships

As in the health sector and to a lesser extent local government (CCT), there is a complex web of relationships between parties to the contracts.

Users are objects of professional analysis within assessment and care management although there are spaces for them and any carer to express perceptions of needs and services. None the less, it is the local authority's assessment, taking into account its resources and the competing demands of other users, which holds sway. A recent judicial review makes clear that the assessment can be revised if the *authority's* financial position worsens, provided individuals are reassessed (Gloucestershire). Authorities are required to have and to publicize a complaints procedure, but, again, challenges to stated priorities would not normally be countenanced within it.

Choice has been especially emphasized for users with high dependency needs. First, intensive care packages should enable a choice between residential and ordinary living environments. This, however, is contingent on the availability of such services and the amount the local authority is prepared to spend, but the transfer of the Independent Living Fund allows them greater leeway. This is designed to augment their normal maximum expenditure in relation to severely disabled people, but is cash-limited. The second form of choice is that users assessed as needing residential care can choose any home they wish, regardless of locality, provided it is registered as suitable for their needs and provided that someone is willing to meet any charges over and above the rate which the local authority is willing to pay.

These individual rights of choice and exit, and the obligation to make financial contributions which the local authority assesses the user is able to meet, as well as 'top-ups', are reflected in the contract arrangements. Otherwise, the contractual arrangements provide only limited space for user influence (for example via reviews of individual care plans) being largely concerned with the governance of relations between the local authority and its providers even if some of those relations concern the quality of service for users. Only a minority of the contracts examined by Smith and Thomas (1993) required users to have a collective voice in homes, for example, although such arrangements were more common in the block contracts negotiated with voluntary organizations. These omissions are modified, to some extent, by the registration and inspection of homes, where the policy guidelines emphasize the active involvement of users or their representatives in both the inspection process and in open access to reports.

The final general opportunity for user representation occurs in the various forward-planning processes: for example, local authorities are required to consult fairly widely about their community care plans and normal practice entails consultation with a range of user groups.

Within our case study sites the structural position of users varied between client groups. At one extreme, a fairly simple standardized contract for the residential care of all elderly people was accompanied by individual care plans which some described as very brief and uninformative. At the other, elaborate, tailor-made contractual arrangements, taking several weeks to set up, were being constructed to allow individuals with challenging behaviour to leave hospital.

Among our case study sites, various initiatives have been taken which reflect each authority's general disposition. However, many of these reflect soft rather than hard forms of influence and in no case was a fully coherent strategy in operation. Examples include:

- publicity brochures and vacancy information about residential and nursing home care (Site I);
- funding independent disability information services and voluntary agencies so that disabled people can employ their own carers (Site I);
- widespread user and carer consultation exercises (Site L);
- users' charters (Site L);
- information services, consultation hotlines, and clarity about user entitlements along consumerist lines (Site J).

Everywhere the most sensitive issues have concerned the exercise of choice over which residential care homes to enter. The new system changed matters in quite fundamental ways. In the past, users and their relatives had a direct relationship with providers, with (usually) medical and nursing staff having a precipitative/facilitating role. Now a social services assessor/care manager has been interposed and local authority homes have come into the same pool.

We return to the management of these processes in Chapter 7. For the present, it is important to note that, structurally, the relationships between users, SSD assessor/purchasers, and providers are inevitably intertwined. Thus, for example, a social worker concerned to enable users and their relatives to make an informed choice among homes has also to bear in mind the requirements for rectitude and for avoiding improper influence—especially when the SSD has an interest in filling its own places or those it has block purchased. It is also worth noting that all the authorities have sought to keep such issues off the agendas of the forums set up to oversee relations between themselves and the providers, managing them informally and at the lowest possible level.

SSDs, as purchasers, have had to establish sets of working relationships with a range of residential care and nursing home providers. The standard means have followed time-honoured arrangements for corporate intermediation, in that representatives of trade associations have been invited to join negotiating forums. The trade associations themselves represent care homes and nursing homes respectively, although the large national corporate providers tend to stay aloof, joining health care associations. Most trade associations are based on local authority areas and are federated to one of a number of national associations. It is through these forums that the initial contracts and their revisions have been negotiated, along with the related information transmission and payment procedures.

The pattern varies, however. In Site I, the SSD was the catalyst for the creation of strong local associations. In Site K, associations have a localized geographical ambit. In Site J associations exist, but they are small and most of the homes with which the SSD contracts are outside its own boundaries. Thus, it has to rely less on this forum and more on larger consultative meetings with its providers.

In relation to *non-residential services*, the market is by no means as clearly delineated or established. As a result, no negotiating forums had been established. Site J had just launched an accreditation scheme for home care providers and Site K's accreditation scheme was at an advanced stage of design. At the time of the research, however, the only operational linkages with such agencies were with local care managers who purchased services on an *ad hoc* basis.

Floated-off trusts have only been created in Sites I and J. These were politically sensitive and complex exercises entailing the transfer of assets and staff, and were planned at a time when central government policies were still evolving. They were handled at the highest levels among both members and officers. According with government regulations, members take up a minority of places on the trust board.

In Site I, a large proportion of the authority's homes were transferred *en bloc*, supported by a four-year contract to purchase at least 80 per cent of those places at a cost higher than market rates. This was done to enable the transition to independent status. A judicial review threatened by the commercial sector was averted by assurances that new contracts would not be on the same basis. Site I uses these block-purchased places for much of its respite care, for which the choice directive does not apply.

The move from local authority control to interdependence represents uncharted territory and there are reports that it has caused tensions on a widespread basis. Site I clearly has a vital interest in the future strategy of its largest (by far) single provider. As one officer said: 'We had a lecture from [an academic expert] and he warned "Whatever you do, don't set up a monster", and the entire management team collapsed with a fit of communal nervousness. We are having some difficulties in exerting our role as purchasers.' The local authority is trying hard to interest the trust in developing specialist services which are in short supply.

Given such a concentration on strategic issues, it is perhaps not surprising that operational issues took a back seat. Local purchasing managers knew little about the contract or the sort of services they might expect, nor, indeed, what the proper relationship should be with trust managers. 'No one had seen the contract, what services we were paying for, where are they, are the day-care places allocated to particular localities? It was all over the place.' The situation has now been clarified, but the status of the trust *vis-à-vis* other providers remains an issue. Being neither flesh nor fowl, it is not welcome at the negotiation forums between the SSD and other providers.

The situation in Site J has been of different choices being made, amid no less tension. Their agency has a different legal form and the decision to transfer services on a large scale was quickly revised amid staff changes at its apex, doubts about the viability of the initial business plan, and disputes about the basis for costings. While a revised financial package was negotiated and there are plans for a gradual transfer of services to it, both purchasers and provider are now very wary of becoming too dependent on the other: 'I'm desperately anxious either to burn off the involvement with the council or to sort it out. They think of us as an arm of the council, that's one of the problems.' From the outset, some of the beds in the trust's first home were purchased by the health authority. As a result, control over access to beds offering different levels of care in the home is split between clinicians and social workers, while there have been disputes about which residents meet which criteria for entry.

Voluntary agencies are a further kind of provider and where these are involved in residential care provisions, they have joined in the negotiating forums along with commercial providers. Such links have simply added to the rich mix of relationships between the more established agencies and a variety of actors within the SSD and the wider authority. Even before the legislative changes there had been a move to formalize relationships: grant aid was being replaced by service level agreements, often with performance targets; the roles of the local authority officers who sat on the executive committees of agencies were clarified; more rarely, the same clarification happened with councillor representatives.

Site J had gone furthest in this direction, conducting formal contract reviews of the services it was paying for. Its new policy was to treat all providers equally, regardless of their provenance. Thus, the accreditation procedures for home care insisted on minimum standards of business competence. Equally, the commercial sector was invited to join the voluntary agencies already involved when the joint planning arrangements with health were revised. Elsewhere, involvement in joint planning was reserved for the voluntary sector. This was particularly the case in Site L which, paradoxically, had moved to reinforce the shift to 'business-like' relations with its voluntary providers.

Generally, however, stark differences in the treatment of the voluntary and commercial sectors remained, perhaps a reflection of the fact that contractual arrangements with voluntary agencies grew out of established grant-aid arrangements and in many ways were seen as extensions of the department. Contractual arrangements were usually for blocks of services, not necessarily specified in detail, so that a direct, more intimate, and proactive relationship existed between the SSD and the agency. This was perhaps most evident in Sites I and K, where we saw examples of officers encouraging agencies to develop new services to fill particular gaps, and also giving close support to small agencies with their business plans—even suggesting that they raise their prices when the level was considered too low to be viable over time. This advisory function was exported to the short-life development agency in Site K.

In part, this very marked difference in approach towards the commercial and voluntary sectors reflects the state of different sub-markets. There was a planned, rapid extension of services for people with mental health needs or learning disabilities—specialist areas in which housing associations and other voluntary agencies had already developed particular strength. In contrast the strength of the commercial sector—residential care of elderly people—was considered to be a market which needed to contract, rather than expand. None the less, such an intimate relationship would not have been countenanced with commercial agencies: officers would have risked disciplinary procedures, while councillors would have had to declare an interest and taken no part in relevant local authority discussions.

Finally, there are in this sector, as in the health sector, *purchaser/purchaser relationships*. All of our case study authorities had had to review their relationship with the reorganized health authorities, those links being affected by amalgamations on the health side, as well as the different balance between purchaser and provider functions in health and social care.

Links were closest in Sites I and K where senior managers on both sides had invested heavily in establishing good relationships. However, the links also varied according to client groups. For services for people with mental health problems and learning difficulties, there was a common strategic interest in the development of resettlement services and various central government grants meant that both sides could bring new money to the partnership, allowing managers the discretion to work together in developing new services. Close working relationships had developed and, while there were no joint contracts with providers, both health and social care purchasers were involved in planning, letting, and monitoring each other's contracts.

Equally, the SSD was involved at operational levels with health providers: in a few cases staff employed by health (provider) trusts working in multidisciplinary mental health teams could initiate purchasing decisions for the SSD by making community care assessments. It could be somewhat disconcerting, then, for health provider managers, working as equal partners with their SSD colleagues, to find those people sitting on the opposite side of the table at contract review meetings with health commissioners! Generally, the pattern was for health trusts, as providers, to be excluded from the high-level joint planning forums, despite their expertise in service provision.

In relation to services for elderly people, interests did not necessarily coincide and relationships were less easy. The pressure points were frequently with hospital social work teams. From April 1993, they controlled access to nursing home beds, while the acute hospital trusts were anxious to increase patient throughput and retreat rapidly from continuing care. Social services managers commented that they suddenly found themselves responsible for a new high priority group, without warning.

Our case study authorities were beginning to make some moves towards the involvement of GPs—especially fundholders—in their local purchasing arrangements. Fundholders were concentrated in the affluent areas, but represented a high proportion of GPs in Sites I, J, and K. By the time of our research, however, none of the SSDs had made significant progress in setting up joint purchasing arrangements. If health was to become a primary care-led service, that was a matter for the future, rather than the initial establishment of the reforms.

In summary, therefore, the considerable ambiguity in the guidance and scope for local discretion in this sector contrasts with the detailed regulation of CCT and the hierarchically imposed limitations as to the organization of DHAs. Factors which have structured the resulting interpretation of guidance include the values held by key actors—particularly the ideological position of the council concerning markets in social care. Strong political opposition to markets and a determination to minimize their incursion left limited space for the influence of more pragmatic considerations or other values. Where market relations were accepted as inevitable or even welcomed, there was more scope for the pragmatic interpenetration of these with other ideas in good currency, such as managerialism, and user-centred or consumerist forms of provision. In this respect, local action mirrored the policy guidance.

Equally, however, various structural contingencies operated to influence the decisions taken—the size of the SSD, its geography, its likely future shape in county areas subject to local government review. So, too, did aspects of market structure, such as the assumed surplus or shortage of particular services and the competitive position and quality of the council's own provision. Lastly, the financial climate markedly affected the authority's room for manœuvre: the threat or reality of charge-capping could drastically curtail any new money for infrastructure or service development and also the purchase of care.

This has impacted on the relationships between key actors but there have also been variations in the extent to which different providers, for example, have been treated, or attempted to be treated, equally.

6

Markets

INTRODUCTION

This chapter reviews our empirical evidence about the extent of and potential for competition in the markets with which we are concerned, taking into account the nature of the services themselves, the institutional rules which frame their operation, and the local contexts in which they are situated. Given the timing and gradual implementation of the reforms, it can only be an interim account, but it can at least explore aspects of market structure and of the strategies which significant actors have adopted or plan to implement.

Other aspects relevant to a discussion of market behaviour, notably the specification, letting, and monitoring of contracts, and the way that asymmetry of information, opportunism, and uncertainty are dealt with will be discussed in Chapter 7.

HEALTH SERVICE

National Framework

Over the past decade, something akin to a global vocabulary has emerged to describe the way in which health care reform around the world has been formulated and implemented. The universal acceptance of 'market principles' is in part owing to common problems of concern in health systems, notably:

a) rising costs of provision;
b) concern about the appropriateness of medical interventions;
c) insensitivity towards the consumer (Collins *et al.* 1994).

The fundamental aim of the NHS health reforms has been to create an internal market whereby the authority and control given to health providers offer an incentive to control costs and to operate as efficiently as possible, whilst the separation and functioning of the purchaser organization facilitates greater consumer choice. The pressure towards a market-based solution is a common force across the public sector and indeed across many countries in Europe. In the case of the UK, at least, the appeal of the market must be understood in the light of frustrations with previous efforts to reform the NHS. Professional resistance has largely remained paramount and as a result ensured that the professional view has held sway in determining the nature and pattern of services available. The NHS has been a provider-dominated organization. An excessive demand for an 'apparently free service' delivered by highly trained specialists with relatively limited alternative supply options combined to create a very one-sided situation (Spurgeon 1993).

However, there are some subtle complexities in the exercise of the consumer role within this context. Historically, the doctor (normally a hospital consultant in conjunction with the GP) has acted via his or her expertise on behalf of the patient. Traditionally, again, this paternalistic pattern has been accepted and unchallenged. Even in a consumer-based market system great difficulties remain for the consumer/patient. There is a considerable asymmetry in the access to relevant information for patient and doctor, with the latter much favoured. Furthermore, normal market exploration by trial-and-error purchasing is not present in health care. As a consequence, the GP has increased in prominence as a proxy for the patient, and so in a contracting situation the power dynamic between GPs (purchasing) and consultants (delivering service) has changed fundamentally.

Further complexities are introduced into these relationships by the degree to which the different agents may value different elements. For example, professionals will still tend to value technical capacity and safety—whilst patients may place greater and conflicting emphasis upon local access and pleasantries of interpersonal contacts.

Formal evaluations of the reforms are scarce and are not appropriate here. However, the inherent tensions within the approach have stimulated considerable debate (Lapsley 1994). The experience of the case study sites examined here reflects many of the tensions and dilemmas of putting market-based reforms into practice.

Market Characteristics

One of the most consistent and remarkable impressions from all sites is a sense of ambivalence about embracing market forces. This impression is not so much a reflection of ethical or value conflicts, although there may be individuals with their own concerns, nor is it to be seen in the rhetoric where there is great emphasis upon statements such as 'ensuring value for money' or 'planning contracts so as to maximize the utilization of public monies'. It is more to do with the practice of how to create and implement a market environment; how to overcome the barriers of geography, local access, and the viability of provider organizations offering services with high levels of interdependence.

Some simple statistics about the nature of the contracts let by each purchaser illustrate the degree of effort and energy needed to move such a structure to a dynamic market situation. Site A places 90 per cent of its contracts with five main, local providers; Site B spends 92 per cent of its budget on standard, routine secondary care in local hospitals; Site C similarly spends half of its total budget with two local hospitals; and finally Site D allocates 95 per cent of its budget with four main providers. It is clear immediately that there is a strong pressure towards inertia, as significant change to these buying patterns would result in major disruption and disturbance to local provision.

It is difficult to discern the real characteristics of markets in health since virtually all contract movement has been at the margin of cold elective surgery, and much of this has been driven by GP fundholders rather than health commissions. This in part reflects the differential orientation to populations. The GP fundholder is typically purchasing for a much smaller, relatively identifiable, set of patients. In contrast, the commission is either purchasing for whole services for the total population, or purchasing an integrated package of services from a provider unit, and, as a consequence, any movement is potentially very disruptive and destabilizing. The constraints, therefore, on market forces for health commissions are much greater.

The more significant changes in acute services are generally returned to a quasi-planning context of rationalization of services. None of the case study sites facing these issues has resolved them via market forces. Most are in the process of review or, in one instance, encouraging providers to offer a rationalized solution. Other services, such as mental health and learning disability, have tended to be less affected by competitive forces, but rather more by central or regional initiatives affecting their service base.

Local 'political' forces, local opinion, and a desire on the part of purchasers to maintain a range of local provision make any attempt to engineer radical change extremely difficult.

Interestingly in Site A (90 per cent local provider contracts), the focus of what might be described as market-led change has focused upon the remaining 10 per cent of the contracts. It is within these contracts that the conditions for market-oriented behaviour begin to come together. Each contract is relatively small, both in financial and activity terms, and therefore potential providers are both able to withstand the loss of such contracts and also have the capacity to encompass the additional work. Moreover, the purchaser has no long-term loyalty to these less local providers. Thus, one form of market that may have been said to have emerged is that of 'peripheral' markets. Although these may also be described as marginal in terms of finance they offer an opportunity, especially where specialist or tertiary services are involved, for the purchaser to bargain forcefully for both price and quality, since alternative suppliers may well exist and they will not destabilize their own local providers.

It is possible to discern perhaps three other forms of market structure within the case study sites. The first of these might be characterized as 'symbolic' markets and tends to be used by purchasers through mechanisms such as market testing or tendering for services (discussed in more detail later). Quite frequently, these mechanisms are used to prepare for major changes in the pattern of services. They rarely produce dramatic movement of contracts, but they do tend to serve notice of the purchasers' intention to examine services seriously and thereby excite positive responses in provider organizations. Thus the action taken can produce useful change by symbolizing the process of market forces at work.

A further form of market force may be captured by the term *rationalization*.

In a number of instances purchasers, particularly in large city sites, recognize a need to reduce the total level of provision or the number of different sites offering similar services. In these cases, the principle of the market should be an ideal mechanism to resolve such levels of over-provision. However, purchasers have largely felt unable to let market forces, unhampered, settle the problem. In part, this is because the market process will not simply impact upon the specific issue required, but have other undesired consequences. For example, the complex dynamic of forces or criteria (local access, quality, relative costs, variation in outcome, unit viability, and so on) are difficult to integrate into a single market decision. A number of initiatives will tend to focus upon quality or cost or a particular feature of a service but will often founder as the other factors come into play in an opposite direction, typically resulting in stalemate. Thus the attempt has been to seek to rationalize services by either enjoining providers to sort it out between them or by moving contracts, usually with intense resistance, to a single provider.

Finally, the last form of market relates to the GP fundholder purchasing function, and might more accurately be described as 'deals'. Here either a single fundholder or multi-fund, perhaps dissatisfied with a specific service, simply agrees a deal, usually within a year, for a fixed number of cases with an alternative provider. Although initially small-scale, such movements can lead to much broader change, sometimes within the deserted provider who reacts by improving its services or by other purchasers following the fundholder lead.

Market Relationships and Strategies

In all sites, virtually all provider units had attained self-governing trust status. The timetable of this process obviously varied both across and within sites. The sooner trust status became the norm, the sooner providers began to operate as independent units and the more 'hands-off' the activities of purchasers. It is difficult to envisage how the principles of a market in health care could operate prior to the separation of purchaser and provider being clearly established. The evolutionary nature of the process of acquiring trust status acted as an important inhibitor upon the establishment of the market. The existence of one or two main providers as directly managed units acted as a significant brake upon the purchasers' capacity to move contracts around. Manufacturing financial crises within units for which one is directly accountable is a strange, if not masochistic, activity. Thus in many instances, historic patterns of service, and thus contracts, were preserved.

The advent of a largely trust environment has enabled the purchasers to address the issue of rationalization of services. This process takes different forms in different locations but is driven by a number of common pressures:

- changes in medical practice which dramatically reduce the length of stay and therefore the need for the existing number of hospital beds;

- the increasing influence of clinical outcome studies suggesting the merits of concentrating resources on centres of excellence;
- a requirement to alter the balance of service provision from the acute sector to primary care.

Once again, these factors are not peculiar to a market economy and it is a contentious issue as to how many such changes would have occurred anyway in a more centralized system. All case study sites are committed to reviewing the pattern of services, and almost certainly to the reconfiguration of services (and organizations) that will alter previously established patterns of patient referral and clinical activity. Despite this commitment, the process of implementation was rather less clear.

Even where purchaser/provider relationships were good, the response of providers to proposals to rationalize services was, on the whole, defensive. On occasions this resistance was manifested through the mobilization of public displeasure at the projected closure of buildings or the loss of local service provision. The tension surrounding this process was exacerbated in those sites where purchasers were in a 'no-growth' situation and thus unable to release resources for alternative, compensatory activities. In such circumstances, there was pressure to reduce the capital estates and to release the money obtained to support developments.

It was apparent that in at least three out of the four case study sites the issue of rationalization of capacity was subject to both national and regional influences. This highlights not only the high profile and sensitivity of the health service but also the degree to which the market, as far as it exists at all, is managed. For example, in order that proposals to move towards centres of excellence for services such as trauma or paediatrics can be implemented, there must be an overriding regional perspective on the appropriate size and location of such centres. In this setting, individual purchasers lose some degree of control, or, at best, become agents of a regional plan or process of managed competition aimed at producing a predetermined outcome.

At a more specific level, purchasers are able to focus upon bringing down costs or improving standards of service in their immediate environment. One of the key strategies used to create immediate changes in the pattern of contracts is that of competitive tendering. The attraction of the approach is speed. Official Department of Health guidelines require that providers are given six months' notice of intention to shift services. This is not required for a service put out to tender.

As part of the process of challenging existing patterns of service, one site put six service areas out to tender. The process engendered a great deal of public reaction, political concern, and provider hostility. In retrospect a member of the health authority described the initiative as 'the initial impact was like we had launched an Exocet missile into the midst of the providers'. In some ways, the initiative could be seen as unsuccessful as the complexity, preparation required, service interactions, and coherence of the service pattern were not sufficiently thought through. However, there were important gains from the process. Providers recognized that there was serious intent to reorganize services and quite specifically sought a) to implement clinical protocols to improve services, and b) to work more closely with the purchaser as they proceeded with more limited tendering of services. Thus, a failed process had great symbolic impact and created a sense of market by identifying potential levers for future utilization.

A further case study site quite explicitly sought to foster the symbolic market. Although no specific tenders were issued, they did adopt a procedure of inviting providers to respond to 'statements of intent' about possible relocation of services.

Providers responded to these documents in a highly competitive style, thus producing a 'think market' mentality. An important outcome of creating the market culture has been a significant movement in the attitudes of clinicians. Whereas they had previously refused to recognize the potential for an alternative service pattern, the publication of a document spelling out the options had a galvanizing effect upon their view that it might really be a possibility. It is not so much an issue of tendering all services—or indeed a significant amount of the total budget—that creates the implied threat, it is the fact that a loss of a small component of a total service will have a consequent effect on prices for the remaining services in order that the total quantum of costs can be covered. Difficult technical issues underlie the problem in terms of how precisely the infrastructure costs of different services are to be apportioned.

Finally, the role of GP fundholders in creating a market has been much praised by the government. The 'deals' described earlier have undoubtedly created movement and a sense of disturbance in the traditional supplier base. On the other hand, this is still a relatively small component of the overall market. The future in all case study sites was one where combinations of GPs (including non-fundholders) come together as consortia or multi-funds. Clearly these combinations create larger pockets of resource and therefore have potentially more impact upon the market. However, it is not clear that this will be the outcome of such structures. In two sites, the objectives of such multi-funds are to encourage primary/community services but importantly to ensure that services, including hospital services, are available as locally as possible. Such a policy might actually result in less competition. The GP multi-fund influence is also uncertain in terms of lack of clarity in processes of accountability.

Summary

Overall it is clear that there is limited development of a market in health. The rhetoric and intention is strong, but so, too, are the constraints. Perhaps the most powerful countervailing influence to market principles is the requirement, reinforced by local views, to maintain locally accessible services. This is in part a political issue with few purchasers willing to risk the political and public fall-out of threatening local providers. Similarly, the difficulty of market capacity and the limitations upon organizations moving in and out of the market has not been solved. The market in health appears, then, to be a source of marginal movement, with other national forces, both political and clinical, being responsible for rather more significant changes in the overall pattern of health care provision.

LOCAL GOVERNMENT COMPULSORY COMPETITIVE TENDERING

Local government services subject to compulsory competitive tendering under the Local Government Act 1988 are refuse collection, street cleansing, building cleaning, vehicle maintenance, grounds maintenance, catering, and sports and leisure management. We begin by considering factors which have a general effect on the nature of markets and the likely level of competition for these services, before going on to examine case study evidence.

It is clear, first of all, that the characteristics of the services themselves differ, leading to a range of different markets (Walsh and Davis 1993). For example, building cleaning is labour-intensive compared to refuse collection which is capital-intensive. The former tends to have low start-up costs. Refuse collection is a highly visible service, being provided to all local authority residents. Grounds maintenance, of a local park, for example, has a less specific impact. Similarly, the position of the local authority as purchaser varies: there is a very strong element of monopsony in relation to street cleaning. While this is reduced for refuse collection, sports and leisure management and grounds maintenance, the council is likely to be the largest single purchaser; this will be least true of building cleaning. These factors will influence the possibility of local comparisons of performance, of competition *within* rather than *for* particular markets, and ease of entry and exit.

Sometimes, market relationships have to accommodate a complex range of contingencies, such as climatic conditions for grounds maintenance or requirements for the instant availability of some vehicles. It is, none the less, possible to set clear specifications and to monitor performance against them, so that the conditions are clear to market actors. A partial exception to this clarity is in leisure management. Here, there is greater discretion over the balance of activities and target audiences—a discretion which some councillors may wish to use in ways which reflect their values (for example, access for minorities, rather than profitability). This may be done both at the contract specification stage or later, with the resultant uncertainties creating features similar to social care and the white-collar services recently subjected to competition. A related problem concerns information asymmetry, once a leisure management contract is let. Given that it is likely to constitute a local monopoly, incumbent providers hold the detailed information about customer preferences and costs, and so are likely to be difficult to dislodge.

The nature of the service will influence the character of provider organizations.

For example, there is less likelihood of capital-intensive services, such as refuse collection, being provided by small-scale organizations, whereas in building cleaning, where start-up costs are low, there is more scope for local companies to compete. The way that services are packaged will also be important. A vehicle maintenance contract which incorporates the whole of the authority's fleet is likely to attract fewer tenderers and expressions of interest than a vehicle maintenance service which is packaged into contracts comprising discrete blocks of work, especially if the former includes specialist vehicles such as fire engines. These decisions also affect the nature of the competition, with discrete blocks allowing a level of competition *within* the service, rather than episodic competition *for* it.

Walsh and Davis (1993) discuss the level of competition for local government services in some detail and conclude that, although there were service variations, generally the growth in competition over time has been fairly rapid, with private providers winning a significant proportion of contracts overall. Measures of competition include changes in the number of:

- providers expressing an interest in bidding for contracts;
- providers being invited to bid;
- actual bids;
- and number and value of contracts awarded to private sector and other authority providers.

Factors contributing to this phenomenon will be discussed in more detail in relation to the case study sites. In general, however, the private sector is becoming better equipped to put in competitive bids as it becomes more familiar with, and obtains more information about, service areas which have traditionally been dominated by local authority providers. Equally, local authority attitudes may have changed as experience of working with the private sector is gained and previously held assumptions (often negative) are challenged. (Of course, there will also be authorities which have had negative experience of working with the private sector which can also influence and reinforce existing attitudes.)

There have also been changes to the legislative framework for contracting. For example, European legislation is becoming increasingly important. The Acquired Rights Directive of 1987, which protects the rights of workers who move from one employer to another, was incorporated into British law by the Transfer of Undertakings (Protection of Employment) or 'TUPE' regulations in 1991, although the circumstances under which TUPE applies are still contested. A further area of European legislation that is important is that on procurement.

There has also been more scrutiny of contract development and processes and the Department of the Environment has set up an enforcement section to monitor performance. In 1993, the Secretary of State issued twenty notices for alleged anti-competitive behaviour, and gave twelve directions, normally requiring re-tender.

These changes impact on what has perhaps mistakenly been called the 'level playing field'. The phrase has been coined to reflect calls for fair competition between public and private sector providers. The artificial horizon, used by pilots, might perhaps be a better analogy, given the shifting fortunes of internal and external providers in relation to competitive advantage.

The various influences on markets will now be considered in relation to the case study sites.

Market Characteristics and Structures

The status of our case study authorities determined the range of services for which they were responsible. Being metropolitan districts, Sites E and H had responsibility for all of the relevant services. As a county council, Site F was not concerned with refuse collection, street cleansing, and sports and leisure management. Site G—a non-metropolitan district council—had no responsibility for providing services to schools and its vehicle maintenance, cleaning, and catering responsibilities were more limited.

In Site E, at the time of the interviews, all 1988 Act services had been won by the in-house contractor. At the opposite end of the scale in Site G, all 1988 Act services had been contracted out via a management buy-out.

There are, as suggested earlier, a number of ways of conceptualizing and measuring competition. There are a set of measures which relate to whether or not there is a 'market' for a particular service which include the measures outlined earlier and used in Table 6.1.

However, markets are also heavily influenced by the behaviour of the various actors in the market. For example, the approach an authority takes to packaging its contracts will be influenced by the stance taken to competition. Similarly, the evidence suggests that providers behave tactically, targeting strategic locations or concentrating on welcoming authorities. These other factors will be explored further below.

Market Relationships

In local government terminology about CCT a distinction is made between purchasers and users. Users are called clients and these may be institutional clients (for example, schools or departments) or local authority residents. Officers purchasing services on behalf of these clients are called client agents. In some cases, a department can be a client and client agent. For example in Site H, the department of engineering and town planning was a client for grounds maintenance and a client agent for vehicle maintenance. In this same example, the department performed the purchasing function for vehicle maintenance, both for itself and other clients.

There are service variations in the client and client-agent arrangements. For example, in refuse collection there tends to be a single institutional purchaser acting on behalf of local residents. For building cleaning there may be several

TABLE 6.1. The local levels of competition for local government services

---

Site G Highly competitive.
No 1988 Act services provided in-house.
Approximately 18 providers applied to go on the select list for building cleaning in the first round of tendering. The total increased to 53 in the second round of tendering.

Site F Level of competition increasing over time.
Five contracts won by private providers (although two of these were subsequently awarded to the DSO).
Approximately 9 providers submitted bids for the vehicle maintenance contract.
In building cleaning there had been 6 bids, in addition to the DSO bid, in the first round of tendering.

Site H Limited competition.
Two contracts awarded to external providers.
There were no bids other than the DSO bid for the first tranche grounds maintenance contract let. Of approximately 11 providers expressing an interest in bidding for the second tranche grounds maintenance contract, three, in addition to the DSO, were invited to tender.
For both the building cleaning and sports and leisure management contracts, two providers (in addition to the DSOs) expressed an interest in bidding, although they did not actually do so. In most other services there was only one bid, other than that from the DSO.

Site E Limited competition.
All 1988 Act services provided in-house.
There were 6 expressions of interest in relation to the sports and leisure management contract, but only one provider (other than the DSO) asked for the documentation, and in the end it did not actually submit a bid. This example was fairly typical of most services in this authority, where there tended to be either a single bid from the DSO or one other bid.

---

hundred clients (including schools, libraries, and so on), whose relationship with purchasers may vary.

One particular group of users who have had a significant influence on contracting are schools. Under the Education Reform Act 1988, the local management of schools (LMS) and the ability of schools to opt for grant maintained status (GMS) has had a considerable impact on the competitive position of in-house contractors by giving power to schools to choose how they purchase. Small schools (employing less than three full-time or equivalent staff in the relevant areas) are exempt from the legislation in the case of grounds maintenance and building cleaning, and can choose whether they want to be part of the contracts or to organize their own provision outside the contract (perhaps from the DSO or by employing staff directly).

The power of local authority DSOs to work for grant maintained schools is both limited and unclear: a common, though not necessarily correct, interpretation of the legislation (Education Act 1993, section 144) is that the local authority can only do work for schools that become grant maintained for two years after they do so.

All of this means that where schools are users of local authority services, they are important stakeholders in the market. In Site F, although 90 per cent of schools felt that the purchaser function for grounds maintenance should be carried out by a central department, the overwhelming majority decided to employ their cleaners directly, rather than paying for a cleaning service to be provided via the DSO. This obviously had major implications for the provider. In effect, the LMS legislation gave schools greater freedoms than other institutional clients (such as libraries, or other departments) and the views of one group of users were being given precedence over others. The authority commented that it would not have implemented such freedoms had it not been compelled to do so.

In Site E, schools' concerns over budget constraints and dissatisfaction with levels of provider responsiveness, resulting in threats to leave the DSO, had contributed to a major restructuring of the purchaser function to make the interests of the user paramount. Councillors on school governing bodies had acted both as a brake on their unilateral action and as a pressure for this change of style. In Site H, it was not only schools, but also tenants' organizations who were influencing contracts to make these more reflective of and responsive to their needs.

Thus interaction between these other pieces of legislation and CCT was not without problems, and the fact that there was little integration with other legislation (the development of the Education Reform Act 1988, for example, was prepared without any discussion between the Department of Education and the Department of the Environment) meant that a good deal of sorting out has had to be done after the legislation was introduced.

The power of schools and tenants' associations to opt out of the general arrangements means that all education and housing authorities potentially face this issue. One way of coping with it, however, is to extend the rights of other users. This would not necessarily have to be in the form of rights of exit or choice, but could include a greater commitment to respond to comments made by users (rights of voice). Similarly, the ability of users to exercise influence or their rights of exit depend on how informed they are. Information was a key issue in several sites in relationships between purchasers, providers, and users: it will be explored in more detail in Chapter 7.

Relationships between providers were also perceived to be significant. The dominant view, held by purchasers and providers, was that private sector providers were colluding with each other against DSOs, forming cartels and fixing prices: 'There are cartels . . . I don't care what anybody says. The big boys are playing the field just like the petrol companies: keep off my patch and I'll put in a higher bid.' There was no hard evidence as such for these beliefs. However, one authority had lost a contract to a private provider whose parent company had been found by the Director-General of Fair Trading to be guilty of collusion in relation to Ministry of Defence contracts. Furthermore, one private provider referred to an unwritten code which limited competition to agreed areas, in the interests of the development of the market. It had, none the less, recently contravened that code.

In another example, a DSO had discovered from one of its suppliers that a private provider had spent the equivalent of one year's income on capital—a move which was perceived to be 'suicide for a commercial contractor'. There were also examples of various companies, either competing directly with case study DSOs or other local authorities, which were putting in 'loss leaders' (i.e. low bids), just to enable them to get a foothold in local authority markets.

Local authority providers also had an unwritten code of practice. One DSO commented: 'We do not tread on other local authorities' toes. The only reason we went to [this area] was because the DSO was a management buy-out and therefore a private company.' DSOs felt considerably disadvantaged compared to their private sector competitors, since the latter were able to access financial information which could assist them in preparing bids (such as the information relating to the specification that has to be provided for a TUPE bid and DSO accounts). DSOs, on the other hand, did not have access to similar information about their competitors.

Attitudes and Strategies towards Markets

Attitudes to CCT varied across authorities. In the metropolitan authorities, it was perceived to have diverted energy to issues which were not seen to be fundamental to the authorities' strategic objectives. In one authority, in the early stages, CCT was seen as: 'the biggest tidal wave that had hit local government for a long time. Every agenda and every discussion was dominated by CCT'.

However, in this authority, over time, 'as the tide has settled it is amazing how competence on CCT has been built into the organization and its management. . . . Now it is just a normal part of the job'. In contrast, the other metropolitan authority had, in reaction to the perceived diversionary nature of CCT, commissioned a council-wide review. This signified a fundamental re-think— a shift from a position of being driven by CCT to a position where the contract process was part of the approach to implementing strategic objectives and achieving a vision for the local area based on principles of accountability, good government, and user-focused services. In this way its reactive hostility to CCT was modified and redirected.

In the other two authorities, the impact of CCT on the wider authority was comparatively less important. In Site G, the effects of CCT had been marginalized to a single department: even the management buy-out had very little knock-on effect on other departments.

Table 6.2 sets out the general attitude to competition in each authority. All authorities were opposed to *compulsory* competitive tendering.

TABLE 6.2. Local authority attitudes to competition

Site E	Hostile to competition and belief that private sector would behave opportunistically. Reflected in: a) wide application of TUPE conditions and elimination of bids which did not meet them, b) only bids lower than DSO bid were evaluated, c) defensive contractual conditions. As the emphasis on quality took hold, however, there was greater willingness to consider private sector contractors where in-house performance continued to disappoint. This quality emphasis reinforced existing support for an internal purchaser/provider split, although some wished to revert to twin-hatted management.
Site F	Pro-competition where this would improve services. Fair procedures emphasized, for example, all interested had a chance to say what would put them off bidding, while 'Chinese walls' were constructed to stop the DSO gaining access to additional information or exerting extra influence over contract specifications. In the early stages the authority had been fairly proactive in its contracting policy (for example, fire vehicles were included in the vehicle maintenance contract). However, with the change of majority party, the emphasis had changed slightly and only those services which had to be tendered under the legislation were put out to tender.
Site G	Pro-competition though not in favour of the 'extreme view that Nicholas Ridley proposed that we are working towards the authority with one chief executive and one leader'. Short-listed contractors were invited to comment on documentation and later to discuss bids and correct minor errors. Attitudes had become increasingly favourable over time as they were reinforced by positive experiences.
Site H	Generally not in favour of competition. DSO closely involved in contract specification in some instances. There was also an implication that where contracts were won by the in-house provider, relationships tended to return to how they were prior to CCT. There were some differences in attitudes between different parts of the authority. For example, although there was general hostility to competition, this had been accompanied by, in some cases, a fairly extreme approach to purchaser/provider roles (such as some schools and other clients treating DSOs as if they were not part of the authority). Members of the Conservative group were also more open to the possibility of contracts being won by external providers, and this view was more generally shared in areas where quality improvements had failed to materialize.

In all four sites, the preferred provider was professed to be the DSO, but Table 6.2 suggests that this preference took various forms. In Site G, for example, initially the authority was supportive towards the in-house contractor. It was only when it came to be seen as unrealistic in the long term to think about retaining services in-house that they were externalized. Sites E and H were both concerned to do everything possible, within the law, to retain services in-house. In Site F, the phrase 'supportive but not protective' was used, although contractor representatives felt there was more emphasis on not being protective than there was on being supportive.

Site G, having no internal providers, enjoyed a greater degree of freedom (since there is no requirement to undertake CCT if there are no internal providers), although it still complied with the spirit of the legislation. It saw tendering as important, but only at relatively infrequent intervals if the relationship was working well, and was prepared to extend contracts by up to the length of the original term, although not indefinitely.

Examples of approaches to the packaging of contracts provide useful illustrations of attitudes to competition and are given in Table 6.3.

Undoubtedly, approaches to packaging have an influence on provider decisions about whether or not to bid for contracts, not least by eliminating smaller operators. However, other factors were important. Private sector providers chose sites for their strategic importance where, for example, a company had won contracts in other nearby locations. Similarly, Site G, as a tourist centre, constituted a flagship for any successful bidder. The attitudes of local authorities were also reported to be influential—at least in the short term—with providers targeting authorities likely to be more welcoming first.

If I was [private company X] I wouldn't target [this authority] . . . when I could choose another authority which would be more welcoming. For example [private company Y] won [a contract] here and it could be made easier for them to develop better partnerships, but certain people don't want that, they want them out.

There was also an implication that in some areas, for example vehicle maintenance, providers would—again in the short term—be unwilling to compete against local authorities for one aspect of the work because they did not want to jeopardize relationships generally.

Some [garages] are reluctant to go against us because if they are seen to be predators they won't get the business of supplying vehicles to us (although that would never happen because of being anti-competitive). It's big business selling vehicles to local authorities. There will come a day, though, when they'll have a go at us.

The perception that private sector providers were concentrating on 'welcoming' authorities in the short term was one important aspect of provider behaviour. Another apparent trend was also significant. In a number of service areas across the case study sites, there were examples of contracts for which there were no other bids besides that of the DSO (see Table 6.1). Objectively, then, there was little or no competition for these services. However, in many of these examples, private contractors had been put on the select list and had been sent the documentation. DSOs therefore believed they were facing real competition and bids were submitted on that basis. It was only when the bids came to be opened that the reality of the situation became apparent. In many cases, DSOs had

TABLE 6.3. Packaging service contracts in local government

Site E   The catering contract included, in one single contract, schools catering (i.e. all educational establishments except special schools), welfare catering (at day centres), and other catering (leisure outlets, golf courses, banqueting centres, and staffing outlets). In effect, then, only very large enterprises could bid. The authority stated that contracts were packaged to reflect the way that services were run, or the need for economies of scale, and not to deter competition. However, one informant admitted that the leisure contracts were written defensively, to cover 'every possible contingency against the private sector'.

Site F   A similar approach to Site E in that packaging reflected the way that services had traditionally been provided. In this authority, it *was* recognized that such an approach might deter some competitors. However, this was felt to be an unfortunate trade-off against the value for money obtained because of economies of scale. Some discussion was under way about whether to break up contracts to attract local firms.

Site G   Packaging decisions were determined by what would attract a good response from the private sector and produce the best quality service. For example, the cleaning of public toilets could have been packaged in a discrete block but was put with public building cleaning because it was felt that it would have come with 'a bit of stigma' on its own. For the same general reason street cleaning was originally subdivided, but was now being brought under one contract.

Site H   There had been some conflict over the packaging of the grounds maintenance contracts. One officer had wanted these to be let on a geographical basis but was overruled by a member who wanted the work in each tranche scattered over the borough on a 'pepper-pot' basis. This was a piece of defensive contracting designed to deter competition, a reaction to perceptions of the private sector as opportunistic. The member responsible seemed to have forgotten that if the DSO was successful, it would have to run that contract. The decision on packaging was contested, but this example is indicative of the attitude of the authority to competition, compared with the other sites. None the less, a national contractor had written a letter of thanks to the authority for the way the building cleaning contract documentation had been put together. Similarly, it had been decided to repackage the single housing maintenance contract into smaller chunks, while it was possible for tenderers to bid for either all or parts of the leisure management contract. Thus, there were indications that tactics hostile to competition were neither uniform nor fixed.

introduced radical changes (such as restructuring, changes to terms and conditions) in response to the perceived competition.

That DSOs were taking the threat seriously was illustrated in Site H, where there was limited 'real' competition. In response to the perceived threat in two service areas, bids had been submitted which subsequently proved to be unworkable: one of these contracts was being re-tendered before the due date, another was in deficit.

Contestability, or the threat of competition, is an underinvestigated area. It would be interesting to examine, for example, the actions of private companies who engage in seemingly irrational behaviour (for example, loss leading or going through the process of being accepted onto a select list and then not submitting a bid). Do these private companies have every intention of bidding for the contract but are deterred by the actual documentation, or is their behaviour part of a long-term rational strategy? Loss leaders, for example, could be viewed as an investment in information, buying a foothold, learning by doing. Using an analogy of direct and indirect racism or sexism, are contractors who do not submit bids, when they have been invited to do so, competing indirectly?

Finally, mention should be made of local authority *provider* attitudes to competition. In many cases, DSOs were not against it. However, many found themselves in very difficult positions, given the constraints they faced. The restrictions on cross-boundary tendering have been outlined above, as have the effects of information provided by tenderers making TUPE bids.

In addition, there were also significant difficulties caused by the dual pressure of operating in a competitive environment and living within local authority and government guidelines. The fact that the term 'level playing field' was coined reflected the idea that public sector providers needed to compete on more equal terms with their private sector counterparts. The perceived unfair advantages relate to the monopoly position of most public providers. However, simply removing that monopoly has not resulted in a level playing field and in reality, perhaps, DSOs are increasingly being seen as disadvantaged in relation to their private sector competitors. Furthermore, unlike their private sector counterparts, DSOs do not have the opportunity to bid again for a contract if they lose it in the first round. To extend the analogy, DSOs are playing in cup matches, whereas their competitors are playing in league games.

Pessimism about DSOs' ability to compete was shared across the case study sites: 'DSOs feel subject to sudden death, if they lose a tender . . . They feel they are constrained by the authority on how they can behave, for example, on external trading and cross-boundary tendering.' It was noted earlier that Site G's decision to externalize its services was influenced by its assessment of the future for in-house providers. There are also further tensions, in Labour authorities in particular, between the perceived need to change terms and conditions to make DSOs more competitive and the desire to be a 'good' employer. That there is an emphasis on cutting terms and conditions is perhaps a reflection of the rhetoric of the inefficient public sector (which lay behind the introduction of competition into the public service). These perceived inefficiencies have (at least in the past) been attributed to apparently higher wages for public sector workers than their private sector counterparts. Interestingly, in countries like Australia and New Zealand (see Chapter 9), a definition of cost-effectiveness does not include so-called savings which derive from cuts to wages, terms, and conditions.

In these difficult circumstances, DSO managers did not regard any meetings they had with their counterparts elsewhere as 'colluding' in the way that they suspected the private sector of doing, particularly since it was claimed that there was no discussion of prices.

Conclusions

Local government CCT services do not contain the same value element or problems of rationing which face other services, nor are they, by and large, experience goods or ones which are co-produced in the interaction between service and user. This makes their specification and marketization easier, although economies of scale and asset specificity may mean that, for some services, *local* competition is episodically *for* the service rather than within it, albeit within a developing regional or national market. Where they faced choices, however, our case study authorities tended not to break up services to encourage local markets, preferring the ease and familiarity of management, the robustness and probity believed to be afforded by existing providers. Only where the framing rules forced a dispersion of decisions did much greater diversity arise. None the less, the contestability of provision did produce significant changes in both working conditions and productive efficiency. Equally, the separation of purchasing and providing, under these contestable conditions, led to a stronger focus on service requirements and, within that, on user responsiveness and quality.

PERSONAL SOCIAL SERVICES

In so far as a market in social care can be said to exist, it has three distinctive characteristics: it is poorly defined and delineated; it contains providers from within and outside the commissioning authority; and it is highly differentiated and fragmented. We discuss each of these features in turn, before turning to the case study evidence.

There are various criteria of market definition and in each case the outcome for social services is unclear. Those responsible for purchasing are not clearly defined, since responsibility can be contested between SSDs, the NHS, housing authorities, the Benefits Agency, and, most of all, family and informal care. Indeed, there are some complex patterns of co-purchasing, as when the SSD recoups charges from people receiving attendance allowance, or relatives 'top up' the SSD payments in order to afford more expensive residential care.

Similar forms of complexity could be outlined when one considers responsibility for provision of services. An example will suffice: as well as family support, a confused and arthritic 80 year-old might potentially receive services from community nursing and physiotherapy, hospital rheumatology, and psychogeriatric services—all of which are free—home care, meals, or day care—subject to charge—from SSD, voluntary, or commercial providers. A decision by the

NHS trust provider to increase patient throughput by reducing lengths of stay and ceasing 'continuing care' can have major repercussions on both purchasers and other providers alike.

Lastly, the definition of services themselves is not always clear cut: 'day care', for example, can mean many different things, some of which have close substitutes in the commercial field, which a local authority would not dream of paying for.

The second key characteristic is the combination of providers, from within the SSD, in voluntary, and commercial agencies. Depending on the local arrangements, the price, the trading currency, the contractual form, and the rules governing trading are likely to vary with the nature of the provider. An SSD will pay for its directly provided services in advance through its base budget: the unit cost is likely to be higher than it is prepared to pay for external services, and the internal trading currency will be in places or hours of services, distributed between local purchasing teams. It will tend to have a block contract with voluntary agencies and floated-off trusts, and so the local trading currency is again places or hours of service. With commercial agencies, where 'spot' contracts are the norm, the currency will be monetary only. The rules allow local authorities discretion over the choice of providers, save for residential care when service users have a choice. However, their grants from central government force them to spend most new money externally. Finally, they are not allowed to provide nursing homes internally.

For all the messiness, however, other conditions favour market relations. By and large, capital intensity varies between minimal and moderate, and asset specificity tends to be limited to a small proportion of specialist staff. The opportunity for competition is, however, limited by a strong preference for local provision, allied to the specialization of user groups: this can lead to a proliferation of small, local monopolies. None the less, comparison with the NHS is illuminating.

We have seen how the vast bulk of acute health care is contained within contractual relations with a very small number of major local providers. By contrast Authority L, alone, has signed contracts to trade under terms contained within that agreement with 239 residential care and 103 nursing homes for elderly people, and 156 residential and 18 nursing homes providing for special needs. Its literature to local care managers gives details of a further 167 homes with which it has no advance contract, but with whom it might trade on terms to be negotiated. A substantial minority of all these establishments lie outside its own geographic boundaries. The statistics above exclude its own provision. While a substantial number of these contracts will never be brought into life, since no service user will choose the home concerned, it is clear that a competitive market exists for at least some social services.

It is important, too, to remember that other aspects of social care affect market relations—especially those between service user, purchaser, and provider. It is pre-eminently an experience good, with an element of co-production between users and providers. It takes place in a relatively closed environment and its recipients are often vulnerable and their capacity to speak out is constrained.

All of this implies that choice at the point of entry is a poor weapon, while there is considerable scope for provider opportunism (which is by no means limited to the private sector). Registration and inspection procedures cover only some services and are an imperfect means of limiting any abuse. Purchasing agents are also seen as an important source of protection, but they also have the responsibility to ration services, so that they interpose themselves between users and providers in a number of potentially contradictory guises. We now turn to our case study evidence, to see how these various factors interacted within various local authority contexts and strategies.

Purchase and Provision of Residential and Nursing Home Care

Care for Elderly and Disabled People   The data needed to map this market are incomplete, especially in respect of overall purchasing. The registration process does, however, provide details of provision and its usage, while there are data about SSD purchasing.

The purchase of residential and nursing home care is split between the SSD, the Benefits Agency for residents protected under the old arrangements, and individuals and families. Users might pay the full amount, or top up their Income Support or SSD payments, and/or be charged by the SSD. Health authorities also purchase a small amount of nursing home care. However, the NHS and Community Care Act means that SSDs are becoming dominant as purchasers, except at the more expensive end of the market. This is in marked contrast to their rapid and continuing decline as providers.

Table 6.4 attempts to summarize the position both nationally and in our case study sites. Some general points stand out. First, local authorities inherited very different sets of market conditions when the new arrangements came into force, as regards the overall level of supply, the balance between supply and demand (both generally and in different localities), and relative market shares. These differences were as much to do with the supply and price of suitable land and buildings as anything else. Within this context, local authority strategies as *providers* varied: Sites I and J tried to externalize provision, with Authority I being clearer that the change was to protect those services and implementing the strategy more speedily than J; Sites K and L attempted to retain services in-house, but both were bowing to spending restrictions and market forces in closing homes. Equally, their strategy as *purchasers* varied considerably. Authority J made most attempt to treat all providers equally and to revise its limited contractual arrangements in the light of messages from commercial providers. Authority K was content to exploit a buyer's market, while Site L made the most energetic attempts to extract value for money from the commercial providers, towards whom its attitude of suspicion persisted. Conditions obtaining in the market markedly modified the impact of such different strategies, however. The clearest example is that the authority most favourably disposed to the market ended up purchasing *least* care in the commercial sector.

TABLE 6.4. Trends in the markets for registered care and nursing homes

	Trends in Purchasing	Competitiveness and Market Buoyancy	Trends in Provision
National	Local authorities becoming the dominant public purchasers: 58% rise in residents they finance (at least in part) to 118,500 in the year 1993–4. Local authority strategies thus an important determinant of market conditions. Limited NHS purchasing of nursing home places. Substantial additional minority of privately funded residents, some in same homes as LA-supported people.	Market consolidation taking place, with public sector and small-scale provision declining and larger operators growing by acquisition and new construction. Significant increase in vacancy rates, but predicted market collapse has not occurred.	Significant decline of local authority share (from over 60% in 1980 to 24% now) with closures and transfer to other sectors. This taken up by rise in commercial and voluntary care home places. No public nursing home provision. Overall growth has kept pace with ageing population. Rapid growth in provision has ceased: slight decline last year. Marked local variation in overall provision and market shares.
Site I	Below average increase in LA-supported residents (51%). Purchase of commercial care home places limited compared with those in externalized trust.	Varies from local shortages in less affluent areas to considerable over-provision in older affluent localities. Shortage of specialist provision. Overall, however, homes have vacancies, some of up to 50% places.	Most local authority places externalized, giving high percentage of provision in voluntary sector. Limited growth of commercial sector, whose share remains below average. Commercial provision virtually non-existent in some localities. Overall rate of provision is below average.
Site J	Despite its 'even-handed' strategy, LA purchases below average proportions of commercial places and these are often outside its boundaries (over 1 in 5 of all purchases). Commercial provision that	High land prices restrict commercial development. Occupancy levels remain high, despite substantial export of customers.	Low overall rate of provision, with commercial sector virtually non-existent in poorer areas. Delayed transfer of local authority homes to trust, but LA decline in market share remains above average.

exists tends to be purchased privately. 65% of supported residents were in LA homes in 1994, compared with 50% nationally. Limited use of nursing homes.

Very high rates of overall provision and some continued expansion. Commercial provision dominates. Very limited voluntary sector. Local authority share relatively low, but its rate of decline was slower: this decline seems to be gathering momentum.

Site K Supported fewer people in care homes than a year earlier, mainly owing to decline in its own provision. Below average overall increase masks a sharp rise in nursing home places purchased. Overall LA spending on residential and nursing care remains high, despite low prices. Residents of K and elsewhere purchase a considerable number of private sector places themselves.

Rural area means that balance between supply and demand and existence of local choice varies greatly. Overall surplus exacerbated by appearance of large-scale providers using aggressive pricing and marketing strategies. High vacancy rates and some closures. Local shortage of specialist provision.

Site L Trends in local authority supported purchasing close to national average, except for limited use of commercial care homes in favour of own provision. Fairly high use of homes outside its boundaries, perhaps owing to tendering exercise. Virtually all short-stays (not subject to choice directive) are in-house.

Vacancies in mainstream provision, especially in local authority homes, bring pressure for contraction. Some shortage of specialist provision.

Despite average rate of decline and continuing closures, LA remains a significant provider of care places, balancing below average commercial provision. Overall level relatively low.

Sources: DoH Personal Social Services Local Authority Statistics, RA/94/1 and RA/94/2.

Care for other Client Groups   Residential provision for other groups is very limited compared to that for elderly people, which accounts for 78 per cent of long-stay and 60 per cent of short-stay admissions. The only other significant amount of such care is for people with learning difficulties (16 per cent long-stay and 35 per cent short-stay). This has seen some growth over the last decade, whereas the very modest amount of provision for mentally ill people has declined. For all client groups, short-stay admissions have been more buoyant than long-stay, reflecting a move towards ordinary living arrangements which the figures fail to show: a substantial amount of special-needs housing has been developed (by housing associations and voluntary bodies), with residential care acting as a back-up.

In our case study authorities, the commercial sector had a toe-hold of 10 per cent and 20 per cent in the residential care of people with learning difficulties in Sites K and L, respectively. The voluntary sector fared rather better, providing virtually all of the care financed by Authority I and minority shares of that in the other authorities. The local authorities remain the largest suppliers. These arrangements reflect a gradual and pragmatic build-up of services, in which contractual arrangements owed little either to political influence or to later orthodoxies of purchaser/provider splits.

Purchase and Provision of Domiciliary and Day Care

The 'market' for care in people's own homes is especially prone to the problems of delineation noted earlier, which bring in their train serious gaps in knowledge. Using the net cost of local authority home care, Wicks has estimated that informal carers contribute £30bn. per annum towards the care of disabled and infirm people (*Mixed Economy of Care Bulletin*, 3 (1994), 15). We know a good deal less about the home care and housework which is purchased directly by its recipients, except that it is also probably substantial, but on by no means the same scale as informal care.

Local authorities tend to take a much narrower definition of the market—that is, the care that they purchase. None the less, these market segments do connect: there is no doubt that one effect of the changes was to transfer the cost of some care from its recipients to the local authority. However, taking the local authority definition, SSDs increased their contact hours by 24 per cent in 1993–4 and the number of users by 5 per cent. This latter figure masks a withdrawal of services from people needing housework-only services in order to concentrate on those with more substantive needs. Since local authority base budgets were under extreme pressure and they were prevented from spending the new money internally, it is not surprising that virtually all of the increase was purchased externally: the market share of voluntary providers rose fourfold to 3 per cent, while that for commercial agencies rose fivefold to 16.5 per cent.

In common with the national pattern, this purchasing was done on a very local basis in our case study authorities, with local teams alighting on agencies who gave a good service and relying on them to expand. Those agencies were themselves very small in scale, often being employment agencies for labour-only subcontractors. The presence of some national franchising operations was reflected locally, but there are few economies of scale in the management of home care, most of such tasks occurring close to the users.

The balance between supply and demand seemed to vary a great deal within authorities: in affluent retirement districts there was likely to be a considerable shortage; and in most areas it was difficult to find home carers willing and able to look after people with challenging behaviour—an especially acute problem in rural areas.

In order to meet these problems of shortage and the limits on its own expansion, Site J was externalizing some of its more specialized services to two trusts. Market-testing of simple services, such as shopping, had shown that they were not viable.

Day care is dominated by the local authorities who provide 85 per cent of it. Voluntary agencies organize most of the remainder, but their provision is rising more quickly, as is that of the currently very small commercial sector. It is here that there is perhaps greater scope for the diversification from residential services which the government is seeking. However, home owners have been rightly cautious: transport problems and the managerial and sometimes architectural challenges arising when a new group of outsiders enter the semi-private space of long-stay residents can act as disincentives. Some home-owners see day care and even local domiciliary care as a means of ensuring customer loyalty to their own services. They are especially chary of domiciliary care however: it requires intensive operational management and staff cannot be supervised directly, so the risk to their reputation is greater.

Strategies and Attitudes towards Markets

Wistow *et al.* (1992) note that when the reforms occurred, market development was foreign to most SSDs' understanding of their 'enabling' role: they saw social care as qualitatively different from marketized services; they were proud of public provision; they doubted that many new actors would enter any new market; they believed that many trusted agencies were unable or unwilling to become competitive businesses; they worried about the impact of commerce upon volunteering and informal care. Such attitudes were by no means confined to Labour authorities, but that party's electoral successes did nothing to increase enthusiasm for market reforms. Furthermore, there were competing priorities—the Children Act, local government reform, complaints procedures, community care plans, assessment procedures—much of which could be implemented without too much attention to market strategies.

However, other pressures were also in play. People had ambitions to meet needs and develop services, using whatever means and incentives were at hand:

their first contacts with the commercial sector and use of contracts had often arisen from the opportunistic expansion of accommodation for people with mental health needs, or learning disabilities, using social security funds and specific grants. Similarly, even hard-up Labour authorities were planning to float off services to trusts in order to shunt costs onto the DSS and also attract private finance needed to improve standards in residential homes, until this option was closed by Circular LAC (91)12.

Such contingencies influenced policies. None the less, Wistow *et al.* (1992) found as many 'conscientious objectors' as 'proven enthusiasts' for market solutions among their sample of 24 authorities, with most adopting cautious and incremental positions between these extremes. Many were cautious because they acknowledged the Audit Commission's view that they lacked the knowledge, information systems, and technical skills needed to behave competitively as suppliers, or to manage markets as commissioners (Audit Commission 1993*b*). They criticized the limited national investment in infrastructure.

Overall, then, the approach was to get things moving, to talk to and do business with suppliers in the main existing market (residential and nursing home care), and to achieve a smooth transition, while relying on trusted suppliers for other services. In this, DoH and Audit Commission advice undoubtedly had an influence.

The reaction from the voluntary sector was equally mixed. Many saw marketization as antithetical to the philosophy and ways of working of voluntary bodies; some feared that the further incursion of monopsonistic local commissioners, driving ever harder bargains, would truncate their identity and independence; others, particularly some 'voluntary corporations', saw it as a positive opportunity to stabilize funding and exploit market advantages, so that they could grow and develop their professionalism.

The private sector was perhaps most suspicious of all. The DSS system had been a licence to increase demand: many did not welcome a cash-limited 'enabling'/rationing agency—especially in the form of a competitor, staffed by social workers having little knowledge of, or sympathy for, business imperatives. Concerns about the absence of a 'level playing field' and calls for standard national contracts were widespread, but particularly sharp where there was a potential oversupply. Amid this concern, some were looking for expansion and business opportunities in the wider social services market, while others were attempting to escape from it, trading up to that segment which was purchased privately.

Among our case study sites, L exhibited most signs of conscientious objection. Attitudes among majority party politicians varied from cut-throat hostility to resignation: those among officers encompassed these views but ranged wider, with some seeing the changes as a positive opportunity to replace current modes of operation. Strategically, it attempted to defend itself against any incursion of market forces beyond those which it is statutorily forced to accept, refusing to countenance contracts for other than residential and nursing home places. For example, enquiries about potential commercial investment were rebuffed and there was a political veto on the regularization of relations with private home care suppliers, even though this was seen to be technically necessary. Purchasing of home care was only possible because it took place at the periphery of the organization, because assessed needs could not be met internally, and because small-scale providers, being almost akin to informal carers, could creep under the boundary fence which the authority had erected between 'market' ('untouchable') and 'non-market' forces.

Authority L had attempted to impose stringent interpretations of the registration conditions—not entirely successfully in areas of acute shortage. The policy backfired to an extent: its own provision had to be reduced to fund improvements in the remaining homes so as to meet those requirements. Furthermore, it was concerned to ensure both value for money and good standards for its citizens, regardless of their financial circumstances. In consequence, it banned top-up payments for homes with whom it had a contract; and it also undertook a tendering process, accepting only those providers who met quality standards and were prepared to impose the most competitive prices. Subsequently, some differential pricing for extra quality in physical conditions and in staff training was allowed for, as well as for residents having 'special needs'. The process could not be watertight: if a potential resident chose a 'non-contract' home, the local authority was obliged by law to pay its minimum contribution and allow that to be topped up.

The attempts to manage the market in this active way led to protests and acrimony from providers. It is perhaps for this reason that a decision to maintain the market in a steady state for the first year was made. In the event, our conscientious objector purchased a higher proportion of its care from commercial providers than any of the other authorities in the sample.

The voluntary sector in Site L was defined as 'non-market', and thus not subject to 'contracting'. Instead, service level agreements governed relationships. Notwithstanding these politically important semantics, relations with voluntary providers had become much more formalized and arm's-length in recent years, with a stress on performance targets, value for money, and a belief that the paymaster should call the piper's tune. Notions of equal partnership were rejected, even when those agencies undertook assessment work ('purchasing') on the authority's behalf.

As a result of CCT, Site L's SSD did have some trading relations which were internal to the authority as a whole. However, even with the projected separation of purchaser and provider elements within the SSD, there is no indication that there will be a move towards internal trading relationships within the SSD. A clear distinction has been maintained between the operation of internal and external budgetary systems.

While it could not be described as a 'proven enthusiast', Site J exhibited the most favourable attitudes towards the marketization of social care among our case study authorities. The dominant approach of politicians was pragmatic and consensus was carefully fostered by an emphasis on customer service and value for money. Much less attention was paid to the ownership of services than in Site L. This was accompanied by a view that officers should be free to manage, and key officers had embraced a model of an enabling department in which a strategic core, purchasing and commissioning, develops even-handed relationships with all providers, using market technologies as the chosen means. There were sceptics at many levels within the authority, but they were much less influential. Movement towards the implementation of this model was necessarily incremental, but there was a strong attempt to impose order and clarity on the process. Thus, formally approved policy documents existed, committing the SSD to provide clear expectations and targets, no shocks, reasonable prices, incentives for innovation, and encouragement of self-regulation in its dealings with 'the independent sector' (note the incorporation of both market and non-market elements, without distinction). In return, providers were expected to offer demonstrable value for money, to share their expertise and the management of risks, to join in strategic planning, and to protect users and promote their interests.

Because it has few residential and nursing home providers within its boundaries —many of whom aim at a more affluent market—Authority J's own provision is not in a competitive relationship with them. Indeed, it has to shop elsewhere, paying a slight premium over the minimum market rate to make itself attractive to outsider suppliers. In consequence, it conducts its relationships in a more individualized way and set-piece meetings with the trade associations are less significant than elsewhere. Early dissatisfaction over its original contract led to substantial simplification.

In line with its general approach, Authority J had made most progress in regularizing its relations with domiciliary care providers, being about to introduce a list of accredited providers who have satisfied criteria about both service quality and minimum business competencies. This process applied equally to commercial and voluntary providers. Indeed, voluntary agencies were generally expected to be well organized and efficient, and we have noted that performance targets and formal evaluation of services were an established part of the scene in Site J. Those agencies were also expected to raise their own funds—even continuing to provide services for 'low priority' groups when the local authority withdrew financial support.

Within the purchasing sections of Site J, there was pressure for the speedy marketization of relations with internal providers: they wanted to have the cash and to be free to trade with internal or external providers as they thought fit. This pressure was being resisted by internal providers and others, on the grounds that transaction costs would increase and that insufficient work had been done to identify the costs of democracy and of providing last-resort services, or to revise inherited terms and conditions of service. Thus, mainstream and external services are budgeted for separately and, save for long-term care, the first port of call was expected to be in-house or to the hived-off trust, with care managers only looking outside if services were 'unavailable or inappropriate'.

However, the externalization of services was being actively explored. The externalization of some specialist domiciliary care, setting up a trust to do so, was to allow for expansion using the STG: had the service stayed in-house, expansion would not have been possible. None the less, these moves were seen as incremental, experimental, and low-risk: the very difficult experiences with the existing residential care trust led to caution on all sides. In that case, both trust and SSD were concerned to limit their reliance on each other.

Perhaps not surprisingly in a Labour-controlled authority, the approach in K was a good deal more pragmatic, incremental, and emergent. The stress was upon service improvement in a financially constrained environment. This led to rather different strategies towards external trading. In the relatively new specialist mental health and learning disability teams the approach was entrepreneurial. There were few services available (and hence few vested interests), so packages of funds were put together and providers were actively courted (sometimes these were local, sometimes national or even international) and offered block contracts to develop specific services. Latterly, formal competitive tendering had been tried, but this was a new development.

Such strategies contrasted with those concerning the residential and nursing home care of elderly people. Here (save for local shortages of beds for mentally infirm people) the belief was that supply needed to contract in order to balance with future demand. The SSD strategy was to allow the market to manage itself down, resisting strong demands for specific market signals, and placating complaints from providers about perceived hostility/favouritism among care managers. While there was some regret that good quality, but financially overstretched, providers might go to the wall and that quality might be squeezed, the belief was that market failures could be coped with. Thus, the authority opted for simple contractual conditions and low prices.

Senior managers adopted a similar, rather cautious, and hands-off approach to non-residential services for elderly people, even though the strategy was to encourage their expansion. They could do so—and so minimize their own advance commitments—because the short-life market development agency was there to take on an entrepreneurial stance. It was able to pump-prime, to offer consultancy over market opportunities and business planning, as well as to interpret the local authority strategy to enterprises who expressed a interest. It concentrated most of its help on small cooperatives and on trusts set up to take on the assets of cottage hospitals as they were closed.

Within Site K, there was a growing sense of the emergence of a corporate, commissioning core of the department, seeking to impose rational, broadly market relations on the network of social care agencies. Thus, there was talk of turning community care plans into commissioning documents, accreditation systems for home care agencies were in an advanced stage of development, and the move towards trading relations within the department was contemplated as the logical extension of this process. The political constraints which might be imposed on such a process were a matter for conjecture.

We have noted how Authority I stepped back from radical approaches to the community care changes at both political and official level. In some senses, this radicalism was an aberration, since across the political divides there was pride in public services and sponsorship of voluntary agencies as worthy causes. Indeed, the externalization of much of the authority's own residential and day care and the generous trading conditions imposed can be seen as a means of protecting supply and creating a body capable of diversification, while maintaining a vestige of control and public service ethos. By the end of our research, there appeared to be no further plans either to externalize services or to develop internal trading relations.

Traditional forms of partnership with the voluntary sector have continued in this environment and the STG provided opportunities for the growth of new services under block contracts. Relationships vary from trusting delegation to paternalistic support, depending on the perceived professionalism and business competence of the agency concerned. We saw examples of officers giving detailed support over financial and business planning to a degree which was only matched elsewhere by the arm's-length enterprise agency in Site K. This support extended to protecting agencies from themselves when they proposed prices thought to threaten their viability or service quality.

The introduction of commercial organizations into this world of decentralized informal networks among 'people like us' caused difficulties on all sides. Commercial agencies were suspicious of local authority protectionism and professional hubris—to the point where judicial review was threatened to force disclosure of the terms of the contract with the trust. None the less, as elsewhere, there was shared recognition that working relationships needed to be developed, with the local authority supporting the formation of trade associations as the legitimate negotiating bodies and then attempting to construct a working partnership with them. This partnership has gone further than elsewhere, in that the contract (and its revision) have had a stronger element of joint design, while it is the trade associations who operate a bed-vacancy information system and who developed the publicity material for which the local authority paid. Similarly, the associations have worked on the development of common quality assurance systems.

Within Site I, there has been considerable debate about whether managing markets is either logically possible or practically feasible. For example, a modest hike in the price per bed did not have its intended effect of raising quality. In general, the conclusion has been to avoid 'messing with hidden and powerful forces', except to try to clarify short-term commissioning intentions through the community care plans. In all this, there has been a tension between strategic direction and local discretion. For residential and nursing home care it is hoped now to develop stronger links at local levels—levels which, according to commercial informants, are weakest and still characterized by suspicion. For home care the challenge is reversed: it is to gain greater strategic control of multifarious local circumstances and arrangements, in order to provide protection against adverse selection and to limit other risks.

Relationships with the Health Service

Two sets of organizations, one sometimes under threat of dismemberment (the Local Government Review), the other of amalgamation, and both undergoing radical internal reform, none the less had to redesign and reinforce the means by which they worked together. There remain many areas in which responsibility is shared, but the precise allocation of duties is uncertain or contested. The successful implementation of strategic policies is contingent on close working, but the performance targets of managers may or may not take account of that interdependency: those for long-stay services, such as the resettlement of people with learning difficulties, are more likely to do so than those relating to acute care, such as shortening waiting lists and speeding up throughput.

Thus, in the multiplicity of links between health and social care professionals, the reforms have created both major challenges to and new opportunities for the development of collaborative relationships. One challenge relates to widely differing definitions of purchasers and providers: in health most clinical staff making diagnostic decisions about patients are classed as 'providers', whereas in social care they are 'purchasers'. Being 'providers', managers and professionals in health are excluded from some joint planning forums, yet the social services staff with whom they work closely take a lead in those forums. The extreme case arose in Site K. The respective health trust and social services managers developed mental health services jointly: at the contract review meeting between trust and health purchaser, that same social services manager was on the other side of the table. The GP fundholder model is closer to the social services definition of purchasing. However, none of our case study authorities had yet developed close working relationships with them and, when they do, relationships with other health purchasers will become more complicated.

In two of our cases, district health authorities had been or were being merged; in all they were merging with FHSAs to form health commissions. Everywhere, too, there was a very heavy preoccupation with the organization and reorganization of acute health services: one set of reform proposals soured relationships with the local authority as a whole.

In such an environment, close personal links at chief executive/director level were seen to offer the best prospect of progress. These were particularly evident in Sites K and I. In K there was some joint commissioning and also close working relationships in joint mental health and learning disability teams: staff from health trusts undertook community care assessments, thus initiating social care purchases. Similarly, strategic managers from health and social services in Site I were working in very close concert over the resettlement of people from long-stay hospitals, coordinating their purchases and their contractual relations with providers. These close working relations were under some threat, as the SSD reorganization implied that, in future, this work would be spread among the five geographical divisions.

In Site J, the greater concentration had been upon reordering the procedures for strategic planning, and so relationships were closest with health commissioners. Those with the health trusts were somewhat less close and more prone to friction.

In Site L, the pattern is more mixed. Certainly some joint purchasing does take place, but it tends to be confined to joint finance monies. Strategic planning forums tend to focus on matters on which agreement is mandatory, such as hospital discharge.

Conclusions

Overall, it is possible to discern three broad types of market conditions and relationships emerging in the social care field.

The first concerns a very wide range of small-scale specialisms, usually based upon a mix of target group and technologies (counselling and advice, day care, short-term rehabilitation, sheltered housing). Here, the strategic enabling role is familiar to social services, though sometimes it is shared with health. And the structure is locally monopolistic in relation to purchasing and providing. There may be a diversity of providers over the local authority as a whole, enabling comparison of price and performance (and some SSDs have deliberately fostered a bounded diversity) but this varies according to economies of scale and scope. In general, then, relationships tend to be more hierarchical, with a strong element of coordination, rather than competitive. Within this segment, the institutional framework allows local authorities considerable discretion: it is bounded only by the tightly constrained financial environment, the incentive to externalize services created by the STG, and the need to exploit partnerships and mixed forms of funding in order to expand. As it is seen to become technologically redundant, or as its price is seen to be higher than alternatives, local authority provision risks being gradually run down.

The second concerns residential provision in registered care and nursing homes. Here SSDs continued with their registration and inspection role and had the choice of continuing to make direct provision. In addition, they rapidly took on the responsibility for purchasing virtually all care bought by the state. Here, the institutional rules imposed much greater constraints: there are national guidelines for registration and inspection; the directive on choice for residents limits their discretion over purchasing; the STG and the rules over housing benefit provide disincentives to continue as large-scale providers. Similarly, the market conditions inherited by local authorities have had a marked impact upon their strategic choices, both as providers and purchasers. The two key conditions have been the extent to which the SSD is the monopoly purchaser and the balance between supply and demand. Overall, the general pattern has been of a halt to overall expansion, a shift towards market consolidation, a risk of some market failure where supply substantially exceeds demand, and a continuation of the adverse terms of trade which have occasioned the steady decline in the local authority market share. We have seen, however, that these conditions have varied considerably, both within and between our case study authorities. In the face of these imperatives, we have observed both similarities and differences in local authority strategic choices. There are similarities in the way that they have developed a *modus operandi* with independent providers, and in the fact that their pricing systems all used the old DSS rates as a benchmark. There are differences in their enthusiasm to defend their own provision, in the tactics adopted to do so, and in the experience of implementing those tactics. There are differences in their overall stance towards commercial provision. None the less, both their strategic choices and the impact of these choices have been substantially limited by the combination of institutional rules and market conditions.

The final market segment concerns domiciliary care. The institutional framework is very similar to that of the first segment, allowing local authorities a great deal of strategic discretion. However, market conditions differ considerably: here the market is less well defined; relations between a variety of providers from SSD, voluntary, semi-commercial, and fully commercial agencies are potentially competitive; it is growing rapidly, the constraint being what local authorities can afford to purchase, which raises the issue of the confused balance between state purchasing and charging, as opposed to private purchasing.

It is in this segment that SSDs were facing challenges in several directions. What should be the relationship between users, purchasers, and providers? How could contractual relationships be framed to limit risk (especially of adverse selection and opportunism) and promote quality? What was an appropriate pricing policy, given that expansion was needed, quality was variable, and in-house costs were generally higher? Should the local authority seek to remain as a major provider and at what premium on costs? Our case study authorities had made very varying progress in addressing these issues, but in no case was the strategy fully developed, let alone implemented.

7

Managing Contracts

INTRODUCTION

In Chapters 5 and 6 we examined the structure developed to undertake contracting, and the nature of the contract/markets in which this takes place. This chapter will consider the ways in which contracts have been implemented, and discuss specifically how aspects such as risk management and service-quality issues have been addressed.

LOCAL GOVERNMENT SERVICES

We have discussed the structures for local government contracting (purchaser/provider structures and the framework for contracting) and the context in which contracting is carried out (the nature of the market and attitudes of the major players to competition). We have seen that there is a highly prescriptive and centrally imposed framework in which the development and letting of contracts takes place and that this level of prescription leaves little room for discretion at a local level, at least in terms of process.

The main focus of the first part of this chapter will be on the roles of different players, particularly users, in the development and implementation of contracts. The second will consider how risk is allocated and managed under contracting, how failure is dealt with and who is responsible for failure. This also has implications for members. The last part of the chapter will consider user satisfaction and will identify sources of dissatisfaction.

Developing and Implementing Contracts

The level of user influence on the development and implementation of contracts varied between sites. The integrated client-agent organization in Site E comprised two main sections: client liaison and client contracts. The relationship between these sections was very complex, at least on paper, although it seemed to work well enough in practice. For example, complaints by users would be handled by client liaison in the first instance, who would liaise with users and providers to get problems put right. Where problems persisted and the default procedure needed to be formally invoked, client liaison would also involve client contracts.

These complex relationships were necessary, however, to make the currently professionally orientated purchaser culture more user-focused. Just as the client-agent organization as a whole was to be firmly allied with the interests of the user, within the client-agency organization, client liaison was to be the users' champion ensuring that their concerns and needs were considered. In both cases, however, there were 'critical' links with, in the first case, the provider and, in the second, client contracts. Just as the provider had to have an input to (but not an undue influence on) the contracts, professionals also had a key role to play in developing contracts.

Managing these various relationships was highly complex and required particular skills, since although there had been considerable progress in challenging traditional approaches, there was a legacy of distrust which needed to be overcome.

In the second round of contracts there has been some improvement but there is still dissatisfaction. For example, some things have been included that the schools did not ask for and they want to know how it got in, on whose authority. There is always a suspicion that it comes from an interest in meeting the needs of the DSO rather than the school.

Part of the problem arose from a 'we know best' kind of attitude where client-agent staff acting in a professional capacity believed they were able to take a broader picture of what was necessary. However, as one person commented: 'You may know best but you have to present that knowledge in ways that don't put the other person down'. Problems associated with a 'we know best' kind of professionalism were also an issue in another of the case study sites. In Site H, the client agent's decision to change the form of the vehicle maintenance contract, from a time-based bill of qualities with costs per hour identified for specific vehicles to an annual single figure covering servicing and repairs for each vehicle, had been met by 'a bit of resistance in some of the client departments'.

There were a number of concerns and some users had been so opposed to the changes that they had taken legal advice on the possibility of preventing them. Both client agent and users had their reasons for proposing or being opposed to the change. For the purposes of this discussion, those reasons are, in a sense, not relevant. The example illustrates rather, an approach to contracting which was professionally driven and an exercise in communication which might have been handled more constructively.

In Site F, a consultation exercise aimed at giving schools the opportunity to select from a menu of options relating to how services were purchased, resulted in confusion for schools when some clients and contractors treated the consultation exercise as a marketing campaign. This is an issue for customers in a market-based system. In this particular example, schools felt that they were given a lot of information about their options but were not clear about which was the best option. They did not feel sufficiently comfortable to make a decision.

In this case, the decision was not a product decision where the client could be reasonably confident about advice given by the client agent, but a purchasing decision—how was the service to be purchased which would have implications for interested parties in the authority. Neither clients nor contractors were neutral. For example, contractors had a clear interest in persuading schools to choose the option which would give them the work as of right. Client agents had an interest in persuading schools to remain with a contract let centrally.

Not surprisingly, therefore, there were complaints about the presentation of the options from both interested parties. A contractor representative commented that information presented by the client agent was 'slanted' and that 'schools do not really know what they are being asked to decide and they fall in with the most obvious option in terms of the way the literature was slanted'. A client agent, in turn, commented that DSOs were not averse to using propaganda: 'The DSO sales campaign to explain to schools the benefits of staying with the DSO was no more than a series of threats. For example: "You realize that if you don't have us we will take your machinery off you".'

In Site G, the purchaser function was initially split into two sections: service design which was similar to the client-contracts function in Site E in that it incorporated responsibility for producing contract documents. Unlike Site E, however, reviewing how the service was provided, and in some cases obtaining user views on this, was also part of the function. The level of user input varied across services. In sports and leisure management, user groups were given an opportunity to feed into the process. In other areas, for example street cleansing, contracts were influenced by the views of professionals: 'People weren't that keen to be stopped in the street to fill in a questionnaire and [so] to a large degree it was our perception of what people wanted and what was a reasonable standard.'

There was also a service-implementation function covering all other aspects of contracting (i.e. pre-contract meetings, monitoring, financial control, keeping up to date with service development, and so on). Following the MBO (managerial buyout), however, the service design and service implementation functions were integrated completely and responsibility for all issues relating to a particular service area was reallocated to different officers within the technical and amenities department.

Roles for members varied across the case study sites. In all sites they performed formal roles which included ratification of specifications, approval of select lists, making broad strategic decisions on packaging and contract lengths, receiving monitoring reports, and so on.

The extent to which contracts were explicitly driven by policies set by members, however, was related to the management style of the authority—the extent to which the authority was officer- or member-led (see Chapter 4).

For example, in Site E, members were extremely influential and also had an informal role exercised via private meetings. This reflected the explicit stance adopted by the authority that contracts should be driven by policy and not the other way round.

Members were influential to varying degrees in the other sites. In Site F, the change of administration had produced a desire on the part of members to get more involved in contracting. This was a source of concern for some providers who were worried about confidentiality issues and perceived interference on staffing issues. It also produced a broader change in member/officer working relations. Under the Conservatives, members had tended to be 'hands-off', setting policies at a broad level and leaving officers to implement these. Under the Labour administration, members were becoming more hands-on.

In Site G, members were reported to be involved at a strategic level, leaving the detail to officers. With the externalization of services, they had been persuaded by officers (using the argument of delegated powers) that all ad hoc contact with contractors should be made via the client. Although members still had the opportunity to meet contractors on a periodic basis (for example, at committee meetings), the former system where members accessed contractors directly in response to comments or complaints from their constituents, no longer existed. The perceived loss of control resulting from this was an issue for some members. There were similar issues in Site H where members' reluctance to delegate, even to chief officers, reflected their concern to safeguard their representative role. One person illustrated the issue by commenting that members couldn't give a damn about the contract and won't give up what they see as their right to see that something gets done in a particular way or at a particular time.

In evaluating tenders, there was also little scope for discretion. Although there was no explicit requirement in the legislation for local authorities to accept the lowest tender, the implicit assumption was there. Local authorities need to have very good reasons to refuse a tender and award a contract to the DSO where the DSO's tender is not the lowest. Such reasons might include doubts about technical competence but as Flynn and Walsh (1988) point out, arguments that a tenderer may not be capable of doing the work may prove difficult to make, particularly for complex services.

Therefore in local government contracting, price is a primary consideration. The implications of this for quality gave cause for concern at a local level. Site F was an authority that was in favour of competition where this was in the interests of the authority and strove to be fair to all providers. However, it perceived the highly prescriptive nature of the legislation to have acted as a constraint in relation to the tendering of four grounds maintenance contracts. Three of these contracts were awarded to the lowest tenderer: a private contractor. However, if the authority had been allowed to use its discretion, it would have chosen to award contracts to the lowest tenderer where there were clear differences in prices submitted, but would have retained the preferred provider for any contract where the difference in bids was not significant.

The grounds maintenance DSO was highly regarded, but was not sharp enough with its bid and lost narrowly. Since the margin was very narrow, the authority would never have accepted the external bid except in the unique circumstances or CCT.

We were saving small amounts of money but at the expense of throwing out tried and trusted contractors within the organization. Anybody else, not having to work to CCT regulations, would have gone to the DSO and asked them to reduce their price a bit.

Officers in Site H were also concerned that processes for checking the performance of tenderers were not sufficient to reveal problems.

In Site G, where there were no DSOs for 1988 Act services, the authority was not bound by the regulations. It used a two-stage evaluation process. The first stage was used to draw up a select list and providers expressing an interest in bidding for the contract were awarded points if they met a wide range of criteria. The authority attached importance to the status of incumbent contractor and points were awarded in the evaluation process for this.

The refuse collection contract—which had not been tendered for ten years—was subject to tender. The incumbent and preferred provider should have had an advantage in tendering and if it had won the contract marginally, officers would have advised members to continue with the known contractor. However, the tendering exercise resulted in a new contractor offering a significantly lower price and the contract was therefore awarded to the lowest tenderer.

Managing Contracts

The allocation of risk in contracts is reflected in the form of contract adopted, the approach to variation, and, more broadly, in the way that decisions are made and dilemmas resolved.

The most common form of contract in our case study sites was a bill of quantities. The majority of work carried out under the contract was covered by this form which attempts to state the price of a unit of work and how many units are required, and therefore constitutes a guaranteed income for providers. Bills of quantities were generally supported by schedules of rates for specific jobs or hourly rates for work that cannot be specified to cover variations and contingencies.

However, in Site E, in response to user demands reflecting users' own needs for flexibility in relation to expenditure, forms of contract had been changed to effectively schedule of rates contracts or, as one person put it, bills of quantities with no commitment to the quantities. This constituted a major change and shifted risk firmly on to the provider. When a DSO won a contract, 'all it has done is won a franchise to trade with schools—there is no requirement for schools that have made other arrangements, to use that service'. This was also a feature of some contracts in Site H but not in Sites F and G, although in the former, users were pushing for more flexibility, less up-front commitment on their part in financial terms, and increased powers of exit.

The distinction between major and minor variations in Site E also effected a significant change. Major variations effectively constituted a break clause giving clients the right to exit from the contract for any reason (although in practice only schools had the absolute right of exit). The authorized officer had absolute discretion to determine what constituted a major or minor variation.

In Site F, there was some lack of clarity over how the variation clause was to be operated (different stakeholders had different views) and also in the extent to which users were aware of or understood their rights under the contracts. In practice, non-grant maintained schools were only able to exit from the contracts

with the council's permission and had to 'choose to be in or out for the whole
contract period. The contract does technically allow them to withdraw for bad
performance but that is not realistic in practice. If schools withdrew . . . then
they would have to go through the whole CCT exercise themselves'.

DSOs in Sites E and H were struggling to cope with the burden of risk. In
Site E, the DSO had not anticipated the extent of the changes. Even if it had
accommodated these via higher prices, it was likely that the contract would not
have been awarded to the DSO, being comparatively too costly. The position
was further exacerbated by the attitudes of some clients.

We expect contractors to be able to adjust their costs to income. If there is only £2m
of work then they may have to cope with any likely cuts.

My grounds maintenance contract is coming up for renewal and I can get anything I want
done at no extra cost. [The provider] is doing the right sort of thing and being seen to
be obliging. They realize that if they don't we can move out.

An external contractor has the choice of deciding whether or not to bid for the contract. I
don't have that option, I have to bid for it knowing that parts of it are non-deliverable.

In Site H, cuts to schools' and other users' budgets were having a major impact
on DSOs and several had already shown deficits or were predicting them at the
time at the research. One was in danger of being closed down.

However, not all the problems resulted from changes to workloads. Some
related to the withdrawal of a subsidy, an action about which one interviewee
commented 'nobody quite appreciated the impact on the supplier'. Falling demand
(down by 57 per cent in one area) following restrictions to the specification
and price increases was also a factor.

The straw that broke the camel's back was a requirement by the authority
for DSOs not only to achieve similar levels of overall profit in 1994/5 to those
forecast in 1993/4 but also to meet additional targets to mitigate budget reductions needed to avoid capping.

DSOs are expected to accommodate reductions in workload as a result of client budgetary considerations without financial recompense or redress by the client even where
a DSO may be confronted by redundancy costs. A private contractor would undoubtedly
seek recovery of direct loss and expense and loss of profit from the client under the
terms of the contract.

It is interesting at this point to consider Site G, where the cost of major variations was not seen as an issue for the authority but rather as part and parcel
of the new arrangements: 'within the framework of the contract you can do most
things. For example on refuse the contract was let on a back door collection
but we have a mechanism to change this to wheelie bins if necessary. It will
cost and we accept that'. This raises questions for authorities in financially difficult situations. Can they afford to compensate a private contractor for changes
to the level of service purchased in response to budget reductions? It also reflects
the advantages and disadvantages of employing contractors of different status

(i.e. internal and external)—considerations that legally are not able to be considered in the tender evaluation process.

A further risk related to the paucity of information systems. This was mainly an issue for Site H where this was not only a source of frustration for users but had also contributed to the loss made by the vehicle maintenance DSO. At the end of the 1992/3 financial year, based on the information available, the DSO appeared to have achieved the required rate of return. Six months later it was discovered that it had made a loss.

A second major issue in managing contracts is who is responsible for failure. The general public does not recognize distinctions between purchaser and provider and when things go wrong it is simply a council issue. How then did sites approach default?

In Site E's second-round contracts, a tiered system of monitoring was introduced. Where problems were indicated during the baseline monitoring process, the level of monitoring would be stepped up. Where standards were consistently achieved however, the baseline level of monitoring would be lowered. The increased level of monitoring incurred a cost and the decreased level a bonus. The value of the sanction applied was twice that of the incentive.

Like many local authority contracts, this contract included a range of provisions which could be applied in the event of failure, including the opportunity for the provider to rectify the problem (where this was possible) within a given time period and thus avoid incurring a default notice. Site G operated a similar system but had introduced in its second-round contracts a provision for defaults to be issued automatically for persistent problems, even where these were rectified.

In all sites, the application of default provisions varied across services. In Site E for example, there were very different approaches in sports and leisure management to those generally applied in other service areas. This service area was not included in the new integrated purchaser and provider organizations but was managed on a twin-hatted basis in a single department. The approach to monitoring was also very different: 'We don't inspect at all . . . I have absolute confidence in the DSO manager—there is no point in paying his salary and doing his job for him'. One perceived reason for this was that: 'Housing and leisure are clearly very different. There still needed to be a value-driven focus to leisure and housing (i.e. influenced as far as possible by the values of the council in terms of the provision of a leisure and housing service). In terms of building cleaning there is nothing value-driven about that.' Many schools might disagree with this. Cleaning was perceived to be very different to grounds maintenance for example, and several heads stressed the importance of individual cleaners for the quality of the service:

People like cleaners need to have a share in the ownership of the organization because then they care and want it to be done well. If they don't have a share, they don't feel committed or involved. I'm not saying they don't do their job properly but there isn't the same flexibility or interest.

Our cleaners do far more hours than they should. They are propping up the service because they take pride in their work.

Of course there are also reasons why other service areas are equally 'special' but the underlying issue in these two examples is that traditional public sector values (a shared sense of commitment, trust, and so on) continue to be important and that contracts do not produce that level of commitment: 'We believe that the person who is managing that facility, has to embrace heart and mind the council's leisure strategy and sports development policy and not be doing it purely because they are contracted to do so'. This belief underlies the general tendency for the level of monitoring to be stepped down when contracts are awarded to DSOs. There are tensions, however. In one first-round contract in Site E, not a single default had been applied despite widespread concern among users about quality. One user's comment on this was: 'I don't know if that was collusion or not. People didn't want to use formal procedures—they tried to sort things out in informal ways.' Another person stated that the reliance on informal procedures for dealing with failure had much to do with the fact that the default clause in the first-round contracts had been written defensively. Horror stories from hospitals operating cleaning contracts had contributed to a belief that private sector providers would be cutting corners at every opportunity and that therefore default procedures needed to enable the authority to terminate the contract if necessary. In practice, this meant that there was a reluctance to use the default procedure against the in-house contractor for fear of being forced to terminate the contract. In the second round, the default procedure was changed to make it both more useful as a tool and more meaningful.

Sites F and H operated similar monitoring and default procedures. Monitoring systems were increasingly becoming more sophisticated with users being given more opportunity to register their satisfaction or dissatisfaction. Random sampling was also used and there was an emphasis on giving the contractor the opportunity to put problems right before defaults were issued. However, in both these sites, defining and identifying failure was an issue. One person gave the example of building cleaning where the service was provided to several hundred clients. 'Subjective' definitions of failure meant that there was not one but 300 specifications. Another commented that although a variety of sanctions were available, in practice, 'the way it is structured makes it almost impossible to administer. The cost substantially outweighs any penalties we might levy and as a consequence we don't bother. This is because a default is difficult to identify.'

In vehicle maintenance for example, it was particularly difficult to identify where blame for failure lay. One user's perception of this was that penalties for exceeding down time (the time a vehicle was off the road) were never enforced 'because there was always some excuse' (such as additional work being found which needed to be done).

Interestingly, in three of the sites, contract provisions were either being tightened up over time to cope with the perceived threat of private contractors or were being relaxed when contracts were awarded to DSOs. However in Site G, where all providers were external to the authority, approaches to monitoring the contracts and dealing with failure—based on a partnership model—seemed to be working successfully. One contractor commented: 'I have not experienced any defaults here. That is not to say that everything is perfect but there is a willingness to make the thing work. Contractors are proud people and work very hard. We would be upset if they did deduct money. We are not out to sting anybody.' Nevertheless the authority was prepared to take a hard line where necessary. In a case where a provider had received 89 fault notices in one day and the immediate manager had done nothing about this, the contractor's regional manager 'was summoned to the council and threatened with termination unless it was put right'. The manager concerned was subsequently sacked.

The management of contracts is not confined to issues such as risk and default. At a more strategic level, there were questions about the role of members in the new environment. In a context increasingly dominated by purchaser/provider splits and markets, what roles are members to adopt? In Chapter 5 we saw that member structures were tending to follow a purchaser/provider split. However, it was not always possible for members to wear one or the other hat exclusively. Moreover, members are not elected for this purpose and the imposition of client/contractor roles creates inevitable tensions.

There were two main dilemmas. One related to accountability and was illustrated most clearly in Site G. Where members were adopting a strategic role and not dealing directly with complaints from the public or having direct contact with providers, how did this relate to their electoral mandate and need to retain the necessary controls over and knowledge of the service provided?

As one member put it:

I would not expect the Chairman of BT to know where every phone box was or the colour of phone boxes but elected members need that information from the officers if they are to know what is going on. If people come and complain about the bins I cannot say that is not my job, it is the contractor's responsibility. Most people see me as the council in my area.

There are other aspects of accountability which will be discussed more fully below and also in Chapter 10, such as who ultimately is responsible for failure or as one officer in Site G put it: 'at the end of the day, if something goes wrong, the members still see it as the role of the officers'.

Another issue is who decides how the service should be provided. In Site G, preventing councillors from having direct contact with providers had, according to some officers, contributed to a better balance of service provision. Under the previous system where councillors reacted to complaints, service patterns in some areas had been 'a complete and utter anomaly . . . because of complaints—responding to a councillor who had been hot on the phone all the time. Now if a councillor rings you, you can say, sorry, but we cannot do it because of the financial position.' One elected member's comments (in relation to who was in charge and what were the guiding principles) aptly illustrate the lack of clarity in members' minds about how to reconcile traditional public sector values with those of the new public management. The view expressed was that the public had benefited from CCT because council staff no longer had their hands 'partly tied behind their backs because they had committees to answer to instead of making money'.

The second dilemma is how members are to reconcile different interests. This was an issue in Sites E and H. In Site E, the authority was struggling with the need for DSOs to become both more user-responsive and more competitive but at the same time was concerned about the implications of changes to terms and conditions for economic regeneration.

What it has done is to make clear the multiple roles of the organization in the government of the city as a whole: economic regeneration, anti-poverty. You save money and you lose jobs at the bottom end of the workforce spectrum. They are jobs for people for whom it is difficult to find alternative employment, for example people with learning difficulties. . . . The immediate saving is obvious but the on-cost on people's dignity, crime and so on, is high. I find it difficult to reconcile competition and social responsibility.

In Site H (in addition to pressures from the external environment), DSOs were being asked to produce additional surpluses on top of rates of return achieved in previous years, to prevent the authority from being capped. Members with provider hats on could understand the implications of these requirements for DSOs but with other hats on felt they had no choice:

The contractor committee is trying to manipulate the situation and take reports to the various client committees to tell them that the effects of the proposed actions might be the closure of a DSO. At the same time though, that same committee attends a meeting of the council, where as part of the council, they vote and have to agree, as part of the council, to take action to avoid capping.

Quality and Users

Although users and quality have been discussed in Chapters 5 and 6 and also in the earlier sections of this chapter, there are a number of specific issues which should be addressed in their own right.

Quality can be conceptualized in a number of ways but in this section user *satisfaction* will be the focus. There were a number of points at which users were able to register their satisfaction or dissatisfaction with the services provided: through comments, compliments and complaints systems; through user groups (although there were not many of these and certain constituencies of users were more vocal and influential than others); and for schools, through the small schools' exemption rule where schools employing less than three full-time or equivalent staff could choose from a number of options (for example employing staff directly, carrying out their own CCT, staying with a centrally let contract, or giving the work to DSOs as of right).

Some officers, particularly in Site F, took the fact that schools decided to remain with a centrally-let contract as a measure of satisfaction, a mandate for management. In reality the picture was much more complex. Undoubtedly, many users were happy with the service provided but other comments suggested that users wanted client agents to carry out a contract-letting role but wanted more autonomy over other aspects of contracting.

For example in all three sites invoicing was an issue. Schools and other users had insisted that invoices be sent to them (rather than simply being paid by the client agent) and had negotiated the right to block payments where they were not satisfied with the service provided.

Similarly, decisions to opt out of a centrally-let contract were not necessarily indicative of dissatisfaction with the quality of service provided. In building cleaning for example, more and more schools were employing cleaners directly. There were a number of reasons for this. The supervisory arrangements for caretakers and cleaners (which varied in terms of detail across the sites but generally meant that caretakers and cleaners were employed by different sectors of the authority) were perceived to have caused a number of problems, both in terms of relationships and flexibility in service delivery.

The bureaucracy involved in making temporary variations (such as giving extra attention to the cleaning of the school hall before a parents' evening) is a good example of the perceived inflexibility introduced by the contracting system. 'Where we want to up the quality a bit, we are stuck on the contractor side, because the contractor is sticking rigidly to the spec, has been instructed to do so, and this is quite natural because they are paid and costed on that basis.' Several sites were attempting to introduce flexible cleaning arrangements but there was potential for this to be abused.

In Site E there had been considerable dissatisfaction with the general quality of service in the early stages but there were improvements over time. The main issues were that services were not sufficiently responsive to users. Users felt that contracts were not sufficiently influenced by their needs both in the developmental stage and also during the contract term (where the lack of flexibility was a major issue).

In Sites F and H, levels of satisfaction varied significantly across service areas though there was general dissatisfaction with the client-agent role. Users were concerned that the client-agent role did not provide value for money (although in Site F the small scale of client-agent units was a constraint on what could be done) and that clients were not provided with sufficient information about the service, particularly the cost of it. The imposition of a third party between user and provider also contributed to high levels of bureaucracy in the contracting process. However, at an authority level, there was more support for a client-agent function. Both authorities recognized the need for a point at which an overview could be taken and the needs of the individual user could be balanced against those of the collective.

A further comment made by users in Site F was that there was a tendency towards more uniformity in quality standards. This also produced more equity in quality standards and might in theory have been a good thing. The problem was that the lack of money meant that in terms of quality standards, the service was delivered to the lowest common denominator.

Satisfaction levels were very high in Site G. There were few complaints and few defaults. This authority was different from others in having no schools as users. However, where users were involved (for example, in the sports and leisure management contract), attitudes had changed from being initially very suspicious to suggesting that there was no longer any need for a user group (which had been performing a watchdog role) since things were so good.

SOCIAL SERVICES

On the whole, local government and the health sectors operate within a highly prescriptive and centrally imposed process with relatively little room for local discretion. In contrast, social care has not been subject to comprehensive structural reform (as in the NHS) or overarching legislative regulation (CCT in local government) so the management of the contracting process is to a much greater degree locally influenced. Because of this degree of variation it is useful to consider social care contracts in terms of specific areas of provision such as in-house services, voluntary agency, resettlement arrangements, residential and nursing home contracts.

In-House Services

We have seen in Chapter 5 that a very substantial proportion of social care provision—that within the SSD—is not managed through a contracting process at all, but through the bureaucratic hierarchy. This was true even in Site I, where it flirted with a radical purchaser/provider split, the absence of any formal agreement giving the purchasers only limited influence over providers. Elsewhere, Site J had gone furthest in considering the possibility of managing by contracts. There was also a local pilot service level agreement in Site L, largely at one manager's initiative.

Voluntary Service

Traditionally, voluntary services have been subsidized through annual grants for loosely defined 'good work'. This minimal relationship was often augmented by a much more intimate involvement in agencies by councillors and officers, who saw it as an extension of their public service. This involvement may or may not have qualified as formal 'work' of 'attendances' on council business. The extreme of this intimacy in our sites involved the local Age Concern—until recently run from council offices by staff paid by the council—but there were other examples:

Our chairman is very strong that we have to defend our voluntary status . . . [He] was a county councillor, a former chair of Social Services and it started with him recognizing that we could offer a service which fitted in with care in the community. . . . He was disappointed that there wasn't any funding last year . . . then they approached us at our AGM with a word here and there and we took hold of it. . . . We had a meeting in November when they asked us what we wanted to do . . . and I proposed a business plan. . . . We got a letter in May giving us £30,000 from April . . . they suggested higher pay scales than in our specification 'to provide a robust service' . . . I don't know how long it's for because, although we're being paid, I haven't seen the contract yet [in August].

In brief, then, links tend to be multiple and often fairly intimate and the contract is a relational one, in which mutual trust and assumed common interests outweigh formal specification. Meanwhile, service monitoring, the development of new ideas, and the exercise of any user influence occurs informally in the course of everyday working relations. As such—and especially in specialist service areas—contracts are but one mechanism for conducting relations within micro 'policy communities' (Marsh and Rhodes 1992*b*). These arrangements may lack something in clarity, in a focus on performance, in openness both to challenge and to new actors with differing values and approaches. On the other hand, they may economize on the management of the system and make for robustness and responsiveness to community interests (Hood 1991). Equally, some voluntary sector respondents spoke of competition between each other, even if this was not formalized.

None the less, as expenditure has grown and a managerial approach has taken hold in social services, so voluntary agencies have increasingly been seen as service subcontractors and there has been pressure both to formalize relationships and to demonstrate value for money. Hence, 'service level agreements' have become more frequent, providing a more complete specification of relationships than previously and setting performance targets. The nomenclature is politically important, both for voluntary agencies fearful of contracts and for councillors opposed to their extended use. Officers involved in contracting see things rather differently.

They are all starting to come together in a similar style. They have different names, but essentially they are the same creature.

The legal department has said that service level agreements are not contracts, but I don't see how they cannot be contracts . . . it's just political . . . it's obfuscation.

In all but Site J, responsibility for managing contractual relations with voluntary organizations was dispersed among various service managers. Contracting specialists might actively assist this process, as in Site L, or might not. One local manager was preparing a contract with an Indian welfare association, for example: 'It'll be my first one. I've been given examples of other service agreements . . . so I'm intending to follow that format.' However, in most of the instances we observed, the onus for proposing terms and conditions of the agreement was placed upon the voluntary agency itself, with the authority perhaps indicating the topics to be included. These were then subject to negotiation, although the local authority reserved the right to impose its own conditions at the crunch. We have already seen, however, that these impositions were not always more stringent than the original proposals.

Common *et al.* have questioned the impact of this formalization, calling it 'playing at shops' (1992: 16), while Smith and Thomas (1993) found that several agreements remained open-ended and incomplete, tending merely to describe existing activities. Equally, the case studies give evidence that the process was beginning to bite, even before the community-care reforms, with annual reviews of performance and even full-blown evaluations in Site J. The change was not all in one direction, however: the reorganizations had disrupted some established review arrangements.

Reaction among voluntary organizations was mixed. Some welcomed the clarification of expectations and performance criteria—even if they sometimes suspected that future funding discussions were no less insecure and might have little to do with their performance. The smaller ones, in particular, were extremely concerned about the bureaucratic burden placed on them to negotiate contracts and keep detailed records of activities and performance: they bemoaned the lack of skilled support, training, and infrastructure. More established ones were concerned about a shift from partnership to imposition on the part of the more forceful authorities in our study: some questioned the SSD's ability to determine what services were necessary when the specialist expertise and close links to users lay with them; others resented the arbitrary withdrawal of funding for some services in expectation that they would finance them from their own resources. Equally, there were instances of the SSD imposing its own model for developing services.

There are four or five [ethnic] groups here. We've been encouraging them to work together to identify areas of common need that would fit with our priorities. Their idea of needs is not the social services idea of needs . . . most of them argue that one project can't possibly meet the needs of such a wide diversity of groups . . . The department's line is not to argue with that.

We found only limited evidence of contract failure or of disputes in relation to voluntary agencies. One organization was not short-listed for a new contract because of its past difficulties with existing services. There were occasional examples of commissioners distancing themselves from problems which small voluntary organizations, on their own, had little power to resolve. Equally, there were examples of commissioners attempting to guide well-meaning agencies into a more business-like way of operating, including revising quoted prices upwards lest services run into debt. The enterprise agency in Site K enabled SSD commissioners to keep a distance from such support.

The resolution of disputes depended upon the perceived distribution of power and determination. Thus an SSD could withdraw funding for a service which rated low in its priorities. On the other hand:

We attempted to introduce our personal relations and sexuality policy. They wouldn't have it. We were saying 'it's part of the contract'. They threatened to return our residents from their homes. That wasn't an idle threat, so after talking tactfully to the residents and carers, people were prepared to live with that, but I still don't like it.

In the main, however, annual or two-yearly revisions of service agreements enable policy development and service variation at the same time as giving the authorities significant deterrent powers when disputes arise.

Resettlement Contracts

The previous section described the adaptation of an established pattern of relationships towards the contracting state. This section concerns the development of new services to replace long-stay mental illness and learning disability hospitals. There are similarities, in that voluntary agencies have been heavily involved in this work. None the less, the development warrants some special attention because it provides an example of overt service and market development under complex conditions. Managers have had to promote the development of new accommodation and supportive services and the reshaping of existing ones, stitching together funding from mainstream DHA and SSD budgets, RHA resettlement grants, housing corporation monies, DSS benefits, and latterly, the mental illness specific grant and STG. In doing so these have involved existing local agencies and developing new relationships with housing associations in particular—as well as attracting established organizations to their area or encouraging the growth of new ones.

This process predated the community care reforms or the establishment of departmental policies on contracting. While there may have been some internal structures—there was a bar on links with the commercial sector in Site L, for example—local service managers have generally been given discretion to develop services and mechanisms for their governance as best they could. The rules attached to funding have had more influence than internal policy rules.

The normal pattern has been to develop relational forms of contracting with trusted partners: typically, the contract is in block form for a number of years, although there may be an element of cost and volume, with payments depending partly on occupancy. For those services where twenty-four-hour residential care is involved, the pattern of contracts may have been disrupted by the imposition of a new standard contract, designed principally with older people in mind and assuming arm's-length, lower-trust relationships with providers. There were complaints that this did not fit services for people with mental health or learning difficulties and some evidence of resistance.

Except for day services, all our developments in the last five years have been out in the mixed economy. We've enabled the organizations to set up and provide before community care came in. I don't take kindly to people saying 'from 1st April we're going to do things this way' when we'd already been doing it for several years.

One manager outlined the gradual development of more sophisticated means of contract construction, letting, and evaluation.

In the early days it was 'Provide five beds for five people'. Then later we broadened it to 'provide five services for five people' . . . The latest one is twenty-five pages long, laying down duties of the landlord, the duties of the care provider, committee structures, quality action groups, user involvement, termination dates . . . they are all specified.

This last contract arose from a formal invitation to tender, a short-listing process based on evaluation of tender documents and past records, and a formal presentation by a range of voluntary, commercial, and health trust bidders. Subsequently, in order to expand the range of trusted providers, the authority was courting a leading US provider: two officers had visited their facilities for a week, being given copies of contract documentation and monitoring procedures, and a reciprocal visit was imminent. Generally, then, formal or informal groupings of preferred providers were developing.

Elsewhere, specialist advice from the National Development Team for People with Learning Disabilities was aiding the construction of a complex multi-part contract to care for someone with challenging behaviour. Such bespoke tailoring contrasted markedly with a much more Fordist approach to the residential core of older people.

However, close partnerships in which managers could control events were not always available to authorities anxious to attract people with resources to develop services: 'They are a national organization and the only contract they are willing to sign was the one they imposed on us . . . It's written very much from the provider angle . . . all the risk is on our side.' In this instance an arm's-length, somewhat conflictual relationship obtained, but the more common pattern was of close working partnership extending to strategic alliances:

With block contracts we have much more of a holding-hands arrangement—coordination meetings, we're involved as far as we can be on their management groups without taking away their independence, we're involved in quality action groups, we've got a presence around the project . . . they'll do training for us, we'll do training for them, they'll be part of our working groups, and we'll reciprocate.

It was through such processes that this authority attempted to raise any concerns of proposals for improving service quality. However, they were also prepared to take more rigorous action when it was deemed appropriate: 'We've described that it's right to invade vulnerable individuals' privacy in their own homes if it's to check that they're getting a good quality service . . . If there's a need to do spot checks we'll do it, on top of what registration and inspection officers do.' Agencies too welcomed close developmental relationships:

The (SSD) mental health team have brought all the agencies together, in that they have done very good work . . . they have broken down barriers that have been in the community . . . they have developed or enabled specialist services to grow, they have brought together small agencies and helped them through the contracting procedure . . . they have a strategic plan for service development based on needs.

None the less, contract forms and procedures did act as barriers to agencies attempting to provide a flexible service to people with various and changing needs. This was especially so for those encountering some residential care contracts.

The first contract . . . was the sort of document that specifies things—equipment and furniture—that wasn't set up for human beings . . . the documentation was quite confusing. One of the managers came to me with this huge document and said 'Gosh, I don't know what they want us to do with this'.

Residential and Nursing Home Care

It is in relation to these services that tensions between neoclassical, arm's-length contracting and relational forms of contracting are most in evidence in social care. We will first outline the pressures in each direction, before exploring how these tensions have been managed.

Commercial enterprises have established a major share of provision in recent years, both supplementing and displacing statutory services. The most usual relationship has been one of incipient rivalry, mutual distrust, and distance. Since local authorities rarely purchased commercial services, their main form of contact was via the regulation and inspection of rest homes under the Registered Homes Act 1984. Even this limited link did not apply to nursing homes, where DHA inspectors remain responsible. The NHS and Community Care Act therefore forced one established agency to develop trading relations with a range of established rivals, from which it had been largely insulated in the past.

Two other elements of the institutional rules also pushed in the direction of arm's-length contracts. First, the directive that—subject to the payment of fees beyond what the local authority was prepared to pay—people should be free to enter the home of their choice, weighted the balance in favour of standardized 'spot' contracts, to be imposed on any home as one of its citizens entered. Secondly, local authority standing orders, designed to prevent fraud, rely on contract specification rather than trust between the parties.

Social care is an experience good, co-produced in the relationships between providers and users, and it is ephemeral, in that particular events cannot be recaptured and subjected to later quality control. Furthermore, the recipients of care in these relatively closed environments are deemed vulnerable. By the same token, local authorities as purchasers are vulnerable to provider opportunism since they lack detailed knowledge of events in homes. There are several important consequences: choice at entry is not a robust safeguard; causal relationships between inputs, methods, and outputs are poorly understood; quality is hard to define and measure; there has to be a strong reliance on self-enforcement. Such features suggest that arm's-length relationships depending on what is specified in advance are likely to be technically and socially insufficient.

Matters are further complicated by the number of actors in the process, making clear distinctions between principal and agents hard to draw within a nexus of contractual relationships. Providers and their agents might come into contact with a care manager (social worker) or the care manager's manager, or someone responsible for overall contract management on the purchaser side, as well as an SSD or DHA inspector and the service user and their relatives (who may be part-purchasers). Contacts and understandings between any two of these actors have to take account of the behaviour of these varied third parties.

Of course the inspection process is one means of managing these issues. It is normally a fairly intensive two-day visit twice a year which will now probably involve lay assessors and consultation with service users. At the extreme, it enables purchasers to eschew any further specification of the service to be provided, concentrating solely on contractual terms and conditions. Equally, it allows purchasers to limit the additional monitoring which they specify in the contractual conditions

A final factor concerns the standard operating procedures developed within social services to respond to the range of clients seeking their help. For the large number of elderly people, staff focus on assessment and the arrangement of services, including placement, with limited involvement thereafter. For the smaller numbers of people with mental health problems and learning disabilities, the involvement is likely to be a good deal more continuous. The former processes point towards arm's-length, the latter towards partnership and relational contracting.

Tables 7.1 and 7.2 outline the way in which each of our case study authorities has responded. Most have veered towards a minimalist approach, which specifies little or nothing beyond the registration standards and which is activated when someone who has been assessed as needing care enters a home. At that point, an individual care plan should be agreed which forms part of the contract, but in practice these plans rarely add further specifications. Any variation at this point is unlikely to lead to much price variation: rather there are standard prices for residential and nursing homes respectively, with the former allowing for two levels according to the individual's need for attention. The only exception to this is when a person (usually *not* elderly) is defined as having 'special needs' and thus outside the normal price or practice which is followed in all sites: 'We have one contract and two pricing systems ... Special needs is out of control ... and the elderly are completely constrained' (Authority L).

In other respects, Authority L has been a good deal more ambitious. It has used its purchasing power to impose a ban on resident 'top-up' payments among providers who must bid competitively in order to be granted trading agreements. Providers may opt out of this process yet still receive spot contracts, if a citizen of L opts to enter their home. Then they may charge a top-up fee, but will only receive a minimum payment from L, nor are they part of the information system about vacancies. The bidding process allows for some leeway above minimum prices, in part to reflect providers' cost structures, and it also allows modest add-ons to acknowledge better quality of facilities, staff quality, and the need for more intensive care.

TABLE 7.1. Approaches to contracting

Site	Contract Process and Form	Negotiating and Monitoring Fora
I.	Spot contract for elderly residents. Some block contracting for other client groups.	Broadly collaborative negotiating fora with representatives of trade associations. Split according to elderly services and others. Subgroups for contractual reviews. Some joint development work. Dispute around market strategy rather than contractual relations.
J.	Spot contract for most elderly residents, with some block contracting for scarce services. Other groups mainly also spot, reflecting market conditions.	Consultative fora, given that many providers are outside the authority's boundary. Revision entailed close consultation with one or two providers.
K.	Spot contract for elderly residents. Other groups more variable.	Broadly collaborative negotiating forum, with subgroup to monitor and review contract. Disputes around price and local purchasing practice, rather than contract.
L.	Tendering process with price thresholds weighted by service quality and client dependency indicators. This leads to an agreement to trade, with contracts let on a spot basis.	Negotiation fora characterized by hard bargaining, brinkmanship, and fractiousness, alongside joint problem-solving and developmental work. These have concerned the tendering process, pricing, contract specifications, and terms and conditions.

This greater ambition in Site L caused a variety of technical and diplomatic challenges:

We went through a long process trying to work out what we should measure . . . but ended up with the few things we did include, that would be easiest. It caused ructions with registration because they had to do something with precision . . . There was a lot of argument and heated letters from providers . . . but disasters haven't occurred.

Similarly the task of evaluating tenders and linking them to purchasing projections 'was awful . . . there was a huge amount of work involved'.

In other respects, L was like our other case study authorities in seeking to develop contracting processes which ran smoothly, which paid people accurately and promptly, and which set out terms and conditions which were clear and reasonable, while limiting the council's risk. Each authority revised these terms and conditions in the light of experience, with some reversion towards a common norm in terms of the topics covered, the language used, and the management and sharing of risks. Such risks included residents dying, entering hospital, leaving unexpectedly, or behaving in ways unacceptable to the provider.

TABLE 7.2. Contract specification

Site	Service Specification*	Terms and Conditions
I.	Very limited, except for any in the individual's care plan.	Not extensive. Incomplete in some key areas (e.g. insurance). Shared risk and confusing layout lead to poor completion. Review improves layout, provides more complete terms and conditions, and allocates risk more precisely.
J.	Specification of inputs, methods, and outputs: some quite detailed and prescriptive. Review limits these specifications, eliminating 'wish lists', and sets out series of more precise improvements to be introduced over time.	Fairly complete. Shared risk. Review results in minor amendments.
K.	None, other than in care plan.	Not extensive, but clearly stated. Review improves presentations. Contract terms and conditions share risk, but low price puts it on providers.
L.	Fairly extensive and expressed in legalistic terms. Review links quality indicators more precisely to different price thresholds for tendering process.	Complex, legalistic, and fairly extensive terms and conditions. Review entails considerable amendment to adapt these to social care and to simplify language and presentation.

* Specifications over and above those required by the registration process.

In one major respect, however, the risk was more firmly placed upon the providers: the public purse was now cash-limited and there was a hurdle of social need, as well as financial need, which potential residents had to jump before being admitted. Thus a significant source of demand was constrained and access modified. Chapter 6 has described how that market varied locally. Here it is only necessary to note that Authority K was in the most advantageous position and sought to exploit it by fixing the price low. It was also contemplating the imposition of higher quality standards, but at least some senior managers disputed the need to raise prices in compensation. Responses to the threat of market failures varied from expressing fairly impotent concern to being hard-nosed: 'We know that there are some people providing a good service who are rocky financially. Should I worry about this?'

The final point to note about contract documentation concerns the way care of elderly people has dominated its construction. It was, none the less, frequently applied to other client groups in more or less modified form. Frequently,

however, those terms and conditions were inappropriate because they were pre-
dicated on patterns of behaviour which did not fit the common experience of
those other groups, for example, the speed of placement decisions, the assumed
length of stay, and times allowed for hospitalization.

The monitoring and enforcement of these contracts occur in a number of
ways. At an individual level, residents' progress should be reviewed after they
have settled in and thereafter at regular intervals. The evidence from all sites
is that authorities are having great difficulty in meeting these requirements,
particularly after the first review. Beyond this, it is up to residents and their
relatives to contact the social services department. The most common queries
concern providers charging residents for services which should be provided as
part of the contract. In such circumstances, they are instructed to stop doing so,
but 'if a client is happy we'd find it hard to do much'. Equally, evidence may
be lacking: 'I couldn't go for reimbursement because there were no receipts,
no evidence of them receiving money.' Lastly, the definition of what is in the
contract price may be insufficient. A resident was being charged considerable
extra sums for Asian food and stronger tea. The contract specifies that culturally appropriate services should be provided, as specified in the care plan. Since
the form of care plans was a matter of dispute in that authority, there was no
care plan and no such specification.

The rules of action were also unclear in relation to procedures. One manager
placed the onus on residents, using the department's complaints procedure. Frequently, the registration and inspection section was involved, but a number of
respondents acknowledged difficulties over role boundaries and around expectations of what could possibly be done, by whom, and on what basis: 'We haven't
got any penalty clauses, we're unlikely to terminate with our current residents
. . . If I was an owner I'd think "what can they do to me?"'

At a collective level, contract monitoring tends to concern financial aspects.
While the contract may specify that various documents should be available for
inspection and access afforded, these clauses are rarely activated. There are two
exceptions. Contracts with nursing homes specified that they submit the inspection reports, since DHA inspectors refused to submit them directly to the
SSD. Secondly, more elaborate specification provided the scope for additional
monitoring.

None of them have submitted evidence of giving thirteen hours care per resident to qual-
ify for the higher band of care, as they were contractually required. We're just writing
to say 'if you don't submit in twenty-eight days you'll be in breach and we will reduce
you and your price to the standard band'. I'm not sure we can because the contract says
you have to mediate . . . none of us has thought it through.

There were some officers in Authority L who anticipated taking on a more active
role in contract monitoring and enforcement and believed that the contract itself
would have to be tightened to facilitate such action.

The most stringent form of collective monitoring is via the registration and inspection process. This lays down standards concerning the physical environment and personal care, staff members and qualifications, management procedures and recording practice, among other things. The division of inspection responsibilities between health and social services does also reflect a difference in philosophy and expectations. One manager had contemplated the possibility of extending his remit to nursing homes: 'They or us are in for a culture shock. I know it's steeped into their own culture, repressed with uniforms and expected to tolerate screams and wards of bed-ridden people.' One of these elements—the existence of mini-wards—breached the contract conditions in two authorities, but not the nursing-home registration criteria. Contract conditions were not enforced.

The enforcement of the registration regulations remained a problem, especially in moving from generalized concerns about care practices to garnering evidence which will stand up to a barrister's challenges in the later stages of the process leading up to tribunal hearings. One officer described the events leading to a successful deregistration, but acknowledged that similar concerns elsewhere could not be proven.

It was superficially a very impressive home, but obsessed by material standards. Stories started to emerge about diets being managed to minimize the risk of people making a mess. People being given food sitting on a commode, and rigid toileting. Eventually we caught them administering medication to people it wasn't prescribed for to keep them quiet.

The larger commercial and voluntary organizations could be particularly intimidating: 'There are some who are little short of dismissive of the registration and inspection process.'

It was the registration and inspection sections who also took a leading role in managing the consequences of home closures, in particular negotiating with creditors and the courts in those cases where commercial law and the homes regulations came up against each other.

We have seen how much of the focus of monitoring and enforcement concerns the protection of the rights of users. What remains to be noted is the way that councils were attempting to develop their strategies for improving and assuring quality of service. Here, approaches were still being formulated, but differences were emerging. As the authority which placed greatest reliance on the contract itself, L was moving on two fronts. First, it was specifying the standards which users had a right to expect of its own services, with the intention that these would become contractual conditions for its agents. Secondly, it was working closely with the other interested parties to develop a series of quality indicators, in the hope that these could be amalgamated into a starring system. Authority J was taking much smaller steps along a similar road by setting out a time-scale of improvements for itself and its agents, but was also considering the encouragement of quality assurance systems within homes themselves—an approach which was also on the agenda in Authority I, not least among the homes associations themselves.

The implications of these differing approaches were also being explored within registration and inspection sections:

At the moment, all inspectors are saying is that this home meets a standard of registration. Once they have the responsibility of making more detailed statements, like deciding whether it's a five star or four star hotel, they are either going to be very popular or very unpopular. You just keep watching what cars they drive.

In all of these processes associated with contracting, the users of residential and nursing homes take on a variety of identities. First, they are defined as active individual agents, entitled to information and choice, to complain, and to leave —which thus means they create risks to other parties which must be managed. Secondly, they are members of collectivities entitled to some say in how the home is run. Thirdly, they are vulnerable people needing the local authority's protection. All of these identities can be justified. What was less clear was that purchasers had thought through a clear strategy, which balanced these identities and which followed the logic of that balance in the contractual process.

Externalized Contracts

We have noted that two authorities—I and J—have chosen to externalize some of their residential and day-care services by creating arm's-length trusts. These were at the same time the most complex contracts—since they involve the transfer of assets—and the most politically sensitive. Chapter 5 details the commonalities of this process, especially the involvement of very senior people in drawing up the contract and later its management as both purchaser and provider representatives. It also notes the very different directions taken, with I using its baseline budget to finance a large-scale transfer of places purchased back under a (broadly) block contract and J attempting to exploit STG monies, but eventually choosing an incremental process of transfer and a (broadly) spot purchasing arrangement.

The difficulties of clarifying and legitimizing the institutional rules and rules of action have been evident in both instances. In one it took the form of a challenge from outside providers and promises to renegotiate contractual terms and conditions. In the other it took the form of disputes around the bases for calculating costs and prices. In both cases, too, rules of action were unclear when it came to the operation of the contract. Initially in I, local purchasers were in the dark about the services on which they had a claim, the contractual conditions obtaining, and the appropriate ways of managing contractual relations. Some of this uncertainty remains, especially when issues are under dispute. In J, too, the criteria being applied to entry to particular facilities were matters of considerable contention.

Contracting for Domiciliary Care

There was no requirement for local authorities to have domiciliary care contracts in place at the time that the NHS and Community Care Act became fully operational. On the other hand, the clear policy imperative was to develop intensive non-residential alternatives, virtually all of the available growth money had to be spent externally, and internal home care services were tightly rationed.

The other major element of the situation was the largely unfamiliar range of usually local, small-scale private agencies, only some of which had clear procedures for training their staff and monitoring and enforcing quality.

In the event, local purchasing arrangements developed, not underpinned by formal contractual conditions. In places, these burgeoned: one local team had over 300 such arrangements, each being invoiced individually. The situation aroused concern:

Domiciliary care is being done without contracts on the delegated authority of divisional managers through invoices. They are wide open to accusations of favouritism and worse, because prices are agreed by them and never tested elsewhere and there is no notification to finance about what it is until the invoice comes in.

A parallel concern was the quality and preparation of the carers, especially those visiting vulnerable and isolated people, including the agencies' inability to do police checks. Three of our sites had either introduced formal contracts or were about to do so. These provided both a service specification and some quite complex terms and conditions, mainly concerned with the management and allocation of risk. That complexity was itself testimony to the vulnerability of the initial arrangements. These authorities were also about to create lists of providers who were deemed to meet a threshold of service quality and financial viability and were therefore accredited to trade with the council. The exception to this trend was L, which had set its face against contracting with the commercial sector except where it was compelled to do so. Given that in-house services could not expand and there were few new service level agreements with voluntary agencies to provide such care, managers would be forced to continue to expose themselves to contractual risks in order to respond to the needs of users.

Nowhere, however, was the new set of processes fully operational at the time of our research and a large volume of business was being managed on an informal basis. In effect, local case law grew up about which agencies were reliable, which could be trusted to make marginal adjustments to the services specified, and which required tighter scrutiny: 'We start to trust them when they come to us and say "this person needs less than she's getting".' These informal arrangements could turn sour: solicitors' letters were exchanged when an agency increased services unilaterally and sent in the bill, because, it claimed, the care manager was never available to be consulted about a volatile and deteriorating situation.

In any event, if responsive, high quality services and value for money were to be ensured contracts, and approved lists of providers did not resolve the issues of monitoring and variation: 'Quality of home care is very much on the agenda, but how do you manage this when you have several hundred packages of care and the number is growing daily? . . . I suspect monitoring isn't being done . . . We have a real problem.'

While the most common response was simply to trust people and to react to problems which became evident, there were other stratagems. Less commercial organizations such as voluntary agencies or home care cooperatives were being encouraged to expand and given some help with costs. One senior manager wanted to move towards block contracts with preferred providers as a means of minimizing transaction costs, encouraging quality, and improving value for money: 'Spot purchasing is very expensive . . . you lose economies of scale and you don't have sufficient clout to lay down the ground rules. For example we know that providers are charging us for an hour, even if they only go in for ten minutes.'

A final stratagem (used in Site K) was to get in-house home care services involved in reviewing and detailed coordination of care packages, since they had the expertise and local presence. The rub, of course, was that, in the long run, these services were competitors. And there was widespread agreement among purchasers that internal services were cheaper and more flexible than external ones: 'There's no shortage of people willing and able to provide good quality care at a good price. What we haven't got is enough money to pay for it because it's all tied up in direct services.'

An Interim Assessment

What may we conclude from experience to date? The enterprise was up and running, with some difficulty and discomfort, but without major accidents. Signs of organizational learning and adaptation were evident, as well as the development of working (if not always trusting) relationships between the parties. None the less, there remained a considerable way to go for authorities to develop clear market strategies as both purchasers and providers, to be clear about the contingencies which require variation within those strategies, to develop forms of contractual relationships which give effect to those strategies, and to develop monitoring and management systems which enable at least the part of the mixed economy for which they are responsible to be steered. Those strategies will have to be based upon partnership and power-sharing with other providers, other purchasers, and service users if sufficient confidence in each other's goodwill and competence is to develop and if risks are to be properly balanced and quality and value for money achieved. The cost of the transactions entailed remains a major open question. The biggest challenge lies in relation to non-residential care—the part of the spectrum of care which is given greatest prominence in strategic policies: here the immaturity which characterizes the social care market is most in evidence and the boundaries which define it are most unclear. The Audit Commission (1993a) recognized that this was an agenda for a decade: that implies a stability in the basic framing rules which, on the basis of recent experience, many would question.

HEALTH SERVICE

Developing and Implementing Contracts

Much of the initial focus of contracting was upon the identification of historic patterns of care with purchasing teams striving to obtain good information on activity levels and costs for previous years. In many instances this data was non-existent or unreliable and hence early contracts could be little more than block contracts based around some very broad parameters as to the shape and pattern of service sought. Even so there could be, as in Site B, up to fifty contracts to be prepared. There developed therefore a rather frenzied approach to agreeing an appropriate language structure for contracting and an associated round of redrafting until an acceptable version was produced.

The focus of contracting in the NHS, perhaps because there was a centrally imposed structure and time-scale, tended to be on simply establishing some mechanism for enabling purchaser and provider organizations to agree a way forward. It was also not clear at the outset how the vast range of medical activities would accommodate the contracting approach. Purchasers were therefore keen to get something in place rather than differentiate services or to establish details of arrangements such as default. Although, as our analysis (reported earlier) of the nature of NHS contracts suggests, a few were lengthy, detailed, and quasi-legalistic, the majority were fairly bland and general, aimed more at being a conduit for a relationship rather than a tight contractual relationship. Essentially, good relationships were seen as the enduring factor which allowed the contracting mechanisms to be achieved and not seen either as too bureaucratic or penalizing. One purchaser described it as follows: 'Contracting is at its best when it is not an end in itself. Unfortunately the paperwork and the target dates take over. Really the contract should be the logical bit at the end of commissioning process; maybe we should only aim to use two sides of A4 per contract!'

This attitude exemplifies the majority view of NHS purchasers and accounts, for the most part, for the absence of detail and specificity in NHS contracts, in contrast with local government in particular. A great deal of uncertainty existed, with purchasing teams being unsure of their own skills and competencies in terms of contracting and regulations and provider organizations being wary as to just what the implications of a contract might be for their own activities. One worker of a purchasing team described this as follows:

Contracting has been said to have replaced the planning function in the NHS and the focus upon yearly contracting rounds instead of longer-term plans is in part an explanation of the sense of pressure and instability created by the contracting process. The yearly contracting round, exacerbated by the fact that the NHS does not know its budget until quite late in the process, makes for a focus upon getting contracts in place (to satisfy statutory requirements) rather than a use of contracts to promote specific change in health services.

Contracts have become so inextricably linked with central government initiatives such as waiting lists and extracting greater efficiency that they (contracts) have not really developed their positive role as an agent of change. There would also seem to be an almost inherent confrontational basis to the way in which the contracting process is managed. The initial publication of a purchasing plan by the purchasers signals the strategic goals of the authority. An initial response to this from providers, in terms of how they might provide and achieve the specified goals forms the focus of a series of discussions and negotiations. The pursuit of cash savings, value for money, and increased activity levels provides ample grounds for dispute. The process is also made difficult by the tight timescales imposed to agree contracts and also by the tendency for initial discussions to be held between staff at a level below board level. As a consequence, the difficult issues can frequently be held over for chief executive-to-chief executive resolution. Typically at this point, the issue is a significant one, it exists under severe time constraint, and even a compromise agreement is likely to provoke renegotiation of previously agreed elements of the contract since the total quantum of costs and viability of the unit may be brought into question by this high-level discussion. The interaction between contracts for different elements of a health service was probably rather underestimated. Small changes in costs or activity levels in a particular contract may lead to renegotiation of a whole set of contracts since the ability of a trust to meet its total costs is based on a fairly accurate balance between costs and activities. Also in principle, as cross-subsidy of a successful product line (health service components) is not acceptable, then a radical change in one contract can only be accommodated by adjusting other contracts. The workload associated with relatively small but significant changes in purchaser targets can be frustratingly significant.

The detail of price, volume, activity levels, and so on requires considerable attention and accounts for the perception that it is a bureaucratic and managerial process not really focusing upon patient care. There is a strong desire in all the sites to make this contracting process a more standard low-key process and to see the focus of work shift to a reconfiguration of services and patterns of care. The latter aspect, the real purpose of change, is in danger of being swamped by the processes needed to establish contracts.

Frustration was expressed by providers in all sites as to the level of involvement offered to them in the specification of contract. They all tended to feel that the contracts were imposed and that they were required to make them work, to make the best of them. Providers were universally in favour of longer-term, more stable contractual relationships. They were critical of the ability of the purchasers to a) be clear about their future goals and intentions, and b) to be able to translate their goals into contractual requirements. In Site D one provider said of the purchaser: 'They have a long way to go as a health authority. They have got to improve their ability to work strategically. They are all values and no action.' The difficulty for purchasers in terms of long-term contracts is that as they do not know their budget for future years they immediately risk an over-commitment which they can only control by cutting back on other services.

Clinicians have felt particularly frustrated at their lack of involvement. Sometimes, it must be said that this seemed to be owing to the provider organization being uncertain how well clinicians might represent collective as opposed to individual objectives. This is, however, an area of change. As purchasers become more sophisticated and specific in the type of contracts set and indeed the nature of the medicine provided, so clinicians have to become more closely involved in the contracting process.

This is clear in Site B where cost-per-case contracts for long-stay clients with mental health or learning disabilities require considerable detail of input from clinicians. This medical exchange can also be a source of disillusionment in itself since purchasers rely mainly on public health for medical advice on a range of specialist services. They can alternatively seek advice from independent consultants from trusts other than the one with which they are dealing. Both approaches have drawbacks and often fail to placate local clinicians who feel purchasers have not understood the specifics of local circumstances.

Risk Management

Within the health service there has been relatively little explicit recognition of the potential output of risk management. Rather simplistic central policy issues here tended to dominate. Purchasers have to some extent been preoccupied with structural changes such as the amalgamation of the DHA and FHSA, the integration of GP fundholders, and the merger of DHAs to form larger commissions. Whilst in principle as cash-limited purchasing organizations they have a requirement to allocate risk towards the provider, they have had to balance this with the need to maintain the viability of local health care services and the potential political outcry from forcing a particular provider or service into financial difficulty. The relative newness of the process has also tended to lead both purchaser and provider to seek compromise and stability rather than attain dominance in the apportionment of risk. The relatively few instances of any provider organizations (trusts) becoming financially unstable suggests that the process of risk management has not yet become a very dynamic force.

Indeed, most risk management in the health service operates through one of two mechanisms: a) the management of ECRs (extra-contractual referrals) and b) the monitoring processes created to regulate and refine activity levels and performance standards.

ECRs require a contingency reserve to be held by the DHA mainly for the kind of emergencies of elective referrals which fall outside the mainstream contracts. The ECR process in effect papers over the cracks created by activities outside the contract agreement. Typically, ECRs have an individual focus with each instance being referred to the Director of Public Health. In order that ECRs do not become a risk to the DHA it is important to obtain good information on traditional referral patterns and to undertake effective needs assessment. It is also important to establish clear guidelines with local GPs so that they do not either attempt to 'play the system' by referring patients outside contract, or indeed become dissatisfied if too many ECRs are blocked or delayed. In Site B, there was a major overspend on ECRs and the authority had to work hard to restore the position. This was achieved largely through relocating outside referrals to local hospitals where contracts and capacity did exist and also on occasions refusing an ECR in cases such as gender reassignment. It is in this area that aspects such as priority setting and rationing of health care has come into focus as authorities have been forced to make decisions about treatment access for individual patients. Although ECRs need to be managed, their focus upon individual cases tends to mean that no overall financial risk exists that cannot be controlled. More difficult is the impact of an increasing rate of emergency referrals on other services. As emergencies increase, other services may have to be reduced which although attracting much adverse publicity still allows risk to be avoided.

Contract monitoring in all sites focused upon activity levels and the ability of providers to meet performance targets, but not to exceed them. The capacity of purchasers to do this related very much to the data capture and information systems available. In Site A, the monitoring processes were very limited. In fact it was in places non-existent and because of this one almost felt that the contracting process had made virtually no input but cost a lot of money to put in place. In most sites, there will be monthly meetings to review activity levels with, as in Site B, a quarterly meeting involving chief executives where a more formal performance review is conducted. The majority of risk management decisions are taken at a relatively junior level so that, for example, fifty extra hernia operations could be agreed by a contracts manager and adjustments or variations in contracts are happening all the time. The finance director in Site B said: 'We know that contract numbers are changing all the time. It just depends whether any changes are required materially to the contracts themselves. The question usually is about whether to substitute, increase, or decrease the volume.'

Thus, risk and variation in health are usually managed out of the system, in part reflecting the relative looseness of the original contract statement. Rather more difficult and unclear is how significant deviations are dealt with. Finance problems that may threaten a provider or detract from future purchasing intentions are not easily resolved. No direct examples of this were observed in the case study site but the general view was that external bodies, such as the regional executive, would become involved. Despite the potential for risk and financial crises, the majority of purchasers and providers have managed to work through these tensions, albeit often with considerable stress and sometimes deteriorating relationships.

More positive aspects such as incentives for meeting requirements of a contract, although considered, are not really feasible within the financial constraints of purchaser organizations.

Quality and Users

Statements of desired quality standards are typically contained within contract documents. However, purchasers often have limited resources to monitor and implement such standards and really have to rely on providers to produce reports and evidence of quality in practice. This is less of a problem than might be assumed as providers are constantly monitoring their own quality standards in terms of user audits and satisfaction surveys. Much of this is driven by the Patient's Charter document which provides a framework and in many instances a specific statement of standards to be achieved. Information deriving from activities based around Patient's Charter standards and surveys provides the basis for much of the quality monitoring conducted by purchasers.

Most organizations have tackled quality issues at a general level by developing a quality framework or specification and asking providers to operate in terms of this framework. Visits to provider sites vary in intensity, the nature of the people involved, and the type of data gathered. Interestingly, as purchasers have no legal entitlement to insist upon changes, the visits are based on goodwill and an implicit joint recognition by both providers and purchasers that they are trying to improve services for patients: 'We have to rely on personal contacts, persuasion methods, and out and out diplomacy because in reality we have no legal powers or authority to insist on any of these quality standards.'

There is in consequence considerable effort expended upon the involvement of user groups. This in effect offers legitimation to the process and makes it difficult for providers to reject the views of their 'clients'. At Site B, the stated aims of quality-monitoring meetings were:

a) to encourage the organizations to demonstrate their ability to do what they say they can do. The quality specification can be used to help them demonstrate aspects of care;

b) to demonstrate what they do in relation to different client groups.

At times, the process seems to focus upon gathering data that is bureaucratic, quantitative, and serves the structural needs of the process rather than qualitative data which illustrates the direct experience of patients. The advent of Patient's Charter initiatives and hospital league tables has rather reinforced this trend.

In addition to this, purchasers have developed their own more individual approaches. Site A has devised a regular monthly quality monitoring meeting with providers where one particular topic of service area is discussed. As this will often involve clinical outcomes, it also provides an opportunity to involve provider clinicians with the public health department from the purchaser. Although there is undoubtedly value in this medical exchange, there is disquiet within some providers that public health represents a particular discipline whereas the provider organization will encompass a range of specialists in different areas, and often disputes can arise over perceived credibility of medical groups.

The complaints system also provides a basic set of information purchasers can use to monitor performance. The reliance upon provider-based information in part reflects the reality of the situation, in that it is providers who have access to users, and also the relatively limited resources available within purchasers to monitor quality. In Site C, an approach to this deficit is being taken by trying to ensure that the quality standards and approach as used by the quality-monitoring staff become part of the thinking of the rest of the purchasing team so that quality becomes an integral part of the agenda rather than an isolated and potentially peripheral issue.

For purchasers, there is a requirement to expand their information sources beyond those accessed by the provider since this tends to mean that data is derived from active service users. This of course is very useful and valid. However, purchasers need to incorporate the views of potential users into the development of specifications of service and ultimately contracts. In this way, both the content and the manner of health services can come to reflect the needs and views of the population served.

Site A has developed an extensive set of consultation procedures to try to involve the local population in determining needs. The majority of purchasing organizations and all sites studied had initiated population surveys, focus groups, or some mechanism to listen to the local population. However, it also must be said that there is still a difficulty in translating these general and often quite diverse views into contracts. This is especially so in terms of priority setting where purchasers are under increasing pressure to obtain value for money and hence prioritize the services bought. They also need to attempt to legitimate these discussions by involving the public. This complex and controversial issue is proving difficult to resolve.

8

The Context of Change

It is now time to begin to draw the threads together. In order to do so, we shall review the evidence that we have assembled in all the earlier chapters of this study about the processes of change that have been driven by the introduction of contracts into the three service areas we have selected for examination. In doing so, we will consider how the evidence (especially the material from our case studies) helps us to answer the questions with which we started our study. From the beginning, as we indicated in our introduction, we have been concerned to identify and analyse the strategies adopted by organizations to cope with change; the new patterns of relationship and cultural shifts that have developed; and the nature of the processes that have been introduced.

UNDERSTANDING THE PROCESS OF CHANGE

In Figure 8.1 we set out schematically an account of the different factors that contribute successively towards structuring the process of change. Equipped with the detailed evidence set out in the preceding chapters, we can now begin the attempt to identify the relative significance of the various factors and trace their impact in the different service sectors at different stages in the evolution of the process.

The introduction of contracts into the different services provides a natural experiment, since a comparable innovation was introduced into each of the three sectors with which we have been concerned. The different rates of development in each sector also help us to make cross-sectoral comparisons about the ways in which relationships have developed.

External Factors

The external environment, as we described it in Chapter 1, has been one of the key factors in determining the form of change. All the main decisions taken by central government spring from the same basic principles. They are the consequence of the introduction into the public sector of what has been termed the new public management (NPM). However, despite this thematic unity, the changes imposed from above have (as we showed in Chapter 1) taken widely different forms in the course of implementation in the different service sectors. Change has also been a 'rolling process' rather than a single 'big bang', although it has provoked some explosive episodes along the way. As Vivian Lowndes shows, the NPM is having a continuous and developing influence as the new procedures

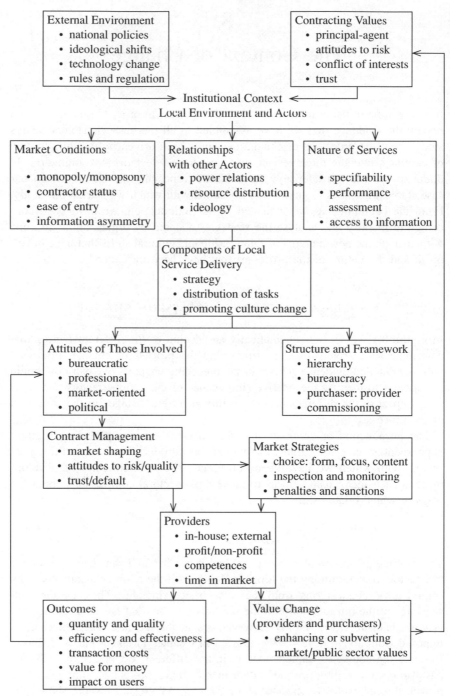

FIG. 8.1. Dynamics of the contracting process

deriving from its introduction begin to embed themselves in institutions in the form of rules, which in turn are changing organizational cultures. These changes are also being maintained in place by a new structure of monitoring and regulation. In addition, she comments: 'as institutional change is hard to control, the NPM may have unintended consequences as new rules are interpreted by different actors in different ways, as they respond to new challenges and seek to further their own interests' (Lowndes 1994: 43).

The situation may be further complicated in a number of other ways. For example, there may be a considerable time-lag as new 'thought worlds' (Mackintosh 1995) establish themselves among the key actors—in this case, assumptions and behaviour patterns deriving from the price-competitive market paradigm. Evidence of this effect working itself through in practice can be seen in our case study material. In it, we also see the consequences of institutional change being grafted on to existing forms but only partly replacing them. This can produce situations in which the changes 'grind against' the survivals of previous forms of organization, producing contradictory outcomes.

Some Imperatives from the External Environment

The impact of external institutionalized environments on the way that public service markets develop is clear from both the uniformities of approach and the areas of variation. Central government has concentrated on different aspects of the system in different services. In the case of local government, there has been strong regulation of the system of contracting and internal trading, and the uniformity of approaches to these issues is apparent. There has been much less concern for organizational structures, and the approaches that have emerged vary considerably, for example in the way that client/contractor splits are organized. In our local authority case studies, different approaches to organization had been adopted in each council, though there were some operational similarities. In the NHS, the institutional pressure is even greater, with a focus both on organizational structures and processes, and on the nature and operation of contracts. In social care, there has been only limited pressure from outside either on the specific forms of organization or of contracts. There is much less agreement on the way that the new processes of the mixed economy of care should operate, and the market pressures have been greater. The main interest of government has been in financial issues on the control of the grant. Issues about organization have only arisen at second hand through the social services inspectorate, and they have been as concerned to work with social services departments as to control them. Moreover, the initial certainties about the value of the purchaser/provider split were strongly questioned, and the social services inspectorate retreated from its initial relatively firm views. It was clear from our case studies that the institutional pressure in social care was less than in other sectors.

The process of contracting in each sector is strongly regulated by central government, though for somewhat different reasons and in quite different ways. In the NHS the purpose of regulation is to push the service along particular lines of development, for example with the encouragement of more sophisticated forms of contract, or to ensure that patterns of provision do not change too rapidly. Regulation is essentially being used for governmental reasons, to retain control in order to ensure that political purposes can be met. In social care, the Department of Health's regulations on the purchasing of care are extremely detailed though they say relatively little about the nature of the contracts that are to be let. The regulation of the market serves a primarily bureaucratic function of setting the rules for payment. The regulation of the market for local government services is extremely detailed, covering how contracts are to be structured and let, and the way that internal markets are to operate. The Department of the Environment's enforcement unit monitors the activities of local authorities closely and frequently intervenes to require local authorities to re-tender, as it had in one of our case study authorities because a default clause was seen as anti-competitive. The Audit Commission has been active in the local government market, pressing for more active market-making by local authorities in the letting of contracts and also in social care through interventions designed to improve the infrastructure and promote strategic development. The purpose of regulation in the local government sector is to control potentially recalcitrant local authorities.

The tendency that has been found in other contract areas for it to be relatively rare to resort to the courts or to formal arbitration procedures was also apparent in our case studies and more general interviews. One of the local authorities' studies had been involved in a case in which the unions took action against the authority when it decided to take work away from an internal contractor and employ a private company, although there were threats made in social care. Elsewhere, there were no instances of either court action or formal arbitration. Resort to the courts or any formal mode of arbitration is rare in either local government or health, although in some cases there are internal procedures. More generally, the sector in which there has been most resort to the courts is social care, over issues of the nature of contracts. This may reflect the fact that the nature of contracts is not regulated as it is in local government, and there is no alternative mechanism available for the resolution of differences. Providers who have resented what they see as the imposition of the contract by the social services department have seen no alternative but to use the courts.

Lack of clarity in the institutional frameworks affected the operation of markets and contracts in the three sectors in a variety of ways. In the NHS, the overlap between the operations of the district health authorities and family health service authorities has up to April 1996 (when they were obliged to merge) limited the extent to which overall health strategies have been developed by purchasers. Formal legal separation has inhibited cooperative working. Joint commissioning with social care has been little developed because of the problems of working across the boundaries of organizations that must work in quite different institutional contexts. As Wistow argues, the nature of the problems that arise is differently interpreted depending on the organizational perspective:

It might be tempting to describe the community care changes as though they were the cause of problems in the health service. From that perspective, local authority funding shortages, assessment delays and other weaknesses prevent the NHS from making the most cost-effective use of its resources.

But viewed from the other end of the telescope, it is change in the NHS which appears to be responsible for placing burdens on the community care reforms that they were not designed to sustain. So, for example, the Audit Commission has concluded that increasing pressure from hospital discharges could cause growing difficulties for increasing numbers of authorities. (Wistow *et al*. 1994: 24)

Where institutional systems overlap then there are likely to be problems of coordination, arising from differences in rule systems and the contrasting and conflicting incentives that they create. For example, if the rules imply that health purchasers deal with social care purchasers, is this limited to the narrow definition of purchasing adopted in the NHS, or the broad one adopted by social services departments? It is common for health managers to argue that social care is poorly organized for the market, and for social care to argue the same of the health service. In fact, they are pursuing different agendas, with health largely concerned for populations and social care for individuals. The agendas of GPs and social services are more congruent—though their interests may differ and also their cultures: it remains to be seen whether this congruence assists collaboration as a 'primary care-led' NHS emerges.

The sectors studied differ in the constitutional and operational rules within which they must operate. In the case of local government, a constitutional system that has been created to make sure that local authorities compete conflicts with political imperatives about internal provision in the case of many authorities. Even so, over time, the influence of the constitutional framework can be seen in the way that attitudes towards internal providers have shifted. The establishment of a client side of the organization has led to that perspective coming to be more important. This is apparent for example in the development of formal and sophisticated procedures for tender evaluation and more extensive monitoring procedures. Other interests—for example, those of staff and service users—also come into play. Thus, institutional frameworks create structures of power, interests, and values that then lead to the emergence of particular patterns of action.

The Culture of Contracting

The impact of externally imposed constitutional and operational rules is not the only external factor that needs to be taken into account. The general influence of the values and procedures deriving from contracting as a process in its own right must also be taken into account as a key 'framing' factor. Also, in the background—but potentially extremely influential—are cultural assumptions about the nature of contracting. As we shall show in Chapter 9, these assumptions vary substantially from one country to another. The British model of contracting implies formality, detachment, and prior specification; it has less space than those prevalent in other countries for the kind of less formal contracting relationship based on long-term collaboration and enterprise for mutual gain. If this formality prevails in an environment also still largely characterized by traditional public sector approaches, in which probity and correct procedures are paramount considerations, there is likely to be much less scope for flexibility in operation.

As we showed in Chapter 2, the lessons from the literature on the working out of principal-agent relationships shows that these relationships are rarely going to remain stable. The parties to them are seeking to maximize their advantage and minimize the constraints—and the costs—that entering into a contract relationship places upon them. But there are a wide variety of techniques open to them in attempting to achieve this outcome and often a range of other factors directly or indirectly involved. This may lead to a need to consider different forms of coalition or partnerships. The continuing stresses that such situations generate is a factor that must be taken into account in any analysis of particular situations involving the letting and management of contracts. Specifically, the contract culture generates particular tensions around the key themes that we identified in that Chapter. These were: how *risk* is distributed and how it can be avoided; and how *quality* can be secured and maintained. In addition, there are potential conflicts about the circumstances in which there is a need for *sanctions* (including default) to be applied and when they will be effective. There are also questions around how the level and distribution of *transaction costs* will be decided.

The problematic character of these issues also helps to explain the different forms of contract that have been employed, as relationships between purchaser and provider evolve in different prevailing circumstances: the arm's-length, neoclassical, and relational. In Chapter 3, we showed how the form, focus, and content of contracts have been adapted to the particular issues arising in the three service areas on which we have focused. We also sought to show how the issues of risk, default, and quality worked their way through in the different sectors and what measures were adopted to cope with them and with what success.

IN THE LOCAL ENVIRONMENT

In each different local situation, the influence of the 'framing' factors will also be supplemented and reinforced by a set of factors that are specific either to those situations or to the services themselves. For, as we have already indicated, the nature of the services themselves will often be a key determining factor in creating or changing the structures for contracting, as will the relationships between the various different agencies involved in the process, both as purchasers and contractors, and the distribution of power between them. These relationships will require particular levels of knowledge and professional expertise. The commissioning bodies, while originally possessing these, may eventually come to lose them, as public bodies progressively come to shed their provider role (we give an example in catering services below).

Within the parameters laid down by central government and the inbuilt constraints in the contracting process, a wide variety of different forms have developed in the various local environments. In Chapter 5 we gave a wide range of examples drawn from our case study material. In many instances, the introduction of the new procedures served to highlight existing tensions and rivalries and call them out in greater strength; in other cases, a pre-existing level of trust survived the changes almost intact. In some instances, a pattern of roles and relationships existed which merely had to be legitimized; in others, a new structure had to be built up virtually from scratch.

Power, Interests, and Values

The challenge that the new systems provided to existing patterns of power and interest varied from sector to sector. The extent to which the change to the existing pattern of organization challenged existing distributions of power and patterns of interest was greatest in the National Health Service. As Harrison and Pollitt (1994: 122) argue: 'The purchaser/provider split has served to justify a level of managerial involvement in what were previously "no go" areas ... the change of organizational environment appears to create new leverage for both purchaser and provider managers over health professionals'.

At the same time, the rate of change was slow and the medical staff retained much of their influence within trusts, without being strongly involved in the details of the new system; they were, though slowly, coming to be more involved in the contract and market process as they saw how it affected their position and interests. The new pattern of organization of the NHS creates a multitude of new divisions and differences between groupings. Some were already present, like those between medical and other professional staff; others have been created by change—divisions between purchasers and providers, divisions within professional groupings, and many others. These cross-cutting patterns of interest and conflict mean that it is particularly difficult for the new pattern of organization to emerge, and the difficulties of creating effective organizational structures were greatest in the NHS. The fact that the changes took place within the existing organization meant that the interaction of existing and new patterns of power, interests, and values was particularly complex. It was not that a wholly new management process was created, but that a new approach was superimposed on existing practice.

In social care and local government, the challenges to existing patterns of power, interest, and value were not so radical. In social care, there was much

less requirement to change the pattern of organization through separating purchaser and provider, and there were fewer overlapping and potentially conflicting interests. The move to contracting did not change the distribution of power
significantly within the social services departments that we studied, in which
the social work professionals and managers largely retained control. However,
their work became much more focused on the assessment process and also more
bureaucratically 'dense'. So while the social work caste continued to control the
overall situation, it was the managers among them who dominated proceedings.
However, even in those social service departments that chose to make a strong
division between purchaser and provider, traditional organizational interests tended
to continue to exist and to be able to reassert themselves. It was much more
difficult for the corporate rationalizers to make radical changes based on the
move to contracts, and those authorities that had made the most radical changes
had tended to retreat from them over time.

Providers in social care are relatively fragmented and weak, and the interests
that are most threatened within the organization are of relatively weak operational staff:

In several areas, different staff were feeling deskilled where the interpretation of purchaser and provider functions were being too rigidly separated at the operational level,
and [this] was proving divisive in terms of building the necessary partnerships between
local purchasers and providers. The most significant loss of skill and function was felt
by some home care organisers who constantly said that when they were commissioned
to provide services, they found the needs of older people were under or over assessed
and most were not involved in drawing up care plans. (Department of Health 1994: 29)

The nature of the change seems to have been more likely to lead to centralization and formalization of management systems in social care, though that may
simply be a result of the early stages of the change. At the time of our research,
the disruption of traditional patterns of power and interests was least in the case
of local government. The services that were subject to contract were either not
core to the organization, or had little power compared to traditionally influential departments such as education. It was also possible to separate contracted
services from the rest of the organization, even where, as was normally the case,
the contract was won by the internal provider. The new pattern of organization
did lead to some growth in the power of the providers, particularly where they
were brought together in large DSOs. Influence is illustrated by the extent of
the use of service level agreements for professional support services, such as
finance, which largely derived from DSO pressure. The client side, while initially relatively weak, is beginning to assert itself more clearly. In each of the
authorities that we studied there had been a growth in the influence of the client
side. The extension of CCT to professional support staff is proving to be a much
more significant challenge to traditional patterns of power and interest, and is
leading to organizational change, and also modifying the role of staff.

Differences of power and interest are most apparent in the approach to the management of information in public service organizations. The importance of information was emphasized in all our case studies, but particularly in the health service, in which contracts sometimes used sanctions when adequate information was not provided. There is evidence of some providers wanting to keep information away from purchasers, particularly about issues related to financial management. Contractors could have significant information advantages, even in relatively simple services; one local authority catering client argued:

The problem of the contract was that it was a new service and we did not know very much. We really did too heavy a specification. Only the catering manager on the contractor side was able to look at the specification when he got it and point out that it was too high ... We wanted five hot meals but that would have been too expensive.

It is natural that purchasers should want to standardize information as a means of controlling the client. Purchasers were more likely than providers to emphasize the importance of robust information in contract management, and health more likely to emphasize information than other sectors.

The impact of the change to contracts and markets is influenced by the pattern of values in the organization. In health, the development of managerialism that had begun with the Griffiths Report has been given a very significant stimulus. The change to contracts has led to further attack on the traditional notion of professional autonomy and the rationing of services through the implicit process of doctors' decisions. In both social care and local government, the introduction of a market-based approach is mediated by political commitments and perspectives. Labour authorities generally oppose the contract movement and are more sympathetic to DSOs, whereas Conservative authorities are more likely to favour the market. These differences were apparent in our case studies. In social care also, there was opposition to contracts in some cases because they did not fit with traditional public service values. Whatever the overall attitude of the organization to the introduction of markets, there has also been a growth in managerial values as a result of contracting and competition. Even those who opposed the change recognized that systems had to be changed to some degree in order to introduce market processes. Whatever the attitude that was adopted towards them, contracts generally lead to an increase in managerial values. There is also evidence of a reduction in the involvement of the politicians in local government or board members in the health service in the management of services in which contracting applies. The introduction of contracts and markets tends to lead to services being seen in managerial rather than political terms.

The result of the interaction of power, interests, and values was most obvious in the case of cooperation between organizations in social care and health. It was possible to establish structures of cooperation at the peak of the organization to deal with policy issues, but much more difficult to change the nature of the working of the organizations involved at the level of service delivery. As the social services inspectorate report on care management argued:

progress was being made from joint planning to joint purchasing, sometimes on a locality basis, but not in integrating micro- and macro-purchasing. This work was highlighting differences in the approach to contracting as between SSDs and health authorities, the former being too tightly drawn and the latter too loosely. In some authorities, practitioners were beginning to develop their negotiating skills in setting up one-off contracts, but the degree of support that they received from newly established contracts units was very variable. (Department of Health 1994: 54)

Health authorities were likely to feel that social services departments were less sophisticated in their understanding of the commissioning process, while social services officers felt that health authorities laid too much emphasis on contracting.

Nevertheless, there were some examples in our study of close joint working and of coordinated micro purchasing, which if not strictly joint, were directed to providing particular packages of care. These examples occurred both in the community mental-health field and in learning disabilities. The key conditions seemed to be a practical commitment by chief officers, the availability of central government incentive money, and a shared strategic purpose, in which both interests and values coincided.

Contracting has generally enhanced the power of the client side of the organization, most in social care and least in the health service. In the longer term, the tendency is for the influence of the provider to grow, as has been illustrated in the case of local government. The values of the market-based approach tend to assert themselves in all the organizations involved whatever the value commitments involved. Many of those where we interviewed argued that the contract world had a specificity that tends to lead to it overriding perhaps more important but less urgent issues.

Finally, a change in the way that language is used—the reference to business planning, customers, the bottom line, and so forth—was common throughout our case studies. Managers had had to learn new languages and professionals were increasingly having to do so as well, not only because managers were gaining power but also because professionals were becoming more managerial. Processes of contracting obviously tended to create their own organizational demands, and became embodied in routines of contract writing, evaluation, letting, and monitoring and management. Structures gave permanence to many of the changes. It was common for those we interviewed to argue that even if there were to be change in the future, because of political decision, it would be very difficult to go back to previous patterns of organization because the level of change had been so great. Contracting had been built into the infrastructure of the system. The fact that contracts had to be written at an early stage gave them a first mover advantage against other aspects of the system such as commissioning, user involvement, or the development of quality assurance systems.

Market Conditions and Strategies

In Chapter 6 we drew together evidence from our case studies which helps to illuminate the processes by which markets have been called into being in the three services. The culture and values of the organizations concerned with these processes vary widely in the extent to which they encourage or work against the creation of markets. Political opposition to the introduction of market procedures will vary from the assertion that market values are alien to the whole character of the service itself to simple statements that the policy objectives are inconsistent with the objectives of the rival political parties.

Other points that emerge from the evidence assembled in our case studies that bear upon the future form and dynamic of contracting include the artificiality of the application of market devices in certain contexts (we compare this to the 'artificial horizons' used to train pilots in flight simulators). Another significant factor has been the extent of competition and attitudes towards it: how far it is being encouraged, and how far the playing field is level for the competitors.

Circumstances vary widely in this and in other respects between and within service sectors—we cite the example of social care here and the contrasts between the different sub-markets, in terms of the presence of possible contractors, their skills and experience, and the potential for encouraging new entrants.

Other changes that are also affecting the dynamics of relationships include technological change and the availability of information. This extends to the growing use of surveys of customer satisfaction as performance measures, though not necessarily to wider access to this type of information.

A final highly significant factor is the presence of users and the extent to which they are active participants in the markets that are being created. This can take the form either of users acting as 'co-producers' of goods or users exercising individual choice about the service being delivered. In addition, the Citizen's Charter and its subordinate charters, which operate over many of the service areas with which we have been concerned, cast users as customers and their complaints as one of the motive forces keeping service delivery up to standard (Prior *et al.* 1995).

Attitudes and Strategies of those involved in Contracting

As we progress through the successive determinants of the forms in which contract relationships are developing, one key factor has not yet been explored in any detail. This is the attitudes of those who have been directly involved in the process. In order to fill the gap, we have undertaken a special study of the attitudes of this group, covering those involved in both purchasing and providing and including key individuals working in agencies of all kinds: statutory, voluntary, and for-profit.

A questionnaire was distributed to a substantial number of managers involved in the contracting process, inviting them to express their views about that process. The schedule consisted of a number of propositions (forty-five in all) to which respondents were asked to express their support or dissent, on a five-point scale ranging from strong agreement to strong disagreement. A total of 576 questionnaires were returned from purchasers of services (the main focus of the study) and from providers. In the latter group, there were 67 respondents from outside the statutory sector, equally divided between those from the voluntary sector and those from for-profit organizations.

The main purpose of the questionnaire was to explore differences in attitude between managers in the three different service sectors (local government (CCT), health, and social care); contrasts between purchasers and providers were also a main focus for attention. Full details are provided in Appendix 2.

More specifically, attitudes towards the market and the policy objectives reflected in their introduction vary quite widely between different sectors and among different actors within them. Both collaborative and competitive strategies have been found; different ways of securing value for money and quality of services predominate in different situations. Rationalizations for these different strategies are variously expressed. These differences are reflected in our study of attitudes towards contracting, which is drawn upon in the next section.

The introduction of contracting involved the development of different organizational structures and processes. In part, these were simply a reflection of the legislative requirements. Both in local government and social care there was a requirement to have a formalistic contract procedure, covering issues of contract preparation, letting, and management. In health, the procedures for contracting were much less precisely stated, and the general approach much less clear, while there were clear requirements on organizational structures and processes, notably the purchaser/provider split. The differences are illustrated in the variety of contracting practice. In local government, where the process of contracting was closely governed by regulations laid down by central government, the pattern of contracting and the nature of contracts was very similar from one authority to another. In social care, the main regulatory requirement was simply that there be contracting out to the private sector, and beyond that very little specificity. The result was that contracts varied considerably as did contract procedures, for example the extent to which competitive tendering procedures were used. The approach adopted was much more conditioned by the state of the market than by a regulatory framework of control. In the NHS, the procedures for the management of the contracting processes were not laid down in great detail, and the result was considerable variation from one organization to another. There was far more room for the play of power, interests, and values. Attempts by the National Health Service Management Executive to influence the form of contracts had only a very limited impact.

It was also difficult in health to develop a clear organizational and process fit between contracting and wider health concerns. There was a desire in each of our health case studies to develop a clear strategic approach to commissioning in which contracts were, at most, a minor part, but it was difficult to do so. As one purchaser said:

At times it feels like this organization is really struggling to achieve its purpose and although strategies like 'Health of the Nation' can help I am concerned that we do not know within this organization about the gap between 'health' and contracts. So how will we be able to do anything about it through such a bureaucratic naïve process?

It was in those cases that had greater permanence of staff that it was easier to develop this sort of strategic approach, but even then contracting tended to dominate strategy. It was particularly difficult to develop long-term strategies when contracts covered only one year.

Contracts are widely seen as having created a more commercialized approach to the management of public services, with much greater knowledge of the costs of services. The changes in organizational infrastructures, notably accounting and information systems, have been considerable. There has been a strong tendency to decentralize budgets, partly as a result of the move to contracting, and this has resulted in operational staff questioning the way that they are supported. Decentralized budget holders, such as schools operating under local management of schools or GP fundholders, are much more willing to change the pattern of their purchasing than are more centralized purchasers. In our local authority case, head-teachers were increasingly concerned to develop autonomy and to use their ability to obtain services where they could do so most efficiently. These developments had pushed DSOs in turn to be more market-oriented, as well as forcing client agents to respond to the needs of their more vociferous and powerful 'customers'. It was here that the tensions between markets and hierarchies were most keenly felt.

Contracts are strongly felt to have made managers more 'business-like' in their approach to the management of public services, though the degree to which this is felt varies from service to service. The overall pattern is illustrated in Table 8.1. The five points on the original scale have been collapsed into three, for greater clarity.

The strong belief in the development of a more business-like approach in local government reflects the fact that the internal market process is clear in that sector, and the influence of professional groups low for the services which have so far been subject to contracting. The difference between the NHS and other sectors in this belief is clear. It may reflect a concern that business values are not appropriate, but, if so, one would have expected a closer correlation between the views of health and social care. It is the difference between purchasers and providers that is most significant. One might have expected that it would be the providers who would have felt that markets and contracts had led to a more business-like approach, and commercial providers in social care did feel that this was the case. Internal providers seem particularly likely to be suspicious of the degree to which contracting has improved management, often suspecting that purchasers are of poor calibre and rely on their organizational position to attain their purposes.

TABLE 8.1. Contracting makes managers more 'business-like' in their approach

	Agree (%)	Neutral (%)	Disagree (%)
Local government	76.8	20.1	13.1
National Health Service	46.7	34.5	18.8
Social care	59.9	26.3	13.8
Purchasers	64.6	23.1	14.5
Providers	46.2	34.2	16.6

TABLE 8.2. Organizations become more commercialized after contracting

	Agree (%)	Neutral (%)	Disagree (%)
Local government	80.3	13.5	6.1
National Health Service	61.0	17.1	22.0
Social care	66.3	26.5	7.2
Purchasers	72.2	20.9	7.0
Providers	64.2	16.6	19.2

Respondents to the questionnaire were more likely to feel that the organization had become commercialized than that managers had become more business-like (see Table 8.2). The change was to the systems of the organization and the way that it operated rather than the people involved.

Again though, there are the differences between the health service and other sectors and between purchasers and providers. Overall, these responses are in line with our case study findings in which the commercial agenda had been picked up more by local government, reflecting the greater ease of introducing contracting for the services involved despite the degree of political opposition. The commercial logic had also had a longer period to work itself out. The more sceptical view of the providers about the agendas of commercialism and business orientation reflects the increasing dominance of the purchasers, but may also reflect the fact that they see the development of a new bureaucracy of the market.

It has been argued that the result of contracting is likely to be an increase in the degree of centralization within public service organizations, but this was not generally thought to be the case by managers in our case study organizations (see Table 8.3).

The perception of centralization is highest in the social care sector. Voluntary organizations in particular are likely to see the degree of centralization as having increased. The perception of centralization is also highly variable, and may

TABLE 8.3. Contracts have led to more centralization

	Agree (%)	Neutral (%)	Disagree (%)
Local government	32.0	35.3	32.8
National Health Service	32.3	29.5	37.9
Social care	39.8	32.3	27.9
Purchaser	30.9	34.5	34.5
Provider	37.9	34.1	28.0

TABLE 8.4. Managers have a more formal role under contracts

	Agree (%)	Neutral (%)	Disagree (%)
Local government	67.7	26.6	5.7
National Health Service	52.4	26.8	20.7
Social care	80.7	15.1	4.2
Purchaser	69.6	22.3	8.1
Provider	60.2	25.3	14.5

reflect the fact that contracting has both centralizing and decentralizing components. Our earlier discussion of the case studies has shown that while there is increased financial delegation to cost centres, there is an increase in the overall centralization related to contracts, for example in hospitals, where the actual negotiation of contracts tends to be carried out by central management, with relatively little involvement of medical staff. Again providers differ from purchasers in seeing the level of centralization as having increased.

Contracting is clearly seen as having increased levels of formalization within public service organizations. It might be argued that this was a part of the point of the exercise, in that there was seen to be a need to break down the informal controls that were operated by professionals and develop a more managerially oriented approach. More negatively, formalization can be seen as a form of bureaucracy.

On these views formalization is highest in the social care sector and lowest in health, with purchasers being more likely to see formalization as having increased than providers (see Table 8.4). This may reflect that fact that the respective role of purchasers and providers—for example in the assessment process—differs between sectors. The differences are also likely to be a reflection of the nature of the contracts regimes in the different sectors, with social care and local government operating under more explicitly controlled regimes. Health has retained a greater degree of informality, which may reflect the greater influence of the medical staff.

TABLE 8.5. Contracts do not provide greater managerial control over services

	Agree (%)	Neutral (%)	Disagree (%)
Local government	32.4	29.9	37.7
National Health Service	22.5	32.9	44.5
Social care	44.8	29.1	26.0
Purchaser	31.6	27.0	41.4
Provider	33.9	39.8	26.3

The differences in the degree to which contracting has been governed by an explicit legal framework is reflected in attitudes towards whether contracting had made organizations more legalistic. Social care organizations were most likely to see contracting as having led to increased legalism, and the health service least so. Providers were more likely than purchasers to see contracting as having increased legalism. The framework of constraint that governs social care contracts is more concerned with bureaucratic detail over payment and it is not surprising that the result should be a perceived increase in legalism. Social care is also the sector in which legally enforceable contracts are dominant, since there is an external market there, parts of which are, in turn, subject to registration and inspection.

It is generally felt that contracts provide greater management control over services than had previously been the case. Again though, there are significant differences between sectors (see Table 8.5).

The balance of attitudes is reversed between social care and the other two sectors. While in the health service there is felt to be greater managerial control, this is not the case in social care. This would support the argument that the managerialist agenda is most explicitly developed in the health service, and that professional control persists in social care. Those managing contracts in the social care cases that we studied were likely to be at a more junior level than in the health service. It is also purchasers who are likely to feel that managerial control has increased rather than providers. Commercial providers and voluntary agencies are particularly likely to feel that managerial control has increased. The limited perception of managerial control also reflects the difficulty of specification for social care services.

There are, of course, different forms of control; and the extent to which it can be exercised over outcomes, rather than processes, may depend on the available technologies, which in turn vary between the different service sectors.

Contracting was seen as having made budgeting easier particularly in local government. The local government contracting system, with its relatively long contract periods, leads to the cost of services being set for a number of years. This gives purchasers in particular a degree of certainty of their spending, though at the expense of a degree of flexibility. In health, there is also a degree of certainty over budgets, but, because contracts are typically only for one year, that certainty is limited. In social care, the feeling that budgeting had become easier was much less, which is to be expected given the fact that most purchasing is essentially done on a spot basis. The rate of turnover of people in care is relatively short, and getting shorter, and the increased levels of dependency make it difficult to predict need. Moreover, the level of care that is needed is strongly influenced by the decisions of other organizations, notably hospitals. The problems are clear from the crises that hit a number of social services departments in 1994–5, when they ran out of money to provide for community care.

Providers were much less likely to feel that budgeting had been made easier, since they must earn money and do not start the year with any guaranteed level of income, though they can be much more sure of the position in local government and health than in social care. Voluntary organizations and commercial providers were particularly likely to feel that their budgeting position had been made much more difficult. This pattern reflects the way that the development of contracting in the public service has tended to shift risk from the client to the contractor side. Managing under contract reduces the certainty of incomes for the provider. The development of contracting shifts the emphasis in organizational decision-making in the public service from an interest in budgets to an interest in financial control. In the past, for most managers there was little need to consider the balance of income and expenditure, but simply a necessity to stay within a set financial allocation. Managers on the provider side must now be concerned for their income as well as their expenditure, and for the management of assets.

MANAGING CONTRACTS

A final area which will have a vital influence on structuring the outcomes of the contracting process is the way in which contracts are being managed and the objectives that those managing them (and those who are being managed through contracts) are trying to meet. Here, the overarching values associated with contracts generally, come into play. These are the tensions embodied in the principal-agent relationship and the issues of risk, sanctions (default), and trust, to which we drew attention in Chapter 2. But they are mediated through the local circumstances and the way in which organizations operate and the attitudes of the individuals responsible for managing the process. (We have presented some evidence on these issues in Chapter 7.)

The main actors concerned, in addressing these issues in specific local circumstances, could be described as following the 'logic of the contract worlds'.

The Logic of Contract Worlds

Different public service sectors, while they each faced the introduction of contracts, had to operate under different logics of action. In all three sectors the importance of trust and cooperative working was emphasized, as was the need for informality and responsiveness. The extent to which these values were achievable was influenced by the context within which each sector had to operate. The play of power, interests, and values varied according to the regulatory and other constraints faced. The initial starting position also served to create constraints on the path that could be followed. Contracts are a source of conflicting pressures and demands, with the desire for cooperation and long-term perspectives tending to conflict with the immediacy of the demands of contract. Different strategies are likely to be adopted, depending on the nature of the decision being taken—operational decisions may invoke a different response, in terms of choice between collaboration or conflict, to strategic ones.

The logic of the contract worlds that were faced in different sectors may be considered in terms of a number of key factors: risk, sanctions and trust, information availability, the specificity of the assets used, clarity of principal-agent relationships, and the extent to which the introduction of contracts was linked to other factors. The way that these factors interact will influence the sorts of contract approach that are possible, and the way that organizational systems develop over time. For example, the extent to which it is possible to set up a monitoring system for contracts will depend upon the ease with which service performance can be assessed—its observability. The ability of the purchasers to monitor will tend to enhance their influence against the provider.

In the case of local government, the risks that are involved in contracts, both for client and contractor, are relatively clear, and can be actively managed, for example through processes of insurance and the operation of performance bonds. Clients can make fairly accurate judgements of the problems that are likely to arise and can take action to ensure that they are covered by contract conditions and specifications. The general approach has been to shift a considerable proportion of the risk onto the contractor. Contractors can make relatively accurate assessments of the level of risk that they face and can adjust their prices to take account of it. Contractors have a clear commercial perspective outside the local authority, and in the case of larger contractors tend to be risk neutral, and inside have become increasingly commercially organized.

It might appear that the local government contract world will be one of distrust, conflict, and tension, given this ease of identifying responsibilities and interests, and the relatively clear identification of principal and agent. Sanctions are certainly used, but both our own and previous research has shown that their use is limited (Walsh and Davis 1993). It was commonly argued to us in case study interviews that sanctions were not used much in practice and that it was quite possible to have cooperative relationships with providers, whether internal or external to the organization.

However, our evidence suggests that the situation in local government is slowly changing. The sorts of relationships that have developed for services that are subject to competition under the Local Government Planning and Land Act 1980 and the Local Government Act 1988 are relatively cooperative. The extension of competition to professional services raises more difficult issues (Walsh 1995*b*). First, there will be much greater linkage between contracts than has been the case before. Information technology contracts, in particular, will overlap with others. There will also be a greater diversity of interests involved, for example the tenants in housing management contracts. Finally, the services that are involved are much closer to the core of the organization. The logic of contracts is becoming more complex, but there is no sign that this will lead to the type of enabling authority propounded by Nicholas Ridley, and the signs are that the competitive authority will have its own contract bureaucracy.

In social care, though providers have generally had to bear the risk that is reflected in a fixed price, there is more tendency for risk-sharing and cooperative approaches than in local government, particularly when dealing with voluntary organizations. The perception widely held in the voluntary sector has been that the introduction of contracting has disadvantaged many organizations, especially smaller community-oriented groups (Deakin 1996). However, this perception is not shared by the social services departments nor by the voluntary sector's competitors in the for-profit sector.

Social services authorities have seen it as their responsibility in part to make the market, which has sometimes involved the purchasers establishing intermediate organizations to make it easier for the providers to operate. Despite the clarity of the separation of purchasers and providers, there is a search for cooperation and trust. It is difficult to monitor performance in the case of social care and the purchaser tends to rely on the requirement for quality assurance systems and the monitoring of records.

Contracting itself in social care is relatively clear; though there is a problem in identifying the principal and agent, the user tends to play an ambiguous role, and it has been difficult to define the position of the user as opposed to the purchaser. Value systems in social care have led the purchasers to be concerned not to let the market operate in a totally free way, but the indications are that in the longer term there will be a significant degree of entry into and exit from the market. There is also increasing complexity as the number of services covered by contracting increases and the contract world of social care becomes more complex.

In health, there is greater complexity than in the other cases, because of the totality of the change and the unwillingness of the government to let the contract world operate. The overarching values of commissioning are not easily reflected in the contract process. There is a strong tendency to share risk between purchaser and provider, though the trend is towards shifting risk to the providers. Sanction-based approaches are being adopted as time passes, a reflection of the difficulties of cooperation that are created by the pattern of separation of the purchaser and the provider. The difficulties of information asymmetry are apparent in the strong emphasis on the need for the providers to provide adequate information for monitoring. The conflicting pressures for cooperation and control are shown in the advice of the National Health Service Management Executive.

Concern has been expressed by some purchasers and providers that the use of sanctions may undermine the development of contracting relationship. A mature working relationship being based on collaboration rather than coercion. The NHSME has encouraged purchasers and providers to make greater use of sanctions and incentives—they need, however, to be agreed and understood by both parties and explicit in contracts. Their use needs to be considered within the context of 'shared risk'. (NHSME 1994)

This is a clear expression of the danger of the contract world undermining the set of values that is seen as being needed for it to operate effectively.

The clarity of the principal-agent relationship is being obscured as more purchasers enter the market, notably through the devolution of control to GP fundholders and multi-funds. Medical staff in hospitals also continue to play a purchaser-type role by virtue of the fact that they make decisions on care. Ultimately, it is difficult to change patterns of provision because of the highly specific nature of the assets involved in health care. The market is likely to work to reduce the number of providers over time, but at any given time the position is likely to be one of monopoly provision. The monopolistic nature of the service, with the high level of political interest, means that the level of regulation is likely to stay high. The separation of the purchaser and provider role in health raises more acutely than in other cases the issue of how the two are to be brought together again, given the limited willingness of participants at all levels to let the market logic dominate.

CONCLUSION

A whole series of market-based theories of organization have been developed over the past twenty years (Harden 1992). These have characteristically focused on issues of property rights, transaction costs, and the relationship between principals and agents. Our study of the operation of markets in the public sector shows that these theoretical approaches do have some explanatory value. However, their applicability is limited because of their assumptions, both about individual behaviour and motivation and about the way organizations in the public sector operate and how their roles change.

Property rights theorists argue that achieving clarity in the identification and distribution of property rights will lead to greater efficiency. This, it is suggested, will reduce the need for explicitly political decision-making about the rationing and distribution of resources. A 'price-competitive, budget-limited market "thought world" ' (Mackintosh 1995) will develop its own legitimacy. But the application of this approach in the public sector has significant limitations. These derive not only from the public nature of many of the goods but also from the problem of defining services in terms of commercial exchanges. There is a collective interest to be considered as well, in terms of property rights enjoyed as citizens, which may conflict with individual rights arising from personal entitlement. In the case of social care, the role of the user (whose needs and circumstances are difficult to fit into the contracting framework) is especially problematic.

Yet authoritative decisions on rights and resources and how they are identified and allocated cannot be avoided—they will always remain (potentially, at least) politically controversial. Recent court cases brought in some shire counties about levels of spending on community care are symptomatic of this problem. They raise fundamental issues about the nature of individual rights and the way in which political decisions are taken and implemented. In the health service, too, resource decisions and their political implications continue to be highly relevant to the ways in which markets are to be managed. The process is not just about efficiency and value for money; it is also an expression of political necessities.

As a result, many of the markets that have come into existence are hybrids. Often they are incomplete, leaving more local discretion than those who originally designed them intended. Competition is frequently minimal or even purely symbolic; and the outcomes that they deliver are often unpredictable. Information is unevenly distributed between purchasers, providers, and users. Managing in these circumstances is a far more complex task than the market-based templates would imply. Moreover, some of these templates are themselves suspect in their simplicities. The replacement of hierarchy by outsourcing through contracts in the corporate sector is a much more complex and incomplete process than some accounts would suggest.

Nevertheless, some of the key issues identified in market-based theories are clearly relevant—for example, the issue of transaction costs. We found many examples of high costs of installing and running contract-based management. Many of the developments that occurred in the cases that we studied can be best seen as the result of attempts to reduce transaction costs—for example, the stress laid on quality-assurance mechanisms. There were a number of examples of cases of attempts to shift costs and risks between purchaser and provider, not always on the basis that one particular outcome was the most efficient.

Various patterns of division and integration between purchaser and provider can be identified as being a result of transaction cost issues. The limitation of an approach based on this perspective is shown in practice by the way in which the solutions reached reflect the distribution of power and interests within and between organizations rather than narrower efficiency issues. In general, the organizational forms that have emerged do not reflect the predictions of transaction cost theorists (Dowd 1993). Transaction cost approaches will go some way to explaining some small-scale changes but do not help us to predict which large-scale institutional forms will predominate or the nature of interorganizational relationships.

Principal-agent theory assumes that each participant in a market will act to maximize their own self-interest and that the organizational forms adopted should therefore carry built-in safeguards to limit opportunistic behaviour. In our case studies, there were certainly numerous cases of self-interested behaviour by many different participants. But generally, it is not helpful to view contracting in the public service as narrowly as this model would imply. It is important to understand that the public services involve a multiplicity of principals and agents, with a diverse and complex combination of overlapping, conflicting, or consistent interests. In these circumstances, a variety of different strategies is possible. Competition is about one set of interests prevailing over another; but collaborative approaches may yield a more positive result for all participants (the 'win-win' outcome to which many of our respondents referred).

There is also a need to extend the basic approach of principal-agent theory to comprehend the existence of a much broader range of relevant interests. It is also important to recognize that some of these interests are not purely financial. Government, to take an obvious example, has an interest in ensuring that the system does not operate in such a way as to produce political embarrassment. Government's other interests may also have contradictory effects: balancing their objectives against one another—economy and value for money—for example, may be quite a complex exercise. And given that the predictive value of market theory has not so far proved to be very great when it has been applied to public sector practice, uncertainty of outcome is likely to be a dominant feature of the situation for the foreseeable future.

In short, the introduction and management of contracts in the public sector creates both dilemmas and paradoxes. There are dilemmas about the choices that arise between control and cooperation; and paradoxes that follow from attempts to operate contracts effectively which are undermined by the process of contracting itself. If we are to understand the pattern of change that is emerging, we need to be able to draw on theories that do not rely on a purely economic dynamic but recognize the crucial role played by the operation of power and interests. We also need to be able to test out these theories in a variety of different locations where power and interest are differently organized and distributed.

9

The Contract Revolution:
The International Experience

A 'competition prescription' (Kettl 1993: 1) has been applied across the British public sector. In Chapter 1, the changes to the National Health Service (NHS), social care, and other local government services were outlined in some detail and set in a broader context of public sector reform, with reference, for example, to changes in central government. Metcalfe (1993) sets the UK changes in the context of global trends of reform in public services, which, though prompted by particular national concerns, also have in common three factors:

First, the deterioration of economic performance from the 1970s onwards made it difficult to allow increasing governmental demands on national resources. Second, there was a feeling that public expenditure was running out of control because of growing statutory entitlements to specific benefits and escalating costs of services. Third, there was the apparent inability of the civil service to respond to these problems by improving efficiency and effectiveness of service delivery and the management of public expenditure. Criticisms went beyond the standard complaints of bureaucratic inefficiency to accusations of lack of competence in managing resources. (Metcalfe 1993: 352)

Various labels have been applied to these reform programmes including new managerialism (Pollitt 1993) and new public management which also comes complete with acronym (NPM) (Dunleavy and Hood 1994). The use of labels to describe these changes implies, first, a degree of coherence more likely to have emerged with the passing of time than inherent in the reform design (see Chapter 1); and secondly, a degree of uniformity, when the reality in relation to the UK, but also true of other countries, is that different combinations of components have been selected from the menu in individual reform contexts (a process described in Chapter 1 as the breeding of a hybrid). The ideas associated with these labels also imply consistency. For example: 'The New Public Management represents elements of neo-Taylorism with all the problems that scientific management models of the past have displayed (Pollitt 1990). For example it tends to argue that there is one best way to manage in all circumstances' (Gray and Jenkins 1993: 22).

Moreover, as we discussed in Chapter 2, the power of discourse in shaping new identities and practices (Townley 1994; Newman 1994), regardless of the degree of implementation 'success' (Marsh and Rhodes 1992*a*) is also relevant. The language of markets, or of ' "enabling" (Ridley, 1988) has now become established within the public sector, so that, even if one wishes to argue against the new orthodoxy, one must start from its ideological presuppositions. The failure of traditional approaches is taken as axiomatic, even if on limited evidence'

(Walsh 1995: p. xv). Language is also influential in the sense that critics not only have to be able to get to grips with the ideology of the new orthodoxy but in addition, with a new language (for example, economics) to use in their argument.

This chapter examines one key aspect of global reform—the contract revolution in public services—more closely. To what extent *are* there common drivers for change? Are the approaches adopted in particular national and institutional contexts as similar as they appear? Are we really comparing like with like and how can we benefit from the international experience?

POLICIES/MODELS FOR EXPORT — A WORD OF CAUTION

An interesting side-effect of global change lies in the exchange of ideas and experience that has taken place between countries. Dunleavy and Hood (1994: 15) refer to the dangers of 'inappropriate cloning' evident in public policy-making and management where organizations are pressurized into jumping onto the reform bandwagon and uniformly adopting 'fashionable management models'. There are clear parallels at the international level.

Gray and Jenkins (1993) in their discussion of the emergence and extension of NPM in British central government, local government, and the NHS, comment that although the question of coherence implied by this concept is open, there has developed a momentum for reform (illustrated by *their* use of language) associated with a set of tenets which

have been *seized upon* by a variety of governments in Europe, North America and Australia. As a result it is too early to see [NPM] as simply a product of governments of right wing free marketeers. In the Netherlands, New Zealand and Sweden, for example many of its ideas have been pursued with almost *missionary zeal* by governments of the centre or left, while countries in Eastern Europe, aided by western government and western management consultants, are proceeding in a *headlong rush* to privatize state activities and train their administrators to appreciate the ways of markets and efficient management. (Gray and Jenkins 1993: 21; my emphasis)

The fact that a national programme of reform sits in a wider context of parallel changes on a global level, does lend some legitimacy to that programme which in turn legitimizes other programmes in other countries.

The 'export' of fashionable policies/models can also be considered in terms of the concepts outlined in Chapter 2. These explain change in the public sector linked to the adoption of organizational approaches (in this case markets and contracts) that are taken as the hallmark of good practice. This may be voluntary, as part of attempts to demonstrate effectiveness (see Chapter 2) or imposed by an external authority in the form of regulation or normative pressure. An example of such imposition in the international context includes the relationship between developing countries and the World Bank (Walsh 1995b). The result of this process, according to Di Maggio and Powell (1983), is institutional isomorphism (where different organizations performing similar roles develop similar characteristics).

At a very basic level, the problems centre on context and the issues of exchanging public sector reform programmes between countries with different:

- *population sizes and geographical distribution*: for example New Zealand has around 3 million inhabitants and covers nearly 104,000 square miles compared to the UK, a country with around 57 million people living across just over 94,000 square miles (Hutchinson Encyclopedia 1992);
- *patterns of government*: for example, Australia has three tiers of government (commonwealth, state, and local) compared to a unitary system of government in New Zealand. The average size of a Swedish commune (or unit of local government) is 30,000 inhabitants compared to 1,500 in France and 75,000 to 125,000 in the UK (Von Otter 1994);
- *welfare systems*: for example, the Italian system of social welfare is a mixed one in that under most parts of the system, welfare provision entitlement is only for workers or retired persons compared to 'universal' welfare models operated in the UK or Sweden. Also in the Italian system, there is more emphasis on money transfer for meeting social needs rather than on direct service provision (for example, transfer payments account for 92.5 per cent of public expenditure (Barbetta 1994)).

More generally, patterns of government and the nature of the welfare state are influenced by historical factors such as wars (Giddens 1985) and the role of religion, particularly Catholicism (Esping-Andersen 1990). These factors will influence the scope for contracting and organizational approaches.

There are also issues about the nature of the good or service. The approach taken to contracting for refuse collection for example, cannot be neatly applied to social care and hence, as we saw in Chapter 1, even the UK government has varied its reform programmes for different service contexts. In the international context too, countries vary in the extent to which contracts have been comprehensively applied. For example, Australian experiences of contracting, for services such as building cleaning, are reported to be positive but in terms of contracting more broadly, 'core services are usually considered to be sacrosanct' (Domberger and Hall 1994: 7).

A more fundamental difficulty relates to the point made at the beginning of this chapter which is that in spite of the presumed consistency in terms of global solutions to common problems, what is actually understood by contracting is highly variable: contracting means different things in different cultures.

For example, in the UK and Sweden, public sector contracting implies a degree of competition or at least contestability but in Italy and the USA, social care contracts are often sole source and negotiated contracts. In Australia, a distinction is made between competitive tendering and contracting (CTC) to refer to contracts awarded with competition between agencies and without competition (i.e. sole source or negotiated contracts) respectively.

It appears that, broadly speaking, there may be an Anglo-Saxon variant of contract which is strongly related to notions of individualism and reflects the influence of neoclassical economics; and a 'continental' version which has more to do with notions of citizenship and the rights inherent in this. For example, the French view of contract is very different to the British view. The former is very loose, being based on minimal specification (perhaps about a page) and founded on a number of background assumptions (for example, that renegotiation is an essential feature of the operation of the contract). The British model, particularly in the local government context is very tight and the emphasis is on covering every contingency and therefore only doing what is stated in the contract. The opportunity for French-based companies to bid for British refuse collection contracts or to buy into English water companies is having an impact on the nature of French contracts.

The different meanings attached to contracts will be explored in more detail later but for now the point to be made is that the language of contracting is very flexible—on the international stage you can do almost anything and call it a contract—which suggests that contracts are not a very precise solution to the problems to which they are attached.

Finally, in this section, a further reason for caution before we jump on the—everyone else is doing it so it must be right—bandwagon, is that in actual fact there is very little evidence that this is the 'right' way to go.

In their papers on Sweden, France, and Australia and New Zealand, Von Otter (1994), Sorbets (1994), and Domberger and Hall (1996) all comment that there are very few studies on contracting in these countries and that where data exists, it is not routinely and systematically collected.

There are also difficulties in attributing causality. For example, in the UK local government sector it has sometimes been difficult to separate the effects of the introduction of compulsory competitive tendering (CCT) from those of the local management of schools (LMS) initiative under which schools are now able to manage their own budgets (Deakin and Walsh 1996). Also, Robinson and Le Grand (1994) discuss the NHS reforms and the difficulties in identifying evaluation criteria and 'the considerable difficulties of isolating the precise effects in these areas . . . when other major changes have been taking place at the same time' (Robinson and Le Grand 1994: 11).

Similarly in Sweden, problems have been experienced in isolating the effects of quasi-markets from those of austerity policy more generally (Von Otter 1994).

We also need to be careful that what we are seeing is not simply a Hawthorne effect, a point of particular relevance to the construction of surveys designed to assess the impact of changes on staff. For example, if this is the first opportunity some of those staff have been given to express an opinion, this may influence the results, since this opportunity may be seen as a positive development in itself.

The evaluation issue is a crucial one and relates back to Walsh's point (Walsh 1995*b*) about the new orthodoxy. The case of the UK health reforms also suggests a more disturbing side to the lack of evidence on the effectiveness of these programmes. In this case, despite the magnitude of the reforms, no official provision was made for evaluating the changes (Robinson and Le Grand 1994). In a sense the motivation for such a position—which may or may not explain the lack of attention to evaluation in other countries—is unimportant. Whether it springs from the foolhardiness of 'conviction politics' or is a reflection of something more sinister (a possibility which might appeal to conspiracy theorists) —the fact remains that the lack of attention to evaluating these reforms, which are being carried out globally, makes the apparent legitimization of national programmes even more disturbing as well as making before and after comparisons very difficult.

Happily, the UK government has, in other instances, adopted better practice with research on CCT (Walsh 1991; Walsh and Davies 1993) and its recent wide-ranging review of its Competing for Quality programme in central government (*Financial Times* 1995), the report of which is to be published shortly.

Given the caveats expressed above, there are clearly examples where policy imitation has taken place and where experiences can be usefully exchanged. Gutch (1992) for example, takes this line in his paper on contracting lessons for UK voluntary organizations from the USA. Although there are important differences in third-sector contracting between the two countries, there are, he concludes, sufficient similarities for useful lessons to be learned. This chapter tries to identify such lessons, both in terms of good practice which may be transferable and of pitfalls to be avoided or dilemmas to be resolved.

Before doing so, it is important to set out in more detail the context for contracting—the background to public sector management reform. What are the drivers for moving to contracts? Economic constraints? Ideology? Empirical evidence that contracting 'works' (although given the limited extent of evaluative data and debate about appropriate evaluation criteria, such as the balance between objectives of economy, efficiency, and effectiveness, this seems unlikely)? In doing so, the chapter draws on evidence from a range of experts, using this to illustrate various points.[1]

CONTRACTING FOR PUBLIC SERVICES: BACKGROUND

The drivers for change will be both a product of national context and influenced by external factors such as global trends. However, just as difficulties have been reported in establishing a causal relationship between public sector management reforms and public sector performance, there are similar problems in isolating drivers for change. These are both multiple and dynamic. Few doctors would make a diagnosis based on one symptom and the same principle should be applied to the study of international changes. For example, it is too simplistic to assert that fiscal pressure creates cultural readiness for change or can be treated with a competition prescription. If that were true, wouldn't Third World countries be contracting?

Nevertheless fiscal pressure is clearly important. Dearden (1991) comments that in response to pressures such as the largest overseas debt per head in the OECD, 'the New Zealand government had to do something about its economy and therefore its social services, which it could no longer afford. This is the something' (Dearden 1991: 15).

Moreover, as Domberger and Hall point out: 'It is noteworthy and certainly no coincidence, that the most fiscally sound government in Australia [Queensland] has no CTC policy nor intentions to implement a broad strategy' (Domberger and Hall 1996: 3). Fiscal pressures are certainly not the whole picture, however, as the Queensland example shows, since Queensland was the first state in Australia to operate a 'private' prison.

In the Netherlands, cost containment was a driver in the proposals by the Dekker Committee in 1987, for the complete restructuring of the insurance-based health care system based on the introduction of market influences (Flynn and Simonis 1990). The reforms set in place by the 'Dekker plan' are not yet fully realized. Van der Grinten *et al.* (1994)—in an important case study, not only of the management of change in a particular context but also of the problems of successful policy implementation *within* the context in which a policy has been designed—show how the reform design and development has been influenced and constrained by the boundaries in the policy structure and policy culture of the Dutch health care system.

For example, to facilitate the control and influence required for cost containment, fragmentation in the existing systems and structures—a reflection of historical and cultural factors including ideas about the role of the state—has had to be addressed. In the Netherlands, only 10 per cent of public funding comes from taxes; 90 per cent of medical specialists are self-employed and independent from institutions such as hospitals; and private (non-profit and for-profit) institutions are the dominant actors, not only in the health field but also in education, housing, and social care.

Fragmentation is also a feature of the Italian social welfare system both in relation to the definition and distribution of responsibility for welfare action and the complexities of the funding system (Barbetta 1994). Public institutions existing at different governmental levels (including national, regional, and municipal administrations) are variously responsible for the administration of money transfers (mainly carried out by national and regional bodies), policy direction, and direct service provision. There has also been some transference of responsibilities between tiers of government (for example, state and regions). Variance is also a feature within tiers of government: the extent of direct service provision relates to the size of comuni (municipal administrations), with smaller comuni sometimes relying on larger comuni for service provision.

In addition to public bodies, private, and in particular Catholic, organizations and semi-autonomous national institutions also have a role. The influence of the Catholic Church is an important feature of the Italian social welfare system. Like the distribution of responsibility, the relative importance of players is also dynamic. Barbetta (1994) suggests that tensions between the state and the church have contributed to the changing configuration of the public sector. The complexity of the non-profit/for-profit distinction in Italian notions of 'private' providers is illustrated by the example of the *IPABs*. These service providers originated from private organizations known as the *Opere Pie*—most of which were created and controlled by religious congregations—which were drawn into the public sector by means of the so-called Crispi law. This ruling, however, was declared unconstitutional in 1988 and new arrangements for existing *IPABs* and new social welfare providers have been set up.

In Italy, therefore:

The result of different layers of legislation enacted in different periods is a strange and chaotic mixture of a publicly-regulated social security system (old age pensions, industrial accidents, unemployment etc), run on an insurance basis and covering the working population, and a National Health System sheltering the whole citizenship. (Barbetta 1994: 3)

The introduction of markets has, in part, been inspired by a belief that the private sector is more efficient than the public sector. In the British central government context, evidence that this belief is a further driver for change is clearly illustrated by the shift in emphasis from market testing (competition between an in-house team and external providers) to strategic contracting out (competition between external providers only).

Von Otter (1995) discusses quasi-market reforms in Sweden and comments that half the counties 'developed planned market experiments; others have focused change on new management systems, process re-engineering, and similar concepts . . . [and] studies have failed to establish meaningful relationships between the insertion of market mechanisms and cost control. Counties which have adopted other strategies are doing as well, sometimes even better' (Von Otter 1995: 5). The tensions between the desire to effect change from within a sector and the opening up of a sector to external competition illustrate the importance of ideology as a driver. We have already referred to the concept of 'enabling' which refers to the separation of core and peripheral functions with the latter being discharged elsewhere.

However, the conceptualization of core and peripheral has been problematic. In Australia, the definition of what is core—and by implication not appropriate for the competition prescription—does not include services such as refuse collection, building cleaning, and other so-called 'simple' services (Walsh *et al.* 1996). However, this definition is starting to be contested. In Victoria, for example, consideration has been given to the use of CTC for welfare services. Of course the definition of core may have less to do with the inherent nature of the good and more to do with its political saliency, or the nature and strength of traditional providers, with local government officers, for example, being seen as a softer target than doctors.

The nature of providers is relevant in another sense which suggests that for all the discussion that has taken place in recent years about the blurring of boundaries between public and private, in practice distinctions are being maintained.

In the USA, for example, where contracting for health and social care is extensive, non-profit providers dominate in the provision of human services, such as child protection, home care, and residential care, provided for the chronically mentally ill, developmentally disabled, and people with AIDS. In Sweden too, the preferred approach has been the introduction of public competition and internal markets between public providers (Von Otter 1994).

Of course, the dominance of non-profits in particular markets is a more complex issue than implied above (see for example Smith and Lipsky 1993), but of crucial importance, it is suggested, is the perceived trustworthiness of non-profits in comparison with for-profits. Although aspects of this trustworthiness are questioned by Smith and Lipsky, such perceptions persist. For example in the UK very different and more favourable contractual forms are used by local authorities in their contracting with voluntary organizations compared to private residential homes (Smith and Thomas 1993).

Part of the explanation for these trends may lie in the fact that however wholeheartedly governments appear to embrace the competition prescription for their varying ills (ranging from dissatisfaction with service quality and concern to reduce the power of traditional service providers in Italy; through to a desire to make the political function more representative of the public (as opposed to agencies and their employees) in Sweden), they still have reservations about letting the invisible hand of the market run rampant. Therefore conceptualizations of core and non-core, as implied above, reflect the political saliency of the services.

A further ideological feature has been the rhetoric of responsible government, where responsibility is to the taxpayer: 'government, when purchasing on behalf of its citizens, has a responsibility to provide value for money' (Domberger and Hall 1996: 6). Most governments might be expected to sign up to the need to be responsible, and political administrations on the left and right can apparently live, to varying degrees, with an acceptance that direct provision is not always essential. In Sweden, 'the political controversy between left and right is not, whether to move in the direction of competition and contracts, but how far' (Von Otter 1994: 11).

There are parallels in Australia where CTC is only partly a function of political persuasion (Domberger and Hall 1996) and in the UK as 'new' Labour adopts some of the language of the market (*Sunday Times* 1995*b*). However there are clear differences of interpretation and degree. In the UK, as Deakin and Walsh (1996) point out, there are two underlying assumptions: that without market disciplines, the state cannot deliver services efficiently and that all activities involving the delivery of goods and services can be carried out more efficiently and effectively through the market. In Italy, however, the move to an enabling role for government in the provision of social care has been accompanied by the increasing role of private organizations in service provision. However, these private organizations are mainly non-profit agencies (Barbetta 1994).

Deakin and Parry (1993) also consider the rhetoric of responsible government in their chapter on the role of the UK Treasury. Just as national governments across the world are concerned, in response to environmental factors, to act in a responsible way and to secure value for money, the UK Treasury is the self-appointed 'custodian of good sense and clear thinking against complacent lower calibre spending departments which have usually been captured by interest groups' (Deakin and Parry 1993: 33). However it is not, as it claims, value-neutral since the management of social expenditure implies an implicit social policy or 'criteria for judging the desirable means and ends of government intervention in personal behaviour and life choices' (Deakin and Parry 1993: 29).

Effective *marketing* by politicians (and the use of this word is deliberate given the above comments) of environmental conditions can create the cultural readiness for change. In the UK, pronouncements about apparently infinite demand for health care and finite resources have produced changes in service provision. Explicit choices are being made about what should and should not be provided as part of a National Health Service (*Sunday Times* 1995a).

So, to summarize, although different countries may be motivated to reform their public services by similar concerns—such as economic constraints or a desire to provide services of a quality that is required by service users rather than deemed appropriate by service providers—these concerns or symptoms, while leading to similar diagnoses, produce very different prescriptions when considered in terms of other factors (such as national context—what can be achieved, what there is to work with—and political objectives such as a desire to be re-elected), just as some people diagnosed as suffering from depression might be treated with ECT (electroconvulsive therapy) when others may receive drugs or counselling. The next section examines these treatment regimes in more detail.

CONTRACTING FOR PUBLIC SERVICES: THE APPROACHES EXAMINED

It is not possible within the confines of this chapter to provide a full discussion of approaches to contracting in different countries and therefore a few 'cases' will be presented.

Contestability in Sweden

In Sweden, a purchaser/provider split has been introduced in just over half of the county councils and, in relation to community care, in one in eight communes. The use of contracts as a managerial instrument designed to replace traditional, hierarchical modes of ordering, is set in a framework of other reforms such as government-prescribed, short-term policy objectives specific to individual agencies. Also important are the concepts of voice (political articulation of needs/wants) and choice (between options for exit and lateral re-entry), with the latter being seen to empower the former.

To ensure contestability—and 'a contestable market does not require the actual presence of a competitor; rather it is the threat of new entrants, or in this case even of a totally new delivery system, which works as a stimulus' (Von Otter 1994: 21)—a target for tendering has been set at 20 per cent of the volume of public services during the first three years. Rationalization is presented in terms of a more strategic public agenda (i.e. fewer objectives) which has meant that there has been a reappraisal of necessary functions with some being closed down and others transferred to voluntary organizations.

In practice, experiences of contracting have varied widely across the country according, for example, to levels of competitive intensity. Von Otter (1994) identifies three dominant models. These models each comprise a different mix of market and policy components and are based on different planning incentives: 'contracting is a composite of two design elements: clear cut and rational *incentive* structures from the market repertory; and public *accountability* from the sphere of planning and regulation' (Von Otter 1994: 5).

These are the mixed-market (also known as the internal market) model, the public competition model, and the consumer choice (also known as the voucher) model. In the long run, these models steer existing public services in different directions. For example, the mixed-market model is different to public competition since, with the latter, choice is restricted to public providers. In Sweden, the Dalarna commune (an example of the mixed-market model) is unusual in seeking a range of providers—in most other examples there is only one alternative —although, over time, the trend is to greater pluralism.

Challenging Insurer/Provider Relationships in the Netherlands

In the Netherlands, the Dekker proposals entail a range of new relationships between insurers and providers which vary on a continuum from purely administrative relationships (i.e. insurers simply pay the bills presented to them by providers) through to relationships where insurers control the delivery, organization, and financing of health care.

The negotiation of contractual terms between insurers and providers takes place within a limited set of bureaucratic arrangements for the delivery of health care. In practice, negotiation is constrained by debate about legitimacy. Increased discretion at regional levels has raised questions about who should legitimately take decisions about the configuration of health services—democratically elected bodies or private institutions such as insurers and providers. Hence, it is a regulated competitive health insurance market, also known as a managed market.

Van der Grinten *et al.* (1994) identify three kinds of contractual instruments:

- selective contracting: this covers the extent to which an insurer can decide which provider to contract with and also the grounds for ending a contractual relationship. Under the previous situation a sickness fund, for example, was obliged to contract with all providers in a region at nationally determined uniform conditions (Schut 1992);

- financial incentives: including bonuses, sanctions, and the sharing of surpluses and deficits within a basic plan for provider payment;
- instruments to influence the delivery of health care: including channelling patient flows to services to improve the fit between patients' needs and care received; and tools for quality assurance and management such as clinical protocols and peer review.

However, the scope for using contractual instruments, for example selective contracting, varies considerably and is influenced by both the general and specific context (Van der Grinten *et al.* 1994).

Pragmatism in Australia

In Australia, the line taken at commonwealth level is that CTC is one part of the broader microeconomic reform agenda and should be considered if it contributes to the efficiency of programme delivery and can be shown to be in the public interest. CTC implies a portfolio of policy-implementation tools and there is certainly an element of selecting the most appropriate approach for specific contexts.

Only one state has introduced *compulsory* competitive tendering (Victoria) with local authorities being required to subject increasing proportions of annual expenditure (from 30 per cent to 50 per cent between 1994 and 1997) to CTC (Domberger and Hall 1996). Therefore in Australia, there has been a gradual and pragmatic approach to the use of contracting and competition with CTC encouraged but not (in most cases) compulsory. Within this overall framework, the level of prescription versus discretion in the application of CTC has varied. Generally, states other than New South Wales and Victoria have not moved very far on developing general guidelines nor are they inclined to drive the process centrally (Domberger and Hall 1996).

Substantial gains from contracting—mainly in the form of savings (see below) —have undoubtedly contributed to the increased uptake of CTC. Also relevant is the lack of legislative compulsion (as the earlier example of Queensland suggests). Generally, the emphasis on voluntarism appears genuine, although there is some evidence to suggest that CTC is being used in response to indirect compulsion (for example, to achieve savings as a means of avoiding outright privatization (Domberger and Hall 1996))—a case of CTC being used as an incentive for improving performance within the public sector.

Shifting Risk in the USA

In the USA, four periods in the history of contracting for health and social care can be identified. Before 1960, contracting was not used as a strategy but in the 1960s and 1970s a big increase in contracting occurred at all levels of government, although at this time contracts tended to be broadly specified with little detail. In the 1980s, the use of contracts as a means of combating inefficiency was promoted and was accompanied by widespread competition among non-profits and an increasing role for for-profits organizations. The nature of contracts changed too in this period; they became more formal and risk was shifted to suppliers. This has been taken further in the 1990s to include an emphasis on the rationalization of government at all levels.

Regulating Purchaser/Provider Relationships in Italy

In Italy, relations between purchasers and providers are usually regulated—in the absence of national rules on purchasing—by a *convenzione*. Private organizations have to meet certain criteria before being allowed to enter into a *convenzione* or contract and there are usually registers of eligible organizations. These criteria relate mainly to organizations' legal status and character (for example, not seeking profit; being constituted with a legal act; having been operating regularly for a given number of years; including suitably qualified operators or systems and so on) and are often a substitute for real monitoring: 'A well entrenched cooperation between a public administration and a private organization carries much weight in fact, so that once a first "*convenzione*" has been signed, the relation is seldom interrupted' (Barbetta 1994: 11).

To summarize, it is clear that contract means different things in different situations. The Italian case, for example, illustrates clearly how the adoption of a contractual approach to service relationships does not necessarily entail a simultaneous adoption of a market model of public services. As Deakin and Walsh comment: 'The metaphor of contract provides an ideal form which can be readily adapted to a whole range of different situations and relationships' (Deakin and Walsh 1996: 1).

PURCHASERS, PROVIDERS, AND USERS: ROLES, RELATIONSHIPS, AND POWER

The second part of this chapter will focus on what we can learn from the international experience. The introduction of contractual forms of management to address various public sector challenges such as those identified earlier by Metcalfe (1993) has brought with it a series of additional issues, some of which may be design issues—resulting from inappropriate policy imitation—and some of which are old dilemmas in new guises.

These include the balance of power between purchasers, providers, and users and the implications of this for service quality; regulation, both of contracts and of markets, and the impact this has on discretion and innovation; issues of equity and choice; the costs and savings of contracting; and ethical issues of accountability and control for governments who are sharing power.

Several countries have introduced competition and contracts to public service management as a challenge to provider domination which is perceived to result in a distorted service pattern, where what purports to be needed stems from the concerns of those working in and producing services rather than those for whom they are ostensibly provided.

The roles of various actors, therefore, are crucial. For example, if purchasers are to act as champions of users, do they have the necessary skills to enable them to do this? To what extent do they have access to information about needs, produced independently from their own providers? Are their relationships with providers adversarial or is there a recognition that providers have a useful and legitimate role to play in identifying needs? How does the role of voluntary sector providers, for example, sit in a context where a purchaser/ provider split has been introduced since many voluntary organizations have traditionally performed a campaigning and advocacy role. Who will represent the user if the voluntary sector comes to be seen as an agent of the state?

Several of these questions have been considered in the UK context during the course of this book. At the international level, these issues seem to centre around cooperation; the impact of reforms on provider staff; and the purchasing role.

In many countries the rhetoric of change has centred on the benefits to citizens, not only as users but also as taxpayers. Many citizens will also be staff affected by the changes involved in a move to contract-based forms of management. In Sweden, one of the levers of the contracting process is the 'emancipation of work' (Von Otter 1994: 6) (though not of workers) through the introduction of flexible work contracts and a move away from standard conditions of employment: 'Personnel policy should be less part of a reward system and more clearly an instrument of management' (Von Otter 1994: 9). Such flexibility is, then, designed to make rationalization easier.

The majority of the impressive savings achieved in the Swedish model (Von Otter 1994) are explained by lower staffing levels or pay. Workers are reported to benefit from less bureaucracy and a more attractive entrepreneurial dimension to their jobs. Whilst this may be true for the new cadre of managers and accountants, an alternative vision to Von Otter's emancipation of work is chronic uncertainty, deskilling, and demoralization leading to a highly alienated workforce. In several countries, this is the reality of moves to decrease provider domination and there are very clear parallels between the Swedish scenario and the UK. In the UK this has often been interpreted as a dilemma for Labour-controlled local authorities, but given that these staff are also the people charged with improving public service it is an issue that needs wider attention.

Other countries' experiences suggest, however, that it does not have to be this way. In Australia, the issue of power generally and the effects of its removal on workers specifically does not appear to arise as there is no sense of any losers. Clearly again, contextual factors are relevant here. Anecdotal evidence suggests that pragmatism is a feature of the Australian culture with the workforce taking the attitude that if they don't like the changes they will find a job elsewhere.

However there are other differences. In New Zealand, the Department of Social Welfare stated in 1990 that contracting is not to be considered a more cost-effective option when based on lower standards of pay and working conditions. This approach may have reflected the ideological position of the government of the time. The replacement of this Labour government with a National one may have been accompanied by a different position. Less up-front is the Australian model where CTC specifications routinely include requirements to employ existing staff, follow equal employment and other affirmative action principles, and promote local industry.

In New South Wales, the government has stated a preference that where activities are to be contracted out, contractors should offer comparative employment to staff who may be displaced (Premier's Department 1993). Hardly earth-shattering but it does compare with the UK government's refusal to make a decision on whether Transfer of Undertakings (Protection of Employment) Regulations (TUPE) apply in the public sector which means that time and money are allocated to this decision in the case of every single contract let.

In Italy, preferred provider relationships are clearly unchallenged. However in Sweden, reform programmes have implications for patient and hence revenue flows. The Dalarna model, for example, created incentives for primary health centres to produce more services themselves. This has had the dual impact of both rationalizing hospital services and expanding primary health care, a policy objective since 1973 (Von Otter 1994). However, as Von Otter asserts, the changes have not been without controversy since local district health boards (budget holders) had close links with local primary-care facilities which produced a bias in favour of those centres.

In the Netherlands, the dynamic of pressure is operating on the insurer rather than the provider side. The reforms were intended to stimulate purchasers to become a more effective countervailing power to providers who have traditionally been paid regardless of the quality of work carried out. However, national and local factors (for example, the debate about legitimacy) are influencing the extent to which freedoms such as selective contracting can be used. In many cases, this freedom tends to apply to professionals rather than institutions (Van der Grinten *et al.* 1994). There is concern that purchasers (insurers) are more likely, as a result of greater competition, to form cartels than to compete with each other in terms of the management of contracts.

S. R. Smith (1994) describes how in the USA free market models, even where modified by transaction cost and principal-agent theories do not reflect the reality of contracting since they are based on the notion of voluntary and mutually advantageous exchanges. Moreover, in practice little genuine competition for contracts has existed and these are usually renewed automatically. Efficiency gains are often elusive and various problems relating to market failure (inadequate information, difficulties in assessing quality, collusion among providers, and so on) have been reported. The reality of the situation is expressed by two questions:

Why do many non-profits enter into a contractual arrangement and remain in the relationship despite deep dissatisfaction, onerous government regulations and payment uncertainties? On the government side, why do government purchasers often promulgate overly complicated, regulations that make their job much more difficult than is warranted? (S. R. Smith 1994: 3–4)

These suggest that although 'contracting . . . has led to a new way of providing public services . . . the structure of contracting appears to be designed to frustrate government purchasing agencies and non-profit providers alike' (S. R. Smith 1994: 4).

Drawing on the work of Krasner (1982), S. R. Smith uses the new institutionalism literature and regime theory in international relations to explain some of these problems. Regimes, it is suggested, are more useful in explaining purchaser/provider behaviour in a public sector context than markets because the public sector is different. This point is made by a number of commentators including Pollitt (1993); Harrison and Pollitt (1992), and Moe (1987; 1991). Crucially it involves winners and losers, so is contested. This political nature of public authority involves uncertainty and compromise which can undermine effective organizational performance. Furthermore, government purchasers are accountable to multiple constituencies and so must devise structures and processes which insulate them from the political uncertainty associated with the nature of this accountability.

Relationships between purchasing agencies and non-profits organizations resemble regimes in that they are 'not based solely on short term calculations of interest' (Krasner 1982: 187), but rather on the sacrifice of short-term interests by one or other party on the understanding that reciprocal behaviour will occur in the future. Therefore regimes are based on 'sets of implicit or explicit principles, norms, rules, and decision-making procedures around which actors' expectations converge' (Krasner 1982: 186).

The advantage of regime theory is that it facilitates the inclusion of the power and dependency element in relationships between public sector purchasers and service providers. S. R. Smith (1994) comments, however, that although there is mutual dependency this is not an equal relationship. The non-profit, for example, has more to lose from the break-up of the relationship. In Chapter 7 of this book it was suggested that local authority providers in the UK are less powerful for the same reasons. There is no second chance if a contract is lost. The provider organization is wound up and staff transferred. There has also been a parallel trend to the US tendency for contracts to be altered to make relationships even less equal as risk is transferred to the provider.

The significance of regimes, as S. R. Smith states, is not purely for descriptive purposes. They also provide a means of ensuring cooperation based on long-term relationships and trust derived from the development of norms and expectations. S. R. Smith identifies two other methods: changing incentives (for example, performance contracting) and coercion (regulations). These will be discussed below.

REGULATION

There are two main aspects to regulation. Given that contracts are themselves a form of regulation (see, for example, Chapter 5), the internal monitoring arrangements are of relevance. Chapters 3 and 7 provide some indication of approaches to monitoring contracts for health, social care, and local government in the UK. A survey of around 100 Italian *convenzioni* found highly variable monitoring arrangements. For example:

- 38 per cent of *convenzioni* examined do not require any periodical report on activity;
- 9 per cent require only accounting reports;
- 31 per cent do not make any reference to supervision or monitoring of activities by a public body;
- 56 per cent of those who do refer to monitoring by a public body do not regulate this (IRS 1990).

At the opposite end of the scale are cases where providers are required to produce excessive amounts of monitoring information. Gutch (1992) quotes the case of a US organization which was required to return seventeen forms every quarter to one funder, each with slightly different requirements.

There are also issues about what is monitored and how the data collected is interpreted and used. This is particularly relevant to performance contracts. Although several countries' reform programmes incorporate an intention to shift from contracts which focus on inputs to performance-orientated contracts, in practice the measurement of performance is underdeveloped and contentious. The role for users in this is a particularly neglected area.

In Australia the measurement of quality has been a neglected area. Where systems are in place, these tend to exist at the individual service level rather than at a state-wide level. Clearly this has implications for equity in that the opportunity for comparison is difficult. More recently, federal accreditation bodies have been established as a means of addressing this issue.

The social and health care context in the USA, which is characterized by the influence of interest groups, illustrates the controversial nature of performance measurement. In this, purchasing agencies are not solo actors but rather are 'immersed in a web of relationships affecting their contracting relationships with non-profit providers' (S. R. Smith 1994: 9). For example, congress and legislators can intervene in the actions of purchasing agencies such as the state mental health authority or the county substance abuse authority. Providers can approach the executive branch to get unfavourable decisions by the purchasing agency overturned. Many private service providers have joined together to form political associations to lobby legislators.

In short, the growth of contracting at all levels of government means that broader political trends are directly affecting the growth of contracting. Contracting should not be regarded as an isolated strategy divorced from the world of politics but inextricably immersed in politics of public organizations in which purchasing agencies, legislators, political executives vie for political control and advantage. In this environment, purchasing agencies will support outside organizations to give them a political edge. (S. R. Smith 1994: 11–12)

In such an environment outcome studies can be political dynamite.

Outcome measures are not objectively constructed but are value-driven. Moreover, in human service organizations the user is a co-producer and this has implications for the construction of outcome measures. What is the role of the user in this; what scope is there for user choice and the production of a range of appropriate measures? For example, who are the stakeholders in determining the desired outcome of counselling?

The measurement of performance in itself, can therefore be very difficult, although this is likely to vary according to whether the service is 'simple' or 'complex' (Walsh *et al.* 1996). When rewards are allocated on the basis of performance this can also produce conflict between purchasers and providers and can lead to goal displacement where the emphasis is shifted to what is measurable.

This is not to say that there is no performance contracting. In the USA, there is increasingly an emphasis on the application of private sector accreditation models to the public sector. In some contracts, rewards *are* allocated according to whether specific goals are achieved. For example, contract agencies receive additional funding from state mental health departments if they meet targets for keeping mentally ill patients out of institutions.

The second aspect in this section is the regulation of markets. This varies across countries and across service areas. There is less regulation in Australia, for example, than in the UK. The focus of regulation also varies. In Australia, the content of regulation includes the costing of contracts and thresholds at which work has to be subject to tendering. In the USA regulations are designed to protect equity and relate to the selection of contractors and the referral of clients. They also have a further added bonus: 'Regulations help insulate government officials by providing a fair and equitable structure to the contracting process . . . In response to the increasingly contested political environment, government regulation of contract agencies has increased at all levels' (S. R. Smith 1994: 14). S. R. Smith states that 'The increasingly contested political environment of contracting can produce overly rigid and excessive regulation of contract agencies' (S. R. Smith 1994: 16). He implies that regulations are designed to protect officials, rather than imposed for the benefit of the service. As was illustrated earlier, the imposition of these regulations is not only a constraint on innovation and the level of discretion available to service providers, but also makes the life of purchasers more difficult.

Managed markets have been a feature of the competition prescription in a wide range of countries including the Netherlands—where the debate about legitimacy is set against insurers' arguments that they cannot achieve the desired outcomes without freedom from regulation by state governments; Sweden—where decisions to close hospitals have not been left for the market to sort out (Von Otter 1994); and, Australia, the USA, and the UK.

The Australian position is indicative of many governments' desires (including the UK (P. Smith 1994)) to retain some form of control: 'The major advantage of CTC policy is that it allows governments to obtain the best of both worlds. Contractual frameworks introduce the discipline of competition while retaining the capacity to control and regulate outcomes in terms of quantity and quality of service' (Domberger and Hall 1996: 17).

USERS, EQUITY, AND CHOICE

The notion of a user is in itself problematic in the comparison of international experiences of contracting. For example, in Italy state provision and assistance is very much part of the culture and there is no tradition of empowerment. In this climate, people are unlikely to see themselves as users or to complain. In Sweden with its very long tradition of Labour government, the middle-class oriented Conservative-Liberal coalition of 1991–4, stressed the importance of choice and voice, as a long-term strategy to empower the public against what they saw as an overly paternalistic welfare bureaucracy.

Choice, according to Von Otter, has emerged as the essential component for accountability in health care reform. Issues of equity are also tied up with the kinds of choices that are acceptable. For example, the voucher model, initially a preferred alternative of the political right, resulted in several different home care firms working in the same building with different clients. As well as being ineffective, it was unacceptable in that accountability was to no one other than the voucher holder. Von Otter has commented that the creation of a choice mechanism puts the collective logic of the political process at risk. The dangers inherent in a voucher system—in addition to structural inefficiencies—are that the redefinition of previously defined collective goods into individualized goods will produce a decision process in which not everyone has a balanced set of choices. In other words, such a system is more likely to benefit the articulate and informed sectors of the population who are better equipped to bear any costs of entry/exit and social disruption.

Von Otter argues, however, that choice exercised by a few has benefits for the majority. For example, in Stockholm in 1988 the decision by one in ten mothers offered a choice of hospitals, to switch to alternative maternity-services providers, resulted in major clinics having to become more responsive to patient demand. In other words, not that many people have to be choosing actively since changes at the margins have a ripple effect.

Choice costs, however, and therefore the value placed on choice is highly contingent, partly on political culture and partly on the nature of the good. It is crucial therefore that all stakeholders are involved in decisions about the value of that choice. For example in the Netherlands, the Dekker reform was sold on the grounds of promoting diversity when in reality it was accompanied by an end to 'open-ended' finance (Flynn and Simonis 1990); compulsory amalgamation of sick funds (which reduced choice (Flynn and Simonis 1990)) and greater homogeneity in the basic insurance cover (which meant that if you wanted extras —or more choice—you had to pay).

COSTING CONTRACTING

Although the problems associated with evaluating contract programmes were outlined earlier (for example, the lack of data collected on a routine and systematic basis; the contested nature of such information where it does exist; and the difficulty in making before and after comparisons), some information is available.

Domberger and Hall (1994) present results from a range of surveys which consider the extent of contracting. For example in 1990–1, services worth $1.2b., equivalent to 15 per cent of departmental running costs, were contracted by the commonwealth department (MAB-MIAC 1992). Figures are also provided for the number and value of contracts for Western Australia and New South Wales. Of these, the New South Wales surveys reported average savings for the budget sector of 20 per cent. However, in terms of effectiveness and quality standards, the picture is more mixed, although again the evidence is patchy.

Transaction costs are perceived to be high in the UK. One explanation for this is that the contracting framework is based on neoclassical models (see Chapter 5) which attempt to cover all contingencies within what will always be an uncertain environment. Transaction costs in the USA are also high as Gutch's examples earlier illustrate and this is one reason why contracts often evolve into long-term relationships. Trust is cheap. This refocuses attention on the potential benefits of hierarchies (see Von Otter 1995).

In Sweden there appears to be more information on contracting costs. Studies show substantial improvements in cost-effectiveness over time (both before and after the reforms) with higher degrees of 'success' (defined as any cost improvement) being found in areas adopting a more pragmatic approach to the market. Also for the first time, costs per capita in major branches of the public sector (except those relating to unemployment) are decreasing (Folster 1993). The point was made earlier, however, that these studies, according to Von Otter (1995), cover a range of models. All studies show cost improvements including those where no purchaser/provider split has been introduced.

SHARING POWER

The move to contract-based government has been variously described as 'third party government' (Salamon 1985) or government by proxy (Kettl 1993). Kettl sets out not to argue that contracting *per se* is good or bad but given that it has become an integral part of governance in the USA comments that 'public reliance on private markets is far more complex than it appears on the surface. In these relationships, the government inevitably finds itself sharing power, which requires it to fundamentally rethink not only how it manages, but also how it governs' (Kettl 1993: pp. vii–viii). In the light of this, he emphasizes the need for governments to become 'smart buyers' or, in the British equivalent jargon 'intelligent customers'. These relationships, he states, cannot be left to manage themselves; the idea of a self-governing market is, he believes, a myth given imperfect competition, information asymmetry, and bounded rationality: 'If the markets in which the government operates were more nearly perfect, the government could indeed rely on them to produce quality goods and services at the lowest costs. Market imperfections, however, mean that the government must assert strong control over the markets' (Kettl 1993: 36). As the debate about what is core and not core shifts, this becomes even more crucial.

Sharing power, however, is not new. A feature of the Dutch health care system, for example, is that aside from the formal responsibilities of parliament and government these already share policy power with a range of actors: hospitals, insurers, physicians, employers, a situation that can produce policy paralysis or inertia: 'no one has the power to change the system itself . . . So, one has to negotiate on problem definitions and solutions and one is condemned to find consensus to reach goals' (Van der Grinten *et al.* 1994). In balancing interests, there is a need for everyone to 'have regard for the total effect' (Coase 1960: 44). The issue of accountability has been addressed in different ways by different countries. Again, notions of accountability are coloured by political culture and are dynamic (as the example of the UK health sector illustrates in the sense that emphasis is laid on different lines of accountability, for example to Parliament rather than democratically elected managing bodies; to the Secretary of State rather than to local people).

In the Swedish system, considerable attention has been paid to the issue of accountability in public services and a new model is emerging. Traditionally, accountability has rested on representation rather than participation. Although the democratic electoral process, legal controls, and professionalism continue to be important, two additional notions from the market repertory have been added with the objective of increasing accountability to the public: choice and contestability. As in Australia, there is a belief that the chosen system—in the case of public quasi-markets and in particular the public competition model which includes a user-choice element to increase accountability unlike the mixed-markets model which performs only on effectiveness—produces the opportunity to capitalize on the best of two systems.

However, as we have seen, there are issues. In a political environment, performance on some but not all policy objectives (for example, effectiveness, accountability, choice) is sub-optimal. Moreover, the so-called best of both worlds scenario in Sweden is being jeopardized by a fragmenting market system. In the UK, the relentless extension of contractual approaches has meant a shift from management by contracts to management of contract.

In a contracting system which is explicitly based on discharging functions there needs to be clarity of responsibility. There is a danger that the situation is becoming not only fragmented but so complex that no one can understand what is going on. As one frustrated French commentator stated:

> Nowadays, no one understands anything about the situation; people no longer know who does what, who pays what, who is responsible for what, since the planning contracts have re-established all cross funding. Worse still, they have been followed by a multitude of other contracts relating to the town, the river proper, the country, rural development etc, without mentioning the 2000 university plan. (*Le Monde* 1994)

All this has the effect of obscuring the situation and preventing the user from participating. This has been illustrated in earlier chapters in the UK local government context. Local authorities cannot abdicate responsibility when things go wrong because, in law, they are the responsible body. In the central government context similar examples emerge—although there has been a blurring of responsibility, particularly in the move to establish executive agencies, an issue that we shall return to later.

Having said all this, the Italian and US models are not without problems. The Italian model copes with the accountability conundrum with a variation of the trust hypothesis in contracting with non-profits organizations for human services. However, this trust is often a substitute for real monitoring and control. Furthermore, there is the issue of how explicitly notions of trust incorporate users. In the UK it is the GP or local authority client officer that is often a proxy for the user.

In the USA, cooperation is achieved through trust in the form of reciprocal norms and expectation, but reciprocal and mutually dependent relationships between purchasers and providers are often unequal with each seeking to gain advantage by recourse to various interest groups.

CONCLUSION

In one sense, therefore, contracting does not appear to be a precise solution to the problems of managing public services in an uncertain environment but is rather the key to the door to a whole new set of problems to be managed.

To conclude, we have seen in recent years a contract revolution, the international scale of which appears to legitimize the new paradigm. What is meant by contract, however, varies in different cultures. Contracts have been introduced for varied and complex reasons and designed with specific contexts in mind. There is no standard model in spite of policy imitation.

In addition to this, the jury is still out on the effectiveness of these models owing to a lack of commitment (and in some cases outright hostility) to evaluation. The medicine has been taken even though clinical trials are not yet complete.

Although evidence is therefore patchy, there is some indication that contract models can produce significant savings. However, when other factors are considered, such as the costs of introducing and managing contracts and the extent to which they achieve quality objectives, the results are likely to be less spectacular. Performing only on economy and efficiency criteria is not enough in the context of public authority.

The nature of public authority means that many countries are unwilling to allow the market free rein but believe that regulated or managed markets provide the opportunity to combine the best of both the planning and market worlds.

There is a need, as the behaviour of the UK government has recently suggested in relation to contracting for central government services, to take stock and consider how the appropriate balance between regulation and discretion; trust and control; decentralization and fragmentation; user choice and collective gain can be achieved and maintained: 'The market medicine should not be swallowed in bulk, but carefully portioned. Too much might kill' (Von Otter 1994).

NOTE

1. An important data source for this chapter was an international seminar on contracts and public services funded by the Economic and Social Research Council as part of the research project on which this book is partly based.

   The research team commissioned six papers to provide a picture of contracting in seven countries—France, Italy, Sweden, the Netherlands, the USA, Australia, and New Zealand. A small group of interested parties (including the authors) were invited to consider these papers and an additional paper on contracting in the UK. Many of the ideas in this chapter are developments of themes explored at this international seminar and the authors wish to acknowledge the contributions of those taking part, particularly Rob Flynn and Stephen Osborne, whose comments have been extemely helpful.

   Several participants in this seminar have commented on this chapter. The contributions of Casten Von Otter, Patrick Le Gales, Rob Flynn, and Enid Wistrich are gratefully acknowledged.

10
Conclusion

In this final chapter we summarize very briefly some of the main conclusions of our study. We have not set out to produce a systematic evaluation of the whole policy of introducing contracts across the totality of the public sector: that would have required a different and far more ambitious approach than the one that we adopted. But there are sufficient lessons to be learned from the experience of the case studies we undertook to justify an attempt to draw out some general conclusions. These lessons are of two kinds: first, they are about the process of change itself; and, secondly, whether the primary objectives of the reforms are being met as a result of the creation of new structures and processes.

The first lesson is the central importance of the overall framework within which the interaction of the powers, values, and interests of the different actors took place. As we have repeatedly stressed, the introduction of contracts into the delivery of public services occurred in a variety of very different environments, all of them undergoing rapid change, with consequent risk of instability and unpredictable consequences.

There were marked differences between purchasers and providers in terms of power, defined in terms of capacity to determine outcomes—for example, a much greater dominance of providers in health than in local government. Values varied, too; there was a greater willingness to accept the relevance of contracting in the health field than in other areas. This underlines the importance of the political dimension in determining how the contract system worked. Both social care and the other local government services were strongly influenced by the political factor, with Labour-controlled authorities seeking to avoid accepting the market approach. But we also encountered some Conservative-controlled authorities that also retained a strong belief in the public services which they had helped to develop.

In local government services (including in some cases social care), contracting could be isolated from the rest of the organization's activities; this was not generally possible in the health field. Values, in turn, influenced the exercise of power—as, for example, in the actions of councillors and to some extent trade unions in Labour-controlled local authorities, although there was a counteracting tendency for unions to embrace 'realism' in their approach to contracting. The pattern of change also reflected ways in which particular groups were able to exercise leverage: in health, GPs who opted to become fundholding were able to pursue their interests through the framework of contracting. Users of services, and to a large extent staff responsible for providing them, generally appeared to be less able to exercise such leverage.

Equally, attitudes were influenced by the perceived redistribution of interests.

Purchasing managers could see means of altering service patterns which had been resistant to change under hierarchical approaches (skill shortages; restrictive practices; embedded means of organizing and doing). In addition, the definition of the core of the organization changed—lowering the status of providers and placing their continued membership of the organization's core under threat.

Although the existing institutional and organizational context influenced the way in which contracting was introduced, the new structures that were created led to the emergence of new patterns of power, interest, and values. The creation of clients as a distinctive grouping with their own interests tended to lead to a greater degree of control by these clients. The isolation of DSOs in many local authorities led in general to a substantial reduction in the power of trade unions. Values, too, changed as purchasers and providers began to take on attitudes and behaviour patterns modelled on commercial practice. In this way, new structures and processes began to change the culture, as well as being influenced by values already in place.

This underlines the importance of the dynamic of change and the ways in which institutions and individuals adapt to new circumstances, especially when outcomes are difficult to predict. One important lesson has been the difficulty that many public sector organizations have encountered in moving 'from rowing to steering' (Osborne and Gaebler 1992). Since this has usually involved surrendering a degree of direct control—'sharing governance'—this is perhaps not surprising. The form of organization that was created to introduce contracting had its own dynamic, in terms of both structure and procedures. The influence of changed structures can be traced from the specification through the creation of contract-monitoring procedures, methods of pricing and payment, and for resolving differences. Language (both the terminology itself and the ways in which it has been employed) has been important here, in structuring the way in which people have perceived the issues. Furthermore, contracting has its own dynamic, tending to drive out other, less specific forms of organization. This formalization of procedures has often brought greater clarity in operation but may also involve higher costs.

Another important dynamic is the interaction between markets and the operation of contracts. Contracts operate differently, for obvious reasons, if they are placed within a competitive market, depending on the type of competition and also on whether those markets are internal to organizations or external. Thus, in the social care field, social services departments that had a choice of providers and a surplus of provision found it easier to take a strict approach to contracting. These differences have in turn helped to determine the respective influence of such key factors as risk, default, and quality. The behaviour of managers faced with decision-making in these sensitive areas has varied widely between the different services that we examined. In particular, the set of 'framing rules' and the changing power relations created by the interaction between rules and the characteristics of the market itself can inhibit or encourage the adoption by managers of rational techniques of decision-making.

One of the key questions to which our evidence begins to suggest some answers is whether the 'contract world' in the public sector is significantly different to that in the private business sector. It has traditionally been argued that contracts are typically relational rather than discrete, in the case of continuing business exchanges. It is clear from our analysis that the role of trust remains very significant in public services; but also that the degree to which it characterizes relationships varies from one sector to another. In our local government case studies, trust, in the sense of partnerships on a basis of mutual understanding, was highest in the case where all the services had been contracted out. This might suggest that trust may be easiest to develop where there is an explicit structure of values and interests. Clarity of interests may be more important than commonality of interests. Externalization may not be sufficient in itself, however: the mutual distrust about both competence and goodwill which was evident after an externalization of social services largely arose from disputes over whether relationships should be governed by public service or commercial principles and practice (for example, over pricing).

We may also be observing the development of cycles of trust, in which good practice reinforces the development of a sense of common purpose; and cycles of distrust, where suspicion is reinforced by the development of conflicts and the use of sanctions. Le Grand argues that relationships between a monopoly purchaser and a monopoly provider are some of the most difficult to manage, since there may be little that either side can do to resolve disputes (see Le Grand and Bartlett 1993). Several such relationships had been enforced upon people in the authorities we studied and it was in some of these that cycles of distrust were evident.

One factor that will help to bring about the development of distinctive patterns in the public sector is the role of politics, at both national and local level. It seems clear that at national level the politicians responsible for the implementation of the policies of which contracting formed an important part saw themselves as addressing what they defined as a long-standing malaise in the public sector. Public sector managers were to be taught a lesson in management and their textbook was to be the example of private sector practice. Equally, politicians at lower levels in the system saw the introduction of contracting as part of this wider agenda of 'marketization' which they were committed to resisting (on the grounds that 'welfare for profit' is inconsistent with public sector values). However, the imbalance of power between centre and periphery has meant that in the longer term there has been no option but to sign up, though rapidity of surrender has varied between services. Thus, the enterprise as a whole was characterized by relationships of low trust and detailed, if variable, control. It was in this dubious context that the lower-level actors had to develop relationships of sufficient trust to make things work.

The reform process can be interpreted both in terms of the imposition of explicit policy agendas and more broadly as part of a general trend that has been producing sweeping changes. Theorists have postulated a dynamic of

rationalization operating on all organizations and especially those in the public sector, because of the impact of externally imposed change. There were clear
signs of such a dynamic in our studies. Low trust and detailed external controls
pose limits on the extent to which lower-level actors can extend this rationality
and maximize their own utilities in ways which enhance overall efficiency. To
take one obvious example, decisions as to whether to internalize or externalize
particular functions owe much to a calculation of transaction costs in traditional
theory. Such discretion is not open to many public sector decision-makers, since
the rules prescribe what action they may take. At the same time, the multiplicity of principals and agents has tended to undercut this process. In this and
other ways, what is taken to be the rationality of market processes is continually being undermined by other factors—which may reinforce the conclusion that
this form of rationality is inappropriate.

Prominent among other key factors that have emerged in the course of our
study are transaction costs. These appear to have been high from the beginning
of the introduction of new procedures—and this has political implications, given
the stress laid on savings to be achieved through reforms. Information asymmetry was also commonly encountered. Among those suffering from particular disadvantages in this context are users, whose access to reliable information
on which to base crucial decisions is frequently deficient. This adds to the other
problems that they often experience in approaching these decisions, such as a
reluctance to challenge professionals.

Generally, over the period we have been observing, there appears to have been
a growth of commitment to market-type approaches on the part of managers
(this is reflected in our attitude survey, briefly reported in Chapter 8). But their
commitment has often taken the form of game playing: a process of mutually
self-reinforcing delusion. Against this, there is also evidence of some mutual
exchange in the learning process. One example is the willingness (observed in
the USA) for some providers to trade off high transaction costs against first mover
and other insider benefits.

Where value change of different kinds has occurred the roots may still be
shallow (though the process is reinforced by individuals moving from private
to public sector to take on commissioning responsibilities). But commitment may
be reinforced as the procedures become embedded and there is a move towards
greater maturity of markets and from short-term to longer-term contracts. This
will help to cement the partnerships that have emerged and develop relationships of trust. However, in some cases these new relationships are replacing
older ones in which trust was also a significant factor.

Finally, what is being done, in essence, is the introduction of different forms
of managed markets which involve different levels of regulation, competition,
and participation. There is a clear process of organizational development and
change in progress. Many of the outcomes are determined by initial decisions
which tend to have a disproportionate influence on later outcomes. There is also
some evidence of a process of 'lock-in', in which the initial approaches adopted

make it difficult to introduce significant changes at a later stage. The decision to externalize services will in most cases be irrevocable, although internal structures may well change—many social services departments are in a state of almost permanent reorganization.

Although the process of change is still working its way through the public sector, it seems at the time of writing (March 1996) to be unlikely that we will see a wholesale retreat from the market. We may, however, have been observing a particular phase in a process of cyclical development, although it may be taking place at a different tempo in the different service sectors, with their differing market characteristics.

Hirschman (1971) has argued that there are cycles of 'publicness' and 'privateness' in social development generally. One can easily imagine a cycle of bureaucracy being succeeded by a market-led phase, modified in its turn as the problems thrown up by one system lead to reforms that take it back in the direction of the other. However, it is open to some doubt whether we have completed a full phase of development or merely reached a staging post. Here, too, final judgements may be premature.

As for the users of services, the presumptive beneficiaries of the whole process of change, their involvement has taken a variety of different forms, ranging from extensive involvement in choice of services and even in their delivery ('co-production') through to a purely passive role as recipients on the fringe of events of a variety of different funding arrangements. One likely area of further development in future will be increased pressure both by individual users and collectivities seeking to gain improved access. This will encompass not just better information on which to base choices but also involvement in the decision-taking about the nature of services and the extent and terms of access to them.

CONCLUSION

Finally, the experience of contracting internationally, which we surveyed in Chapter 9, underlines yet again the point that the contract world embraces an almost infinite variety of forms. Not only do the cultural, political, and organizational contexts of contracting vary; the introduction of contracts into different situations has also led to a wide range of different outcomes. This, in turn, suggests that 'market imperatives', which are often held to be the main determinant of both the form and the end results of the process, are in practice only one of a complex set of different determining factors. Some of these go with the grain of human behaviour; some against. Some are more consistent with democratic styles of decision-taking than others. Some lead to outcomes that fit the circumstances and needs of services users; others do so to a lesser extent. What is important (by way of final conclusion) is that there are still policy choices to be made and that there are valid reasons for preferring one set of priorities over another. And when taking such decisions, there are legitimate grounds for doubting whether a simple market-driven approach will always (or even usually) meet the wide range of different objectives and interests that reforms might be expected to meet. On this, as on other matters, the jury (as they say) is still out.

APPENDIX 1

Analysing Contracts

The analysis of contracts was a significant part of the research. Contracts were analysed from each of our three sectors: health, social care, and local government services subject to compulsory competitive tendering under the Local Government Act 1988 (i.e. refuse collection, street cleaning, building cleaning, catering, schools and welfare catering, vehicle maintenance, grounds maintenance, and sports and leisure management).

The contracts were analysed along three dimensions: focus (narrow or broad; inputs, methods, outputs, and outcomes), form (real or 'quasi-' contracts; their language and legal content; costs, block or spot), and content (inclusion of default clauses, arbitration provision, quality issues). Our original intention was to formally model the contracts according to aspects such as the degree of specification and the emphasis on formality or informality but it soon became apparent that our ambitions would have to be modified.

There were a number of reasons for this. Although there is a vast literature on contracting, very little of it is based on empirical analysis of the documents themselves. Therefore in the early stages, very little was known about what to expect from the contract documents. A further issue for us was that when we came to read them, we discovered that contracts, for health care in particular, were extremely variable. Also, contracting in health and social care was on the whole a new activity and, in the case of health care, there was very little guidance as to what the contracts should cover and what form they should take (certainly in comparison to local government (CCT) contracts). One fairly simple reflection of this is in the different content and organization of health and local government (CCT) contracts with the latter comprising tender documents, conditions of contract, specifications and bills of quantities, and the former, at least in the early stages, neither using terms like contract conditions nor separating the different sections. There were further issues about the collection of contracts which are covered in more detail below.

So, instead of developing sophisticated quantitative data on the contracts, we produced tables using simple categories relating to key aspects of contracts (for example, what they covered), supported by illustrations from the documents themselves (to show how these issues were dealt with). Broad judgements could be made, for example, about the approach taken to risk (i.e. was it shared, borne more by the purchaser than the provider, or vice versa). These judgements were supported by qualitative data (to illustrate things like the approach to risk/uncertainty; the contract focus – i.e. mainly on inputs/ methods or outputs/outcomes; the approach taken to monitoring, variation, and so on) and were cross-checked by different members of the project team.

Contracts for Health Care

The health contracts were selected from a database of contracts collected by the National Association of Health Authorities and Trusts (NAHAT) which is the representative body for family health services authorities and health authorities and which also has in membership the majority of NHS trusts and GP fundholders.

The contracts were collected by NAHAT as part of a feasibility study into the setting up of a contract database. NAHAT wrote to all purchasers in England and Wales requesting copies of all contracts. The response was varied: some purchasers did not return contracts; in other cases the contracts sent were incomplete (in the sense that quality specifications and other sections were missing). The contracts which constituted our sample were randomly selected only in the sense that they were scanned onto a computerized database in order of receipt by NAHAT from purchasers and according to the quality of the hard or disk copy. We also analysed all contracts sent by GP fundholders. These had not been scanned onto the computerized database but were selected from the database of hard copies of contracts (which contained by no means all contracts drawn up in the first year of contracting).

The sample contained 118 contracts drawn up for the first round of contracting (1991–2). Of the 118 contracts, the purchaser was a DHA purchaser in 67 cases (57 per cent) and a GP fundholder in 51 cases (43 per cent). The provider was a directly managed unit (DMU) in 101 cases (86 per cent) and an NHS trust in 17 cases (14 per cent). Of the contracts where the purchaser was a DHA, 38 (57 per cent) were between purchasers and providers in the same district and 29 (43 per cent) between purchasers and providers in different districts (and in several cases these were also situated in different regions).

A further sample of 58 health contracts, from the third round of contracting (1993–4), were subject to a less detailed analysis to try to ascertain any broad changes over time.

Contracts for Social Care

A database of first-round social care contracts is held with the Institute of Local Government Studies at the University of Birmingham. These contracts were also subject to a detailed analysis along the same lines as the health contracts.

However, contracts from subsequent rounds of contracting were not collected for the social care and local government CCT sectors. This was because at the time of the research, there were only first-round social care contracts available and also because the letting of local government CCT contracts had been phased since 1988 and these contracts were generally much longer than health contracts.

Contracts for Local Government Services (CCT)

A large database of contracts was collected and is held with the Institute of Local Government Studies at the University of Birmingham. Full contract documentation—usually running to hundreds of pages and including bills of quantities and other supporting documentation—was not always sent.

The physical size of local government CCT contracts made the full analysis of such documents more difficult and time-consuming. A pragmatic approach was therefore adopted for this sector in that the detailed analysis of a small number of the local government CCT contracts collected was supplemented with information collected from other sources such as extensive knowledge of this area by Professor Kieron Walsh and by the Local Government Management Board's contracts database.

In spite of the constraints outlined above, the data has been used successfully (see Chapter 3 and Walsh 1995a) to provide a broad comparative picture of contracting in health, social care, and local government CCT. Two sector-specific studies have also been carried out (P. Smith 1994 and Smith and Thomas 1993).

APPENDIX 2

Attitudes to Contracting Questionnaire (ACQ)

Please rate the extent to which you agree or disagree with the following statements by ringing the appropriate number. The range of agreement is from (1)—Strongly Disagree —through to (5)—Strongly Agree

1　There are few improvements for service-users because of contracts　1 2 3 4 5
2　Contracting makes managers 'business-like' in their approach　1 2 3 4 5
3　Contracts often make it difficult to change services　1 2 3 4 5
4　Contracts do not improve accountability to the public　1 2 3 4 5
5　Contracts limit necessary professional discretion　1 2 3 4 5
6　Contracts have led to a better service balance　1 2 3 4 5
7　Standards of service are made clear through contracting　1 2 3 4 5
8　Robust information is crucial to successful contracting　1 2 3 4 5
9　Contracts need clear payment procedures　1 2 3 4 5
10　Contracts have led to more centralization　1 2 3 4 5
11　Quality of services usually improves as a result of contracts　1 2 3 4 5
12　Contracts require clear tender evaluation procedures　1 2 3 4 5
13　Managers have a more formal role under a contracts regime　1 2 3 4 5
14　There will always be work areas where contracts do not readily fit　1 2 3 4 5
15　Contracts do not facilitate user/client involvement in defining needs　1 2 3 4 5
16　Most people can't really understand the point of contracting　1 2 3 4 5
17　Contracts generally enhance the efficient delivery of services　1 2 3 4 5
18　Contracts are valuable in developing quality assurance mechanisms　1 2 3 4 5
19　Contracts create distrust between clients and contractors　1 2 3 4 5
20　Budgeting is much easier under a contracts regime　1 2 3 4 5
21　The contracting approach means more people are involved in decisions　1 2 3 4 5
22　Running on a contract basis is usually expensive　1 2 3 4 5
23　Contracts are not really appropriate in the public service　1 2 3 4 5
24　Contracts improve accountability to the local authority　1 2 3 4 5
25　Organizations become more commercially oriented after contracts　1 2 3 4 5
26　Managers are less likely to take risks under a contracting regime　1 2 3 4 5
27　Contracts promote the involvement of users/clients　1 2 3 4 5
28　Contracts result in much more useful information about services　1 2 3 4 5
29　Usually contracts mean little positive organizational change　1 2 3 4 5
30　Contracts lead to managers adopting a 'legalistic' approach　1 2 3 4 5
31　Contracting places a greater premium on highly skilled staff　1 2 3 4 5
32　Contracting makes co-operative working with other organizations easier　1 2 3 4 5
33　Equality of service access results from a contracting approach　1 2 3 4 5

34	Contracts continually throw up administrative problems	1 2 3 4 5
35	Contracting simplifies the process of management	1 2 3 4 5
36	Contracting creates conflict within the organization	1 2 3 4 5
37	Contracts usually result in more effective services	1 2 3 4 5
38	Contracting usually means less administration	1 2 3 4 5
39	Contracts mean over-emphasis on defaults and sanctions	1 2 3 4 5
40	The contract culture makes organizations less flexible	1 2 3 4 5
41	Contracts place a greater premium on good administrative systems	1 2 3 4 5
42	Contracts make management control over spending more difficult	1 2 3 4 5
43	The contract culture enhances responsiveness to user need	1 2 3 4 5
44	Contracts do not provide greater management control over services	1 2 3 4 5
45	Monitoring performance is a key feature of the contracts approach	1 2 3 4 5

REFERENCES

Adam Smith Institute (1994) *The End of the Welfare State*, London: ASI.

Akerlof, G. (1984) 'The Market for "Lemons": Qualitative Uncertainty and the Market Process', in G. Akerlof, *An Economic Theorist's Book of Tales*, Cambridge: Cambridge University Press.

Alchian, A., and Demsetz, J. (1972) 'Production, Information Costs and Economic Organization', *American Economic Review*, 62: 777.

Alford, R. (1975) *Health Care Politics: Ideological and Interest Group Barriers to Reform*, Chicago: University of Chicago Press.

Allen, P. (1995) 'Contracts in the National Health Service Internal Market', *Modern Law Review*, 58/3 (May), 321–42.

Aoki, M., Gustafsson, B., and Williamson, O. E. (1990) *The Firm as a Nexus of Treaties*, London: Sage.

Appleby, J. (1994) *Developing Contracting: A National Survey of DHAs, Boards and NHS Trusts*, Birmingham: NAHAT.

Arrow, K. (1974) *The Limits of Organisation*, Norton: New York.

Atiyah, P. S. (1979) *The Rise and Fall of Freedom of Contract*, Oxford: Clarendon Press.

Audit Commission (1986) *Making a Reality of Community Care*, London: HMSO.

—— (1992) *Managing the Cascade of Change*, London: HMSO.

—— (1993a) *Realising the Benefits of Competition: The Client Role for Contracted Services*, London: HMSO.

—— (1993b) *The Community Revolution*, London: HMSO.

Axelrod, R. (1984) *The Evolution of Co-operation*, New York: Basic Books.

Baker, K. (1993) *The Turbulent Years*, London: Faber.

Barber, J. (1989) 'Risk in the Method of Construction', in J. Uff and P. Capper (eds.), *Construction Contract Policy: Improved Performance and Practice*, London: University of London Centre for Construction Law and Management.

Barbetta, G. P. (1994) 'The Italian System of Social Welfare: The Role of Nonprofit Organisations and Contracting Out', a paper prepared for an international seminar on contracts and public services, held at the University of Birmingham, 15–17 Sept.

Bartlett, W., and Le Grand, J. (1994) 'The Performance of Trusts', in R. Robinson and J. Le Grand (eds.), *Evaluating the NHS Reforms*, Newbury: Policy Journals.

Baumol, W. J., Panzer, J. C., and Willis, R. D. (1982) *Contestable Markets and the Theory of Industry Structure*, New York: Harcourt Brace Jovanovich.

Beale, H., and Dugdale, T. (1975) 'Contracts between Businessmen', *British Journal of Law and Society*, 2.

Brennan, G., and Buchanan, J. M. (1985) *The Reason of Rules: Constitutional Political Economy*, Cambridge: Cambridge University Press.

Bruce-Gardyne, J. (1974) *Whatever happened to the Quiet Revolution?* London: Charles Knight.

Brunsson, N., and Olsen, J. P. (1993) *The Reforming Organisation*, London: Routledge.

Buchanan, J. M. (1986) *Liberty Market and the State: Political Economy in the 1980s*, Hemel Hempstead: Harvester Wheatsheaf.

Butler, D., Adonis, A., and Travers, T. (1994) *Failure in British Government*, Oxford: Oxford University Press.

Butler, R. (1991) 'New Challenges or Familiar Prescriptions', *Public Administration*, 69/3 (Autumn), 363–72.

Campbell, D. (1992) 'The Undeath of Contract', *Hong Kong Law Journal*, 22.

—— and Harris, D. (1993) 'Flexibility in Long-Term Contractual Relationships: The Role of Cooperation', *British Journal of Law and Society*, 20/2: 166–91.

Casson, M. (1991) *The Economics of Business Culture: Game Theory, Transaction Costs, and Economic Performance*, Oxford: Clarendon Press.

Chalmers, A. F. (1982) *What is this thing called Science*, Milton Keynes: Open University Press.

Coase, R. H. (1960) 'The Problem of Social Cost', *Journal of Law and Economics*, 3 (Oct.), 1–44.

Cockett, R. (1994) *Thinking the Unthinkable*, London: Fontana.

Collins, C., Hunter, D. J., and Green, A. (1994) 'The Market and Health Sector Reform', *Journal of Management in Medicine*, 8/2: 42–55.

Colson, E. (1975) *Tradition and Contract: The Problems of Order*, London: Heinemann.

Commission on Local Democracy (1995) *Final Report: The Commission*.

Common, R., Flynn, N., and Mellon, E. (1992) *Managing Public Services: Competition and De-centralisation*, Oxford: Butterworth Heinemann.

—— —— —— (1993) 'Contracting for Care: Further Developments', paper presented to quasimarkets conference, SAUS, Bristol, Mar.

Davis, J. (1992) *Exchange*, Buckingham: Open University Press.

Deakin, N. (1994) *The Politics of Welfare*, Hemel Hempstead: Harvester Wheatsheaf.

—— (1996) 'The Devils in the Detail', *Social Policy and Administration*, 30/1 (Mar.), 20–39.

—— and Parry, R. (1993) 'Does the Treasury have a Social Policy?' in R. Page and N. Deakin (eds.) *The Costs of Welfare*, Aldershot: Avebury.

—— and Walsh, K. (1996) *The Enabling State: The Role of Markets and Contracts*, *Public Administration*, 74/1 (Spring), 33–48.

Dearden, R. (1991) 'First Welfare State at the End of the Road', *Health Service Journal*, 8 (Aug.), 15.

Department of Health (1989) *Working for Patients*, London: HMSO.

—— (1994) *Caring for People: Community Care in the Next Decade and Beyond*, London: HMSO.

Department of Social Welfare, New Zealand (1990) 'Contracting for Social Services: Principles and Guidelines', cited in Domberger and Hall (1996).

Di Maggio, P. J., and Powell, W. W. (1983) 'The Iron Cage Revisited: Institutional Isomorphism and Collective Rationality in Organizational Fields', *American Sociological Review*, 48: 147–60.

Domberger, S., and Hall, C. (1996) *Contracting for Public Services: A Review of Antipodean Experience*, *Public Administration*, 74/1 (Spring), 129–47.

Donnison, D. (1990) *A Radical Agenda*, London: Rivers Oram Press.

Dowd, S. E. (1993) *Money and the Economic Process*, Aldershot: Edward Elgar.

Dunleavy, P. (1991) *Democracy, Bureaucracy and Public Choice: Economic Explanations in Political Science*, Brighton: Wheatsheaf.

—— and Hood, C. (1994) 'From Old Public Administration to New Public Management', *Public Money and Management*, July–Sept., 9–16.

Esping-Andersen, G. (1990) *The Three Worlds of Welfare Capitalism*, Princeton: Princeton University Press.

Etzioni, A. (1993) *The Spirit of Community Rights: Responsibilities and the Communitarian Agenda*, New York: Crown.

Financial Times (1995) 'Whitehall to Test Value of Contracting Out', 5 Apr., 12.

Flanagan, H., and Spurgeon, P. (1995) *Managerial Effectiveness in the Public Sector: Theory and Practice*, Milton Keynes: Open University Press.

Flynn, N. (1990) *Public Sector Management*, Hemel Hempstead: Harvester Wheatsheaf.

—— and Common, R. (1992) *Contracting for Care*, York: Joseph Rowntree Foundation.

—— and Simonis, J. (1990) 'Cost Containment in Health Care: A Comparison of Policies in the Netherlands and England', *Public Policy and Administration*, 5/3: 48–62.

—— and Walsh, K. (1988) *Competitive Tendering*, Birmingham: Institute of Local Government Studies.

Folster, S. (ed.) (1993) 'Systemskifte i fara?' Stockholm: Industrins Utredningsinstitut, IUI, cited in Von Otter (1994).

Fowler, N. (1991) *Ministers Decide*, London: Chapman.

Fox, A. (1974) *Beyond Contract: Work, Power and Trust Relations*, London: Faber.

Gaster, L. (1995) *Quality in Public Services: Managers' Choices*, Buckingham: Open University Press.

Giddens, A. (1985) *The Nation State and Violence*, Cambridge: Polity Press.

Glennerster, H., Matsaganis, M., Owens, P., and Hancock, S. (1994) 'GP Fundholding: Wild Card or Winning Hand?' in R. Robinson and J. Le Grand (eds.), *Evaluating the NHS Reforms*, Newbury: Policy Journals.

Gordon, R. (1985) 'Macauley, Macneil, and the Discovery of Solidarity and Power in Contract Law', *Wisconsin Law Review*.

Gouldner, A. (1964) *Patterns of Industrial Bureaucracy*, New York: Free Press.

Gray, A., and Jenkins, B. (1993) 'Markets, Managers and the Public Service: The Changing of a Culture', in P. Taylor-Gooby and R. Lawson, *Markets and Managers: New Issues in the Delivery of Welfare*, Buckingham: Open University Press.

Gronbjerg, K. (1993) *Understanding Non Profit Funding: Managing Revenues in Social Services and Community Development Organisations*, San Francisco: Jossey-Bass.

Gutch, R. (1992) *Contracting Lessons from the US*, London: NCVO Publications.

Halcrow, M. (1989) *Keith Joseph: A Single Mind*, London: Macmillan.

Harden, I. (1992) *The Contracting State*, Buckingham: Open University Press.

Harding, T. (1992) *Great Expectations . . . And Spending on Personal Social Services*, Social Services Policy Forum, Paper I, London: National Institute for Social Work.

Harrison, S., and Pollitt, C. (1992) *Handbook of Public Service Management*, Oxford: Blackwell.

Hayek, F. (1978) *New Studies in Politics, Philosophy and the History of Ideas*, London: Routledge.

Heginbotham, C. (1993) 'User Empowerment in Welfare Services', in N. Thomas, N. Deakin, and J. Doling (eds.), *Learning from Innovation*, Birmingham: Birmingham Academic Press.

Heimer, C. (1985) *Reactive Risk and Rational Action*, Los Angeles: University of California Press.

Hirsch, F. (1977) *The Social Limits to Growth*, London: Routledge.

Hirschman, A. O. (1971) *Exit, Voice and Loyalty* Harvard: Harvard University Press.

HM Treasury (1992) *Government Purchasing: Progress Report to the Prime Minister, 1991*, London: HMSO.

Hoggett P. (1990) *Beyond Excellence: Quality Local Government in the 1990s*, Bristol: School for Advanced Urban Studies.

Hood, C. (1991) 'A Public Management For All Seasons?' *Public Administration*, 1 (Spring), 3–19.

House of Commons Social Services Select Committee (1985) *Report on the Future of Community Care*, London: HMSO.

Hutchinson Encyclopedia (1992) 10th edn., London: Helicon Publishing Ltd.

Hutton, W. (1995) *The State We're In*, London: Jonathan Cape.

IRS (1990) 'Convenzioni tra enti pubblici e soggetti privati per l'erogazione di servizi socioassistenziali, Milano', cited in Barbetta (1994).

Jenkins, S. (1995) *Accountable to None*, Harmondsworth: Penguin.

Keen, J., and Packwood, T. (1996) 'Case Study Evaluation', in N. Mays and C. Pope (eds.), *Qualitative Research in Health Care*, London: BMJ Publishing Group.

Kenney, R., and Klein, B. (1983) 'The Economics of Block Booking', *Journal of Law and Economics*, 26: 497.

Kerrison, S. (1993) 'Contracting and the Quality of Medical Care', in Ian Tilley (ed.), *Managing the Internal Market*, London: Paul Chapman Publishing Ltd.

Kettl, D. F. (1993) *Sharing Power: Public Governance and Private Markets*, Washington: Brookings.

Klein, B. (1980) 'Transaction Cost Determinants of Unfair Contractual Arrangements', *American Economic Review*, 70: 356.

Knight, F. (1921) *Uncertainty, Risk and Profit*, New York: Houghton Mifflin.

Krasner, S. D. (1982) 'Structural Causes and Regime Consequences: Regimes as Intervening Variables', *International Organization*, 36/2 (Spring), 185–205.

Kreps, D. (1990) *A Course in Microeconomic Theory*, New York: Harvester.

Lapsley, I. (1994) 'Market Mechanisms and the Management of Health Care: The UK Model and Experience', *International Journal of Public Sector Management*, 7/6: 15–25.

Lawson, N. (1992) *The View from No. 11*, Bantam Press.

Le Grand, J., and Bartlett, W. (eds.) (1993) *Quasi-Markets and Social Policy*, London: Macmillan.

Le Monde (1994) 'The Development of the Region and Satellite Towns', M. Charasse, 3–4 July, cited in Sorbets (1994).

Lewis, J. (1993) 'Developing the Mixed Economy of Care: Emerging Issues for Voluntary Organisations', *Journal of Social Policy*, 22/2: 173–92.

Lincoln, Y. S., and Guba, E. G. (1985) *Naturalistic Inquiry*, London: Sage Publications.

Loasby, B. (1991) *Equilibrium and Evolution: An Exploration of Connecting Principles in Economics*, Manchester: Manchester University Press.

Lowndes, V. (1994) 'Understanding the New Public Management: The Contribution of New Institutionalism', paper for ECPR workshop, Madrid, Apr.

MAB-MIAC (Management Advisory Board and Management Improvement Advisory Committee, Australia) (1992) 'Contract for the Provision of Services in Commonwealth Agencies', Report No. 8 AGPs, Canberra, cited in Domberger and Hall (1996).

McAfee, R. P., and McMillan, J. (1988) *Incentives in Government Contracting*, Toronto: Toronto University Press.

Macauley, S. (1963) 'Non-Contractual Relations in Business', *American Sociological Review*, 28: 55–70.

Mackintosh, M. (1995) 'Putting Words into People's Mouths: Economic Culture and its Implications for Local Governance', *Open Discussion Papers in Economics*, 9, Buckingham: Open University Press.

Macneil, I. R. (1980) *The New Social Contract: An Inquiry into Modern Contractual Relations*, New Haven: Yale University Press.

March, J. G., and Olsen, J. P. (1989) *Rediscovering Institutions: The Organizational Basis of Politics*, New York: Free Press.

Marsh, D., and Rhodes, R. A. W. (eds.) (1992*a*) *Implementing Thatcherite Policies: Audit of an Era*, Buckingham: Open University Press.

—— —— (eds.) (1992*b*) *Policy Networks in British Government*, Oxford: Clarendon Press.

Mather, G. (1989) 'Thatcherism and Local Government: An Evaluation', in J. Stewart and G. Stoker (eds.), *The Future of Local Government*, London: Macmillan.

Means, R., and Smith, R. (1994) *Community Care: Policy and Practice*, London: Macmillan.

Metcalfe, Les (1993) 'Conviction Politics and Dynamic Conservatism: Mrs Thatcher's Managerial Revolution', *International Political Science Review*, 14/4: 351–71.

Meyer, J. W., and Rowan, B. (1977) 'Institutionalised Organizations: Formal Structure as Myth and Ceremony', *American Journal of Sociology*, 83: 340–63.

Miller, G. (1992) *Managerial Dilemmas: The Political Economy of Hierarchy*, Cambridge: Cambridge University Press.

Moe, T. M. (1987) 'Interests, Institutions and Positive Theory: The Politics of the NCRB', *Studies in American Political Development*, 7: 236–302, cited in Smith, S. R. (1994).

—— (1991) 'Politics and the Theory of Organization', *Journal of Law, Economics and Organization*, 7 (Spring 1991), 106–24, cited in Smith, S. R. (1994).

National Health Service Management Executive (1994) *Review of Contracting: 1993–4*, Leeds: Department of Health.

Newman, J. (1994) 'Beyond the Vision: Cultural Change in the Public Sector', *Public Money and Management*, Apr.–June, 58–64.

Niskanen, W. (1971) *Bureaucracy and Representative Government*, Chicago: Aldine Press.

North, D. (1990) *Institutions, Institutional Change and Economic Performance*, Cambridge: Cambridge University Press.

Osborne, D., and Gaebler, T. (1992) *Reinventing Government: How the Entrepreneurial Spirit is Transforming the Public Sector*, Reading, Mass.: Addison-Wesley.

Ostrom, E. (1990) *Governing the Commons: The Evolution of Institutions of Collective Action*, Cambridge: Cambridge University Press.

Pettigrew, A. (1987) *The Management of Strategic Change*, Oxford: Blackwell.

—— et al. (1992) *Shaping Strategic Change*, London: Tavistock.

Pollitt, C. (1990) *Managerialism and the Public Service: The Anglo-American Experience*, (2nd edn., 1993) Oxford: Blackwell.

—— (1993) *Managerialism and the Public Services: Cuts or Cultural Change in the 1990s?* (2nd edn.), Oxford: Blackwell.

Premier's Department, Sydney, New South Wales (1993) *Contracting and Market Testing Policy*, cited in Domberger and Hall (1996).

Prior, D., Stewart, J., and Walsh, K. (1995) *Citizenship: Rights, Community and Participation*, London: Pitman Publishing.

Propper, C. (1992) *Quasi-markets, Contracts and Quality*, Bristol: School for Advanced Urban Studies.

Reiter, B. (1981) 'The Control of Contract Power', *Oxford Journal of Legal Studies*, 1: 347.

Richardson, G. (1972) 'The Organisation of History', *Economic Journal*, 82: 883.

Ricketts, M. (1987) *The Economics of Business Enterprise: New Approaches to the Firm*, Brighton: Wheatsheaf.

—— (1994) *The Economics of Business Enterprise*, Brighton: Wheatsheaf.

Ridley, N. (1988) *The Local Right: Enabling not Providing*, London: Centre for Policy Studies.

—— (1992) *My Style of Government*, London: Fontana.

Robinson, R., and Le Grand, J. (eds.) (1994) *Evaluating the NHS Reforms*, Newbury: Policy Journals.

Sako, M. (1992) *Prices, Quality and Trust: Inter-Firm Relations in Britain and Japan*, Cambridge: Cambridge University Press.

Salamon, L. (1985) 'Government and the Voluntary Sector in an Era of Retrenchment: The American Experience', *Journal of Public Policy*, 6/1.

Schut, F. T. (1992) 'Workable Competition in Health Care: Prospects for Dutch Design', *Social Science and Medicine*, 35: 1445–55, cited in Van der Grinten *et al.*, (1994).

Self, P. (1993) *Government by the Market? The Politics of Public Choice*, London: Macmillan.

Smith, P. (1994) 'The Nature of Contracts in the British National Health Service', paper presented to ARNOVA (Association for Research on Nonprofit Organizations and Voluntary Action) Annual Conference, 20–2 Oct., Berkeley, Calif.

—— and Thomas, N. (1993) 'Contracts and Competition in Public Services', paper presented to the Association of Directors of Social Services Research Conference, Bristol, 25–6 Nov.

Smith, S. R. (1994) 'Transforming Public Services: Contracting for Social and Health Services in the US', a paper prepared for an international seminar on contracts and public services, held at the University of Birmingham, 15–17 Sept.

—— and Lipsky, M. (1993) *Non-profits for Hire: The Welfare State in the Age of Contracting*, Cambridge, Mass.: Harvard University Press.

Sorbets, Claude (1994) 'Contracts and Public Services—The French Figure: Compulsory Figures and the Styling of Authority', a paper prepared for an international seminar on contracts and public services, held at the University of Birmingham, 15–17 Sept.

Spurgeon, P. (1993) 'Regulation or Free Market in the NHS? A Case for Coexistence', in I. Tilley (ed.), *Managing the Internal Market*, London: Paul Chapman Publishing.

—— and Barwell, F. (1992) *Implementation of Change in the NHS*, Harlow: Churchill Livingstone.

Stewart, J. D., and Ranson, S. (1994) *Management for the Public Domain*, Basingstoke: Macmillan.

Stinchcombe, A. (1990) *Information and Organizations*, Berkeley: University of California Press.

—— and Heimer, C. (1985) *Organisation Theory and Project Management: Administering Uncertainty in Norwegian Offshore Oil*, Oslo: Norwegian University Press.

Stockford, D. (1993) 'Purchasing for Health: The Contracting Context', keynote address at conference on crucial issues in NHS contracting, 13–14 Oct.

Strauss, A., Fagerhaugh, S., Suczer, B., and Weiner, C. (1985) *The Social Organisation of Medical Work*, Chicago: Chicago University Press.

Sunday Times (1995a) 'Two-Tier NHS is Born', 1 Oct. 1–2.

Sunday Times (1995*b*) 'Blair Unveils his "Contract with Britain"', 1 Oct. 1–2.

Titmuss, R. M. (1969) *The Gift Relationship*, Harmondsworth: Penguin.

Townley, B. (1994) *Reframing Human Resource Management: Power, Ethics and the Subject at Work*, London: Sage.

Trakman, L. (1983) 'Frustrated Contracts and Legal Fictions', *Modern Law Review*, 46: 39.

Travers, T. (1986) *The Financing of Local Government*, Birmingham: Institute of Local Government Studies, University of Birmingham.

Tsebelis (1991) *Nested Games: Rational Choice in Comparative Politics*, Berkeley: University of California Press.

Van der Grinten, T. E. D., Nooren, J. E. A. M., Breedveld, L. C. M., and Boonekamp, L. C. M. (1994) 'Contracting in Dutch Health Care: The Insurer-Provider Relationship on Decentral Level', a paper prepared for an international seminar on contracts and public services, held at the University of Birmingham, 15–17 Sept.

Von Otter, C. (1994) 'Contracting in the Swedish Public Service—Towards "Creative Destruction"?' a paper prepared for an international seminar on contracts and public services, held at the University of Birmingham, 15–17 Sept.

—— (1995) *Cost Control in the Swedish Health Sector*, Stockholm: Swedish Centre for Work Life Research.

Walsh, K. (1991) *Competitive Tendering for Local Authority Services: Initial Experiences*, London: HMSO.

—— (1994) 'Contracts for Public Services: A Comparative Perspective', paper prepared for Socio-Legal Studies Association Conference, Nottingham University, 28–30 March.

—— (1995*a*) *Public Services and Market Mechanisms: Competition, Contracting and the New Public Management*, Basingstoke: Macmillan.

—— (1995*b*) *Public Services and Market Mechanisms*, Buckingham: Open University Press.

—— and Davis, H. (1993) *Competition and Service: The Impact of the Local Government Act 1988*, London: HMSO.

—— Deakin, N., Smith, P., Spurgeon, P., and Thomas, N. (1996) 'Contracts for Public Services: A Comparative Perspective', in D. Campbell and P. Vincent-Jones (eds.), *Contract and Economic Organisation: Socio-Legal Initiatives*, Dartmouth Publishing.

Webb, A., and Wistow, G. (1982) *Whither State Welfare?* London: Royal Institute of Public Administration.

Willetts, D. (1992) *Modern Conservatism*, Harmondsworth: Penguin.

Williamson, O. E. (1975) *Markets and Hierarchies: Analysis and Anti-Trust Implications*, New York: Free Press.

—— (1978) *Economic Organisation: Firms, Markets and Policy Control*, Brighton: Wheatsheaf.

—— (1979) 'Transaction-Cost Economics: The Governance of Relations', *Journal of Law and Economics*, 22: 233.

—— (1985) *The Economic Institutions of Capitalism: Firms, Markets, Relational Contracting*, New York: Free Press.

Wilson, J. (1980) 'Adaptation to Uncertainty and Small Numbers Exchange: The New England Fresh Fish Market', *Bell Journal of Economics*, 11: 491.

Wistow, G., Knapp, M., Hardy, B., and Allen, C. (1992) 'From Providing to Enabling: Local Authorities and the Mixed Economy of Care', *Public Administration*, 70/1: 25–45.

—— —— —— —— (1994) *Social Care in a Mixed Economy*, Buckingham: Open University Press.

Young, H. (1990) *One of Us*, London: Pan Books.

INDEX